TRANSACTIONAL DISTANCE AND ADAPTIVE LEARNING

Transactional Distance and Adaptive Learning takes a fresh look at one of the pioneering educational theories that accommodates the impact of information and communications technologies in learning. The theory of transactional distance (TTD) provides a distinct analytical and planning foundation for educators to conduct an overarching inquiry into transitioning from mass instructional and management systems in higher education to dynamic and transformational futures that focus on each individual learner.

Based on the TTD, this pragmatic approach offers instructors, administrators, students, and other stakeholders a comprehensive planning method to assess the current state of their instructional, learning, and management practices and to develop alternative models to prescribe future improvements in their institution. This complex, self-organized, and adaptive method includes current and emergent properties of:

- hardware, software, and telecommunications systems that allow faculty, students, and administrators to communicate;
- instructional and curriculum systems that provide teaching and learning environments for faculty and students; and
- management, societal, and global systems that influence how institutions are supported, funded, and managed.

Farhad Saba is Professor Emeritus of Educational Technology at San Diego State University, USA, and Founder and Editor of Distance-Educator.com.

Rick L. Shearer is Director of Research, World Campus at The Pennsylvania State University, USA.

TRANSACTIONAL DISTANCE AND ADAPTIVE LEARNING

Planning for the Future of Higher Education

Farhad Saba and Rick L. Shearer

Routledge
Taylor & Francis Group

NEW YORK AND LONDON

First published 2018
by Routledge
711 Third Avenue, New York, NY 10017

and by Routledge
2 Park Square, Milton Park, Abingdon, Oxon, OX14 4RN

Routledge is an imprint of the Taylor & Francis Group, an informa business

Library of Congress Cataloging-in-Publication Data
A catalog record for this book has been requested

ISBN: 978-1-138-30233-4 (hbk)
ISBN: 978-1-138-30232-7 (pbk)
ISBN: 978-0-203-73181-9 (ebk)

Typeset in Bembo
by codeMantra

The authors dedicate this book to our families who have supported our collaboration throughout the years to explore the theory of transactional distance, its nuances, and practical ramifications. Their support and encouragement helped us move forward on several related projects in the last two decades in researching and developing the theoretical and practical framework of this book.

We would also like to dedicate this book to Charles A. Wedemeyer and Jay W. Forester. Professor Wedemeyer re-conceptualized independent study and correspondence education into the field we know today as distance education. His foundational book *Learning at the Backdoor* and his work with the Open University in the United Kingdom moved the field into a new era of system thinking in education. Professor Forester founded system dynamics as a distinct theory, methodology, and technology and laid the foundation for our thinking beyond the traditional simple cause and effect relationships that so often characterize educational research.

CONTENTS

FIGURES

TABLES

CASE STUDIES

ABBREVIATIONS

Abbreviation	Description
24/7	24 Hours/7 Days a Week
3-D	Three-Dimensional
ACM	Association for Computing Machinery
ADA	Americans with Disabilities Act
AHS	Adaptive Hypermedia Systems
ALEKS	Assessment and Learning in Knowledge Spaces
ALS	Adaptive Learning Systems
AM	Amplitude Modulation
Apps	Applications
AR	Augmented Reality
AS	Academic Senate
ASIST	Approaches and Study Skills Inventory for Students
ASSG	Adaptive Simulations and Serious Games
ATI	Aptitude-Treatment Interaction Analysis
BYOD	Bring Your Own Device
CAD-CAM	Computer Aided Design–Computer Aided Manufacturing
CBI	Computer-Based Instruction
CBL	Case-Based Learning
CBT	Computer-Based Training
CEO	Chief Executive Officer
CGS	Counseling Group Session
CIO	Chief Information Officer
CPS	College of Professional Studies
CubeSats	U–Class Spacecraft (miniaturized satellite)

CUMAPH	Cognitive User Modeling for Adaptive Presentation of Hyper-Documents
D2L	Desire2Learn
DE	Distance Education
DEASM	Detected Emotion based on Active Shape Model
e-Portfolios	Electronic Portfolios
FCC	Federal Communications Commission
FERPA	Family Educational Rights and Privacy Act
GIS	Geo Information Science
H.R	House Resolution–US Congressional Bill
ICT	Information and Communication Technology
ID	Instructional Design
IDT	Instructional Development and Technology
IGE	Individually Guided Education
ILS	Index of Learning Styles
IoE	Internet of Everything
iOS	iPhone Operating System
IPI	Individually Prescribed Instruction
IPTV	Internet Television Protocol
ISP	Internet Service Provider
IT	Information Technology
IT&DC	International Training and Development Center
ITS	Information Technology Service
ITSs	Intelligent Tutoring Systems
ITU	International Telecommunications Union
ITV	Instructional Television
K-12	Kindergarten through Twelve Grade
LAN	Local Area Network
LeaP	Learning-based Adaptive Parameter
LMS	Learning Management System
LSI	Learning Style Inventory
LSQ	Learning Styles Questionnaire
LTI	Learning Tools Interoperability
LTM	Long-Term Memory
MacOS	Macintosh Operating System
MIT	Massachusetts Institute of Technology
MOOCs	Massive Open Online Courses
Mbps	Megabits per second
MHHE	McGraw-Hill Higher Education
NASA	National Aeronautics and Space Administration
NDLE	Negotiated Distance Learning Environment
PBL	Problem-Based Learning
PrBL	Project-Based Learning
PBS	Public Broadcasting Service
PCs	Personal Computers

PLAN	Program for Learning in Accordance with Needs
PLATO	Programmed Logic for Automated Teaching Operations
Q&A	Question and Answer
RHEC	Regional Higher Education Council
ROI	Return on Investment
RTD	Radio and Television Department
SaaS	Software as a Service
SL	Situated Learning
STEM	Science, Technology, Engineering, and Math
TPP	Trans-Pacific Partnership
TTD	Theory of Transactional Distance
TV	Television
U.S.	United States
VP	Vice President
VPAA	Vice President for Academic Affairs
VPN	Virtual Private Network
VR	Virtual Reality
WGU	Western Governors University
WI-FI	Wireless Fidelity (wireless networking)
WM	Working Memory
XML	Extensible Markup Language

FOREWORD

The Fable of Chickens and Owls!

Speaking at a conference a couple of years ago, I questioned what I perceived as unjustified exuberance in university circles about the hoped-for benefits of recent innovations in technology. Of course, I said, developments such as expanding bandwidth, faster download speeds, and a widening choice of social networking applications should help teachers and improve the learner's experience. This case ought not be overstated, however, because once a reasonably effective communications network is in place, the benefit for students of incremental improvements can only be marginal. Indeed, the value added to the student's learning experience of such incremental changes in technology will be trivial by comparison to the quality that can be added by investment in developing the skills and pedagogical knowledge of the teachers who are to use that technology. I said "investment" because the needed changes in teaching cannot be brought about through the actions of individual teachers themselves. They must come about through major organizational and structural change in the educational institution itself. This is only possible when university administrators face up to their responsibility to replace outdated teaching practices and develop new policies regarding such matters as the teaching qualifications for being appointed to the faculty, the provision of compulsory in-service teaching-training, and monitoring of teacher performance. Above all, effective use of communications technology depends on giving up the ancient model of professors as gurus in the classroom and replacing them with teaching teams, applying the principles of specialization and division of labor that have characterized almost every activity except teaching since the Industrial Revolution.

Following my presentation, I was approached by a member of the audience who asked if I would express those same views at a Congressional committee.

Always wary of becoming entangled in political party affairs, I declined the invitation. A few days later, I received a letter from the same audience member containing what he said was "a fable, which Aesop somehow neglected to record." In this story, a hen is sitting on a chicken coop that is being swept down river in a flood. Under these difficult conditions, the hen is trying to teach her chicks about what they can expect from life in the forests ahead where she expected to land. Unsure of her facts, and seeing a wise owl on a tree above the river bank, she called for help. The owl did not want to get involved in this risky situation and pretended not to have heard, and so the hen was left to teach as best she could, as she continued downstream. The sad end to the story is that the coop, together with its passengers was swept right through the forest and was finally dumped in a treeless meadow, where all they had learned about forest life proved to be quite useless. The point of the fable, said my correspondent, was to underscore the responsibility of the owls who know how to make teaching better (like me he insinuated!) to come off their high perch to help the hens, and for the hens to make use of the owls' knowledge, while coping with the reality that their coops are being swept ever faster in uncertain directions, by the current of events.

Braver than I, in the book before us here, two eminent educationists have decided to make the leap, leaving the safety of their academic perch to examine the barriers as well as the opportunities that technology offers higher education, offering to share their decades of knowledge on this subject with the hens on the university coop, teachers, but especially administrators, responsible for developing the policies that will support new teaching practices. It is a bold enterprise, if only because most university administrators owe their positions to success within this outdated structure, and many find it threatening to contemplate radical change. Nevertheless, simply adding 21st-century technology while employing 20th-, or dare I say, 18th-century pedagogies, can only have the effect of landing them, like the hapless hen in the fable, in a future for which their institutions are very inadequately prepared. It is to be hoped that at least a few will consider the suggestions about changing pedagogy and changing organizations that is the purpose of this book.

The Theory of Transactional Distance

The book contains a wide-ranging and comprehensive discussion about all aspects of technology, teaching, and institutional policy and management, but at its core is a very simple theoretical concept. This theory, the theory of transactional distance, is a view of teaching and learning that the authors, "Fred" Saba and Rick Shearer have studied, tested, researched, and applied in practice for over thirty years. What they have helped develop has proven to be a remarkably parsimonious model to aid in understanding the potentially overwhelmingly vast universe of variables that we should consider when we speak of education.

Lying at the heart of their analysis, this theory serves heuristically to uncover many of the key questions that policymakers need to consider in formulating new methods of teaching, and at the same time serves as a prism through which to expose some alternative responses to those questions.

For any such discussion about teaching that involves the use of communications technology, this theory of transactional distance is an especially suitable framework, given its origin as the first pedagogical theory specifically derived from the analysis of teaching and learning conducted through technology, as contrasted to the many theories developed in the classroom.

This is not the place for a full account of the history of the theory nor the theory itself, but a short statement about both history and the theory will help set the stage for the chapters that follow in this book. First, with regard to its history, readers should know that when the theory was first conceived, about fifty years ago, it emerged in what was then the very obscure subfield of education defined as distance education. At that time, although communications technologies were employed to link teaching institutions and students in workplaces and at home, there was no recognition in educational literature, research, or theory of any differences in teaching and learning under those conditions, as compared to what happens in a classroom. The first proposition of a pedagogy of such "distance education" appeared in 1973, with the field defined as

> the family of instructional methods in which the teaching behaviors are executed apart from the learning behaviors, including those that in contiguous teaching would be performed in the learner's presence, so that communication between the learner and the teacher must be facilitated by print, electronic, mechanical, or other devices.
>
> *(Moore, 1973, p. 664)*

It was defining these "teaching behaviors" when the learners are geographically distant from the teachers that became known as the theory of transactional distance, that term being used a few years later (Moore, 1980). However, a key proposition of the theory was that distance in teaching and learning is *not* a merely geographic concept. It is better thought of as a distance of understanding, a gap between a teacher's perception of what he or she wants to communicate and the perception of that message that is received by a learner. Bridging such gaps in understanding features in every interpersonal relationship is the specific focus of the teacher who engages a technology to cross the bridge and is what all educators must study, understand, and manipulate. Challenging though it is for the classroom teacher to cross this psychological and communications gap, it is even more so for those who have to acquire the knowledge and skills needed to do so through the media of print or electronic technology, each of which requires a considerable variety of skills. Untangling this highly complex multivariate environment, to help both researchers and practitioners get a grip on the otherwise overwhelmingly vast range of phenomena was and remains the role of transactional distance theory. It does this by reducing the many variables to three sets, usually represented in the literature as a three-dimensional model. Here is a summary.

The first dimension is a universe of the many ways in which teaching programs can be structured; the second dimension consists of the vast variety of verbal and other interactions between the learner and the representative(s) of the teaching institution that transpire within the teaching program; the third dimension defines those who make up the other side of the teacher-learner dialogue in the infinite variability of the persons who come to learn in those programs. A short account of each of these dimensions must suffice here, but the reader is referred to Moore and Kearsley (2012) for further elaboration.

The first set of variables, the structural variables, are elements in the curriculum and a course's instructional design. Every course consists of such elements as learning objectives, content themes, presentations of information, case studies, audio and video materials, graphics, exercises, projects, and tests; they also include planned interactions between the students and the instructor and usually among students themselves. The quality of instruction depends not only on how carefully these elements are composed but how appropriately they are composed for each *individual* student. A university that has set up a design team to undertake these many tasks might test parts of their course in an experimental group to gauge the suitability of each component of the course in accomplishing each objective. They might even measure the reading speed of their potential students and then tailor the number of pages or screens in each part of the course. Instructors might be provided detailed rubrics and marking schemes to help them ensure that all students meet the standard criteria of achievement. They may design tasks to ensure frequent monitoring of each student's learning performance, providing remedial activities for those who need them, thereby ensuring that every student has accomplished each step of the course in a tightly controlled sequence. The students might be admitted into the course as cohorts, and none may be permitted to move into any content area except at the pace of the whole group. Each student might be required to follow the same sequence of study and activity; audio and video materials could be synchronized very tightly to specific pages in a study guide on the Web while online discussions may be carefully organized so that each student is included in a specific chat room or class blog or wiki, according to a carefully scripted plan. It should be clear that such a course has a high degree of "structure." By contrast, a different course may permit students to explore an undefined set of websites and other resources by arrangement with the instructor, at their own speed, and submit evidence of having met the required achievement criteria, only when they feel ready. They may be told to call or e-mail an instructor or a help desk if, and only when, they wish to receive advice. Such would be a course with much lower structure than the former course.

To describe the second set of variables in transactional distance, the term "dialogue" is used. Dialogue differs from interaction, only in that it describes interactions aimed at bringing about learning and, therefore, it has only positive qualities that other interpersonal interactions might not have. A dialogue is purposeful, constructive, and valued by each party. Each party in a teaching-learning dialogue is a respectful and active listener; each is a contributor and is ready to build on the contributions of the other party or parties. In teaching, the direction of all dialogue is towards the student's developing knowledge and skills; its extent and exact nature are determined by the individual or group responsible for the design of the course, to some extent by the subject matter of the course, and by several environmental factors. One of these is the existence of a cohort of learners and the size of any such group; it is likely there will be more dialogue between an instructor and a single learner than between an instructor and any single learner in a group. Interactions occur, of course, among students within a group, but these are only dialogues in the pedagogic sense when they are managed by an instructor as a resource designed to accomplish specific educational objectives of a lesson.

Focusing on the Individual Learner

The third dimension in the theory of transactional distance enfolds the multitude of variables that make up the learners. In its original form, the theory focused primarily on learners' personality characteristics, and specifically on those characteristics that determined the extent to which students were able to manage their own learning. This propensity to engage to a greater or lesser extent in directing one's learning was labeled as the learner's autonomy. To those who study the history of distance education, it has been abundantly clear that many students are capable of undertaking some of the teacher's tasks for themselves, such as making a personal learning plan, finding learning resources at work or in their community, and deciding for themselves when progress was satisfactory. Indeed, history shows that studying through the medium of a communications technology places an onus on the student to undertake a degree of self-management that is not necessarily essential in the typical classroom environment. So important was this regard for the student's participation in the teaching-learning relationship in past years that what was called correspondence study was renamed "independent study" in the American universities that used that means of teaching. The principal exponent of this label was Charles Wedemeyer, who, in the 1960s and 1970s described such independent study as:

> teaching-learning arrangements in which teachers and learners carry out their essential tasks and responsibilities apart from one another, communicating in a variety of ways for the purpose of ... providing

> external learners with opportunities to continue learning in their own environments, and of developing in all learners the capacity to carry on selfdirected learning.
>
> *(Wedemeyer, 1971)*

The key point here is that from its earliest years, teaching in distance education was focused on individual students (not a class), and it was assumed that students would enjoy some degree of self-direction in their learning. In this tradition, a major theme in research was understanding the personality characteristics of those who were best able to direct their own learning, and how to tailor a teaching program to best suit students with greater ability and how to provide for those with less. Challenging the proposition first forwarded by Dubin and Taveggia (1968) that there were "no significant differences" when students are taught using different methods, other researchers, most well-known being Cronbach and Snow (1977), showed that such a conclusion rests on comparisons of class averages, and that for every individual student, there *is* a best method that varies from learner to learner.

This focus on characteristics of individual learners provides the third dimension of transactional distance and a third dimension for the classification of distance education programs. From this perspective, teaching programs can be differentiated by the degree of autonomy learners are expected or permitted to exercise. This is not a prescriptive position; it does not say that it is always desirable for students to exercise autonomy, nor that all students are fully autonomous, or ready to be autonomous, or that all programs and teachers should treat them as such. Applied in practice, however, when planning their courses, instructional designers may consider the extent to which a student is able to act autonomously and instructors consider what is appropriate dialogue with more autonomous, as compared with the less autonomous, learner. At the present time, there appears to be a fresh appreciation of these and similar questions about the individual learner, now being referred to as "personalized learning." Relevant research explores competency-based education, assessment of prior learning, and the use of learning badges, learner analytics, and adaptive learning.

Reformed Teaching Requires Attention to All Three Dimensions of Transactional Distance

It should be clear from this short discussion that it is the interactions among the three sets of variables represented by transactional distance—structure, dialogue, and learner autonomy—that gives the model its heuristic significance. Among the kinds of researchable questions raised by looking at teaching through this prism, are—as previously mentioned—the appropriateness of a specific application of a communications technology for different learner personalities, or how different course designs ("structure") in a given content area are best achieved through different combinations of an institution's human resources; or, given what is known about the students' degree of autonomy in one course, what should the institution invest in learner-learner interaction ("dialogue") or in student support services, compared to its investment in other courses with students having different degrees of "autonomy"?

Such illustrations should underscore the contrast that transactional distance theory reveals between the relationships of teachers and students in "contiguous teaching" (an unfashionable term one is not likely to use today!) and those in "distance education." Its relevance for discussion about educational policy in this digital age should be obvious, given the indisputable fact that in the 21st century what was the "very obscure subfield" of distance education has become such a major tributary of the mainstream, becoming a preoccupation, often an obsession, of teachers and administrators of educational institutions at all levels, from K–12 to (even) the doctoral programs. What has caused this wave of attention to teaching the student who is *not* in the classroom or on the campus, is, of course, the continuing evolution of online technologies and applications. It is the scramble of education's professionals like others—for example, travel agents, bankers, retailers, and publishers—to defend and protect their business, indeed, to survive, in the face of digitally delivered competition that has caused this unprecedented readiness to consider whether there is need for reform of teaching and ways of organizing institutional resources. The reality is that the problems are all solvable, given the political will to make the necessary changes. The bald fact is that after half a century of research in distance education, we can confidently assert that we DO know how to teach better outside the classroom when using technology, and we DO know how to use human resources more effectively. However, we also know that such improvements depend on a shift from a pedagogical model based on the preindustrial little red schoolhouse of 19th-century folklore, to a postindustrial systems model. In this book, the authors have used one such model to examine the opportunities offered by changing technology and the need for changes in policy and practice to benefit from that technology.

From the safety of my branch overlooking the torrent, I wish them success!

Michael Grahame Moore
Distinguished Professor of Education
The Pennsylvania State University

References

Cronbach, L., and Snow, R. (1977). *Aptitudes and instructional methods: A handbook for research on interactions.* New York: Irvington.

Dubin, R., and Taveggia, T. C. (1968). *The teaching-learning paradox: A comparative analysis of college teaching methods.* Eugene, OR: Center for the Advanced Study of Educational Administration. Retrieved from ERIC data base [ED 026 966].

Moore, M. G. (1973). Towards a theory of independent learning and teaching. *Journal of Higher Education, 44*, 661–679.

Moore, M. G. (1980). Independent study. In R. Boyd and J. Apps (Eds.), *Redefining the discipline of adult education*. San Francisco, CA: Jossey-Bass, pp. 16–31.

Moore, M. G., and Kearsley, G. (2012). *Distance education: A systems view* (3rd ed.). Belmont, CA: Wadsworth.

Wedemeyer, C. A. (1971). Independent study. In L. C. Deighton (Ed.), *The encyclopedia of education* (Vol. 4). New York: Macmillan.

PREFACE

Complexity of Higher Education

The world of higher education is messy and complex. It is driven by a multitude of interlaced key factors and variables. Change in any one variable can have a decisive impact on many other factors. What's more, the many elements that are involved change in time; they are dynamic. Viewing the world of higher education with a simplistic single cause-and-effect lens at one point in time does not reveal its complexity and dynamic nature across the landscape of a university, a college, or an academic department. This is while institutions of higher education are also going through an immense transformation the world over. They have one foot in the modern industrial era and another in the emerging postmodern epoch[1]. As Veletsianos (2016) has demonstrated, many innovative methods and technologies in education are currently "emerging." A new approach is needed to take into account the emergent complexity of higher education during this time of transition.

As an alternative to today's ad hoc piecemeal approach to addressing multiple manifestations of this complexity, this book proposes taking a fresh look at one of the pioneering theories that incorporated basic educational theory and also accommodated the impact of information and communications technologies, a theory known as the theory of transactional distance (TTD). Originally conceptualized and formalized by Michael G. Moore, now Distinguished Professor Emeritus of Education, The Pennsylvania State University, the TTD initially provided a high-level précis and a means of analyzing the transactions between a teacher and a learner in terms of the structure of the curriculum, the interaction or dialogue between teacher and student, taking into account significant variables in the learner's profile and background. However, in this book, the premise of the theory is expanded to look at not only the details of instructional systems but also to provide a fresh perspective on features of other systems employed in an institution of higher education, especially:

- Hardware, software, and telecommunications systems that allow faculty, students, and administrators to communicate,
- Instructional and curriculum systems that provide the teaching and learning environment for faculty and students, and
- Management, societal, and global systems that influence how institutions are supported, funded, and managed.

By looking at these components individually and studying their interrelationships holistically, stakeholders in a university would be able to better understand the complexity of their enterprise at the current time and develop practical plans for its future.

The Purpose of This Book

The theory of transactional distance (TTD) provides a distinct analytical and planning foundation for educators to conduct a systemic and overarching inquiry into transitioning from the current industrial system of higher education to a postindustrial future. The theory not only explains the process of teaching and learning in the era of anytime anywhere learning but it also provides a road map for designing a more effective management system that is conducive to:

- Resolving the chronic problems that have challenged colleges and universities in recent years, and
- Anticipating and planning to confront the issues and problems that may emerge in future years.

Altbach (2016, 1975–83) summarized the contemporary crisis in education in the following paragraph.

The American academic profession finds itself in an era of largely deteriorating circumstances. Financial cutbacks, enrollment uncertainties, pressures for accountability, and confusion about academic goals are among the challenges facing American colleges and universities in the early 21st century. The situation is in many ways paradoxical. The American academic model is seen as the most successful in the world, admired internationally for providing access to higher education to a mass clientele as well as possessing some of the best universities in the world. Yet, higher education has come under widespread criticism. Some argue that the academic system is wasteful and inefficient, and they place the professoriate at the heart of the problem. Others urge that higher education reconsider its priorities and place more emphasis on teaching, reasoning that the core function of the university has been underemphasized as the professoriate has focused on research.

In the last few years, critics of universities have presented a series of issues ranging from lack of affordability and access, to a crumbling consensus on what constitutes a liberal education, to a general decline in the quality of teaching and learning (Blumenstyk, 2015; DeMillo, 2011; Ford, 2002; Hersh & Merrow, 2005; Readings, 1996; Vedder, 2004).

A report of the Commission on the Future of Undergraduate Education (2016, p. 1) summarized its finding in the following:

1. College attainment rates are troublingly unequal: Among 25- to 29-year-olds, in 2015, 50 percent of women had a bachelor's degree or higher compared with 41 percent of men. Similarly, 72 percent of Asian students earned an associate degree or higher compared with 54 percent of white, 31 percent of black, and 27 percent of Hispanic students. In a related study, only 36 percent of students from low-income families earned a bachelor's degree compared with 54 percent of students from high-income families.
2. Many college students are academically unprepared for college: One-half of all college students take remedial courses.
3. More students are borrowing: The proportion of college graduates who took out federal loans increased from about 50 percent to 60 percent from 2000 to 2012; the median cumulative loan amounts increased nearly 25 percent from about $16,500 to $20,400.
4. Students who do not graduate are most likely to default: Students who do not graduate and who take out the smallest loan amounts have the highest default rates.
5. Too few students graduate and too few graduate on time: Only about 60 percent of students earn a bachelor's degree, taking, on average, almost six years to complete their studies. Only 29 percent of students who start a certificate or associate degree at a two-year college earn a credential within three years.

There is a general understanding that higher education is in decline and experiencing a state of crisis. This is despite the fact that faculty have spent countless hours in workshops, seminars, and brown bag luncheons to improve the quality of their teaching, and become familiar with the application of billions of dollars of digital information and communication technologies that have been infused to universities over the last three decades or so to improve instruction.

A major theme of this book is that educational innovations are constrained under the current administrative policies of institutions of higher education. Universities cannot realize the full value of their faculty development efforts and investment in digital technologies as long as policies established more than a hundred years ago, such as crediting students based on seat time in a class-room, are in effect (see Chapter 10, Management Systems). The TTD offers a coherent paradigm to educators to recognize how inconsistencies between instructional practices, administrative policies, procurement of information and communication technologies, and the needs of students to prepare for life in a postindustrial economy and postmodern society have led to contemporary paradoxes in higher education. Moreover, the coherent paradigm of the TTD provides the primary concepts and a specific methodology to resolve these paradoxes.

Therefore, the main theses of this book are as follows:

1. The TTD primarily addresses the process of instructional transaction be-tween the learner and the teacher, and provides the theoretical foundation as well as practical means for making learning flexible and adaptive to the needs of each individual learner.
2. Learners will not benefit from the flexibility, adaptability, and economy that the TTD affords them unless their universities extend the same flex-ibilities, adaptability, and economy to the management processes of the university. The impact of innovations in teaching and learning, such as the use of adaptive learning systems that are conducive to implementation of the TTD, becomes marginalized at the institutional level and the desir-able effects of such innovations eventually dissipate unless management of higher education can also adopt the principles of the TTD.
3. The TTD offers the theory and methodology for educators, university administrators, learners, parents, government agency administrators, law-makers, and other stakeholders to envision the future of a university that is flexible and adaptable enough to respond to the individual needs of learn-ers, plan for such a future, and implement the plan.

To describe and elucidate these theses, this book will:

1. Provide a detailed explanation of the theory of transactional distance;
2. Demonstrate the implications of the TTD for developing and offering adaptive learning systems for meeting the individual needs and aspirations of learners;
3. Explain how the design of instruction based on the TTD influences the management practices of universities;
4. Provide the reader with a planning method to:

    a. Assess and describe the state of their current instructional and man-agement practices in an institution of higher education, and
    b. Develop alternative models to prescribe future improvements in their instructional and management practices as they deem fit.

True to our pragmatic perspective, we are not offering a dogmatic vision of the future. We are proposing a planning process and a guide for its implementation to educators. Ford (2002), a critic of modern universities with an eye on the postmodern, suggested the concept of a "constructivist postmodern university." However, ironically and paradoxically, he went on to specify a particular curriculum for the university of the future. A constructivist postmodern approach would leave such specifications to the stakeholders of institutions who are constructing their future. Forwarding specifications and remaining constructivist are inherently contradictory. Each institution of higher education is unique, and our hope is that each institution remains distinctive despite the inertia of modernism for standardization and uniformity. The TTD, and its native methodology system dynamics, allows educators to map out an exclusive path to the future in their current transition from a modern system of mass education that catered to the exigencies of the industrial era to a postmodern system in which the individual learner is the focus of attention.

Planning for the Future

In light of the TTD, the new future that educators and other stakeholders can envision and build for their institution is in sharp contrast to today's system of higher education: a system that grew rapidly and matured during the modern industrial era. From the vantage point that Kuhn (1970) provided towards the nature of scientific disciplines, the TTD is a shift in the traditional paradigm of higher education (for a discussion of transactional distance as a theoretical paradigm, see Chapter 1). This change not only encompasses how instructors teach and students learn but also how a university is managed. The industrial management system of universities served countless students who were preparing themselves to flourish in an industrial economy in the 20th century. At the dawn of the 21st century, this static system of management is clashing with the dynamic needs of students who would be living in a postindustrial era. In contemporary advanced economies, skills for performing linear, repetitive manual tasks are gradually augmented, and in many cases supplanted, with problem-solving and decision-making competencies that often should be performed in nonlinear, innovative, and discontinuous work flows and environments. As Toffler (1980) posited, there is a "hidden curriculum" in policies and management practices that are in effect in most educational organizations, such as, the credit hour system. This veiled construction fosters compliance to standardized solutions at a time when learners need to develop skills for offering diverse answers that respond to unique problems.

To unmask the rigid system of mass education and begin to focus on the adaptable needs of each learner, each institution is going to develop its distinctive part. However, in reading this book, we ask you to imagine a future for higher education that is fundamentally different than what we have today, namely, a future in which instruction is not mass produced and delivered via digital means of communication in a form of education that Otto Peters (1998) referred to as "industrial." In contrast, education is dynamically responsive to each individual learner not only at the micro instructional level but also at the macro management level of a university. Understanding the theory of transactional distance necessitates setting aside some of our current concepts that have served us well up to the present but must change now to make universities academically and financially viable in the future. A plausible scenario for a new vision would be a world in which:

- Each learner establishes his or her personal program of study and learning calendar under the supervision of an instructor and a counselor. However, s/he may join a group of learners periodically as her or his personal learning program requires.
- Instruction is not based on a set curriculum but dynamically adapts to the profile of each learner.
- Students are credited by what and how much they learn, and not by seat time.
- There are no preset academic calendars, semesters, or quarters; learning times are adjusted dynamically to the profile of each individual learner.
- There are no classes with same student cohorts; learners join lectures, forums, study groups, and mentoring sessions based on their individual needs.

Hopefully, there will be many other alternative visions for the future of higher education. The above scenario is just one attempt to move our thinking from the current framework to a new one. In the next chapter, we will introduce the conceptual framework of the TTD to facilitate the process of visioning alternative scenarios for teaching, learning, and managing. In Chapter 13, details of this process are presented. However, each future chapter offers an important aspect of the process.

Note

1 As we will demonstrate in this book, the American school of postmodernism is pragmatic and constructive in nature and is different from the impractical and deconstructive essence of the dominant French school of postmodernism. It provides for reconciling dichotomies in educational practice that seem to be hard to resolve, such as the degree of faculty-centered teaching vs. the degree of learner-centered practice, or the "right mix" of online learning vs. classroom learning, or the right mix of media presentations for learning. This approach to reconciliation is in sharp contrast to the deconstructive method of postmodernism that has been practiced in academia in recent years, essentially debasing the fundamental role of the university in society and leading it towards nihilism. The American

school of postmodernism, as described in this book, leads to establishing dynamic instructional, learning, and institutional management systems that are congruent with the emergent transition of higher education from the modern era into the postmodern time.

References

Altbach, P. G. (2016). Harsh realities: The professoriate faces a new century. In M. N. Bastedo, P. G. Altbach, and P. J. Gumport (Eds.), *American higher education in the twenty-first century: Social, political, and economic challenges* (4th Kindle ed.). Baltimore, MD: Johns Hopkins University Press.

Blumenstyk, G. (2015). *American higher education in crisis?* New York: Oxford University Press.

Commission on the Future of Undergraduate Education. (2016). *A primer on the college student journey.* Cambridge, MA. Retrieved from www.amacad.org/multimedia/pdfs/publications/researchpapersmonographs/PRIMER-cfue/Primer-on-the-College-Student-Journey.pdf/.

DeMillo, R. A. (2011). *Abelard to apple: The fate of American colleges and universities.* Cambridge, MA: MIT Press.

Ford, M. P. (2002). *Beyond the modern university: Towards a constructive postmodern university.* Westport, CT: Praeger.

Hersh, R. H., and Merrow, J. (2005). *Declining by degrees: Higher education at risk.* New York: Palgrave Macmillan.

Kuhn, T. S. (1970). *The structure of scientific revolutions.* Chicago, IL: University of Chicago Press.

Peters, O. (1998). *Learning and teaching in distance education: Analyses and interpretations from an international perspective.* Sterling, VA: Stylus Publishing Inc.

Readings, B. (1996). *The university in ruins.* Cambridge, MA: Harvard University Press.

Toffler, A. (1980). *The third wave* (1st ed.). New York: Morrow.

Vedder, R. K. (2004). *Going broke by degree: Why college costs too much.* Washington, DC: AEI Press.

Veletsianos, G. (2016). *Emergence and innovation in digital learning: Foundations and applications.* Athabasca, AB: Athabasca University Press.

ACKNOWLEDGMENTS

Many colleagues and students influenced our thinking over the years as we explored the various facets of distance education and systems theory. They all have our deep appreciation although we cannot name all of them. We specially recognize Michael G. Moore, who has been a wonderful colleague and mentor throughout the years. He was always encouraging when we were developing the manuscript for this book. A special gratitude is also due to Gus Root, Professor Emeritus, Syracuse University, who taught the lead author system dynamics and showed him how to use it for modeling complex organizations. Our original research in the early 1980s was greatly facilitated by J. Michael Mahon, then of Northern Telecom (Nortel), who provided the computing and telecommunication facilities that enabled us to experiment with integrated two-way voice, video, and text telecommunications years before these capabilities became available on desktop computers.

Kathryn Krebs Helson, David Twitchell, and John Vitaglione, then graduate students at San Diego State University, who are now outstanding professionals in the field of educational technology, directly assisted in managing complicated experimental procedures, running computer simulations, and developing instructional materials for experimental purposes. Marcie Bober-Michel was particularly helpful with developing data analysis procedures.

Over the years we presented our research and development in its various stages of development in professional conferences. Terry Anderson, Randy Garrison, and Miguel A. Cardenas were among the colleagues that provided us with insightful comments, helpful criticism, and encouragement. Gary S. Lewis and Nancy Moreno-Derks reviewed early manuscript versions for this book and made our sentences and paragraphs smoother and more fluent.

We also greatly appreciate the guidance we received from Daniel Schwartz, our editor at Routledge. He offered tremendous assistance and sage advice at every stage of this project.

1

CONCEPTUAL FRAMEWORK

Introduction

This chapter provides an overview of the principal concepts of the theory of transactional distance (TTD). Primary constructs of autonomy, dialogue, and structure that are essential for understanding the theoretical paradigm of transactional distance are presented in the language of system dynamics. This form of representation shows the interrelationships among the key concepts of the theory and the temporal and dynamic nature of their interaction. The concept of transactional distance is further explained as a measurable construct, a postindustrial idea, and a postmodern notion. This explanation is presented to illustrate how these attributes ground the TTD in the framework of a scientific paradigm. A review of selected literature about the TTD is presented in the Appendix to provide the necessary background for this chapter.

The Theory of Transactional Distance

Conceptualized and developed by Michael G. Moore, the TTD has its roots in adult and distance education (Moore, 1973, 1983, 2013). In his early studies as well as in later publications, Moore stated that in any educational setting, there are four variables present. These are:

1. Dialogue that describes the extent to which, in any educational programme, learner and educator are able to respond to each other. This is determined by the content or subject matter which is studied, by the educational philosophy of the educator, by the personalities of educator and learner, and by environmental factors, the most important of which is the medium of communication. (Moore, 1983, p. 157)

2. Structure is a measure of an educational programme's responsiveness to learners' individual needs. It expresses the extent to which educational objectives, teaching strategies, and evaluation methods are prepared for, or can be adapted to the objectives, strategies, and evaluation methods of the learner. In a highly structured educational programme, the objectives and the methods to be used are determined for the learner and are inflexible (Moore, 1983, p. 157).

3. Autonomy refers to the extent to which learners decide on certain factors such as "what to learn, how to learn, and how much to learn" (Moore, 2013, p. 68). Moore posited that adult learners tend to set their own learning goals and pursue achieving such goals on their own. Realizing that dialogue, structure, and autonomy determine the degree of separation between the learner and the educator in time and space, Moore defined transactional distance as a function of these three variables.

4. Transactional distance is a psychological variable that modulates in relation to three constructs: autonomy, structure, and dialogue. These constructs are measured by the quality and quantity of communication between the instructor and the learner. According to Moore, 1983, p. 158 "In a programme in which there is little structure, and dialogue is easy, interaction between learner and teacher permits very personal and individual learning and teaching" (Moore, 2013) (Figure 1.1). Using the variables dialogue and structure, Moore proposed four possible sets to classify individual learning programs:

− D − S: Programs with no dialogue and no structure
− D + S: Programs with no dialogue but with structure
+ D + S: Programs with dialogue and structure
+ D − S: Programs with dialogue and no structure

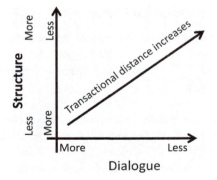

FIGURE 1.1 Relation of course structure and instructor–student dialogue in transactional distance.

In general, where there is minimal provision for learner interaction with an instructor, structure as well as transactional distance increase and attention to individual needs decrease. Conversely, when dialogue increases, transactional distance decreases; learners exercise more autonomy. They engage in dialogue with the instructor and with other learners more often in longer periods of time and with higher quality of interaction. For example, in a relatively small classroom where the instructor allows for learner autonomy and encourages learners to ask questions, participate in discussions, or even set some learning goals, distance and structure are minimized, and dialogue and autonomy are maximized. In contrast, in a large lecture hall where there is less possibility for interaction between learners and the instructor, generally, distance and structure are maximized, and dialogue and autonomy are minimized. In such a setting, learners usually do not have a chance to influence the dynamic of instruction in order to adapt it to their individual needs, unless they have access to classroom response technologies. These principles hold not only in the classroom but in online or hybrid (blended) courses as well. Distance in education, therefore, does not depend on the geographical separation of the learner and the instructor but on the quality and quantity of communication between the two. Transactional distance as a variable that changes dynamically depending on the requirements of an instructor for structure and the needs of the learner for dialogue and autonomy has major theoretical ramifications. These are described in the next four sections.

Transactional Distance Is an Objectively Measurable Construct

Dialogue is measured by variables such as direct or indirect participation of the learner in asking questions, requesting clarification, or demanding explanation for the course content or how instruction is presented. Structure is measured by variables such as direct or indirect control of the instructor in providing guidance, offering advanced organizers, or elaborating and clarifying course content. For measuring these variables, Saba and Shearer (1994) used speech acts of thirty individual learners while they were communicating with an instructor. In this study, the data were collected in thirty separate instructional sessions for each learner. We demonstrated that while the basic dynamic pattern held true for all learners, the interplay between dialogue and structure was unique for each student. It is important to note that since the TTD is concerned with the individual learner, we did not aggregate the data from the subjects. The data from each learner were analyzed separately on an individual basis. To assess the effect of instructional treatments on learners, it is important to study individually the data collected from each learner. Otherwise, individual differences are confounded and the research study may show perplexing results. (For a discussion on trait-treatment interaction analysis, see Chapter 5.)

Other researchers have studied key constructs in the TTD as well (see the Appendix). However, not all of these research projects can be considered to be within the theoretical paradigm of transactional distance. A paradigm is a set of consistent and interrelated concepts that are validated through studies using an identical method of inquiry (Kuhn, 1970). Nonetheless, researchers interested in the TTD rarely, if ever, have replicated research studies. This lack of conceptual and methodological consistency has created confusion and misunderstanding regarding the nature of transactional distance and how to study it. An example is studies in which researchers have measured "perception" of or "satisfaction" with transactional distance instead of transactional distance itself. Another example is studies in which the average score of one group of students who were subjected to an instructional treatment was statistically compared to the average score of those who did not receive the same treatment. These comparative studies completely ignore individual differences among learners. The key concepts in the TTD and their native method of study, system dynamics, provide a comprehensive and unique paradigm to study the teaching and learning process as a dynamic whole with interrelated components. Studies that use other concepts and methods do not completely comport with the paradigm of the TTD.

Transactional Distance Is a Dynamic System Concept

Components of static educational systems have a constant behavior. In these systems, all learners receive the same lecture and study the same instructional materials during the same length of time, and presumably achieve the same predetermined objectives in the same location. This is regardless of individual differences among learners, their prior knowledge about the course content, and their need to have access to different learning opportunities. In dynamic systems, however, learners receive differential instruction depending on their individual profiles, and can exhibit emergent learning outcomes that go beyond the predetermined learning objectives. Dialogue, structure, autonomy, and, thereby, transactional distance are different for each individual learner at each moment in time and modulate interactively as the educational session progresses. These variables affect each other and are affected by each other during a program of study; thus, their value changes interdependently on an ongoing basis. To illustrate the point, the dynamic relationship between structure and dialogue is depicted in the following causal loop diagram.

A short explanation of some of the essential concepts of system dynamics is necessary to understand the diagram in Figure 1.2. In this illustration, the more structure there is in a system, the less dialogue; the more dialogue, the less structure. An instructor and a learner, in this example, optimize their stock (level) of transactional distance as they engage in dialogue (a flow or a rate), while the instructor sets the required flow of structure for that individual learner. Stocks

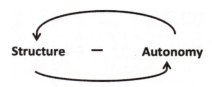

FIGURE 1.2 Dynamic relationship between structure and autonomy.

(levels) in system dynamics are analogous to how much water there is in a swimming pool, and flows (rates) are similar to the amount of water per unit of time that is added to the pool and is drained from the pool. In more technical terms:

> Rates define the present instantaneous flows between the levels of the system. They correspond to activities, while the levels measure the resulting state to which the system has been brought by the activity. The rates of flow are determined by the levels of the system according to rules defined by the decision functions. In turn, the rates determine the levels. The levels determining a particular flow rate will usually include the level from which the flow itself comes.
>
> *(Hadjis & Papageorgiou, 2011, p. 1334)*

Thus, in Figure 1.2, dialogue and structure are conceived as flows and transactional distance is conceived as a stock. (For a more detailed explanation of stocks and flows, see www.systemdynamics.org/DL-IntroSysDyn/stock.htm.)

Relations among the components in a dynamic system are governed by two types of feedback loops: positive and negative. The feedback loop in Figure 1.2 is negative as it is indicated with the minus sign in the middle of the diagram. A negative loop means that there is an inverse relationship between two components: That is, the more the value of a component increases, the less of another component is available in a system. In the context of transactional distance, the instructor receives information about the tolerance that the learner has for dialogue, and the learner receives information about the structure that the instructor has imposed on the teaching–learning process. Thus, the instructor adjusts the flow of structure to respond to the learner's need for dialogue, and the learner adjusts his/her expectation of dialogue to the necessary structure. This dynamic feedback loop determines the stock of transactional distance at each moment of instruction for each individual learner as the process of teaching and learning is in progress.

Figure 1.3 shows an example of a positive feedback loop in which it is indicated that the more resources available to an institution, the more can be spent on curriculum and organizational development efforts. In turn, a more developed organization performs better and attracts more resources to that organization for further development. The positive loop is highlighted with a plus sign in the middle of the diagram.

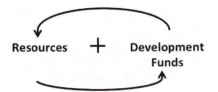

FIGURE 1.3 Example of a positive feedback loop.

Positive feedback loops, combined with negative feedback loops, provide control mechanisms in a system.

In Figure 1.4, more enrollments lead to increased student population in a positive feedback loop.

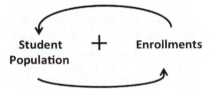

FIGURE 1.4 Example of positive feedback loop showing the effect of enrollments on the total student population.

As shown in Figure 1.5, the more students graduate, the less the student population (a negative feedback loop).

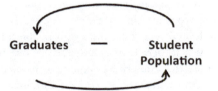

FIGURE 1.5 Example of negative feedback loop showing the effect of graduation on the total student population.

The control process includes a positive feedback loop that consists of enrollments and a negative feedback loop that involves graduation (Figure 1.6).

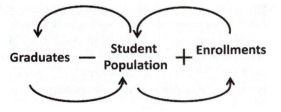

FIGURE 1.6 Example of a negative and a positive feedback loop as a control mechanism.

There is no inherent value in these loops. A positive loop is no better or worse than a negative one—they have different functions and they play specific roles in various circumstances. Positive loops tend to amplify changes in a system and often produce exponential growth, and negative loops tend to negate changes and move the system towards equilibrium (Hadjis & Papageorgiou, 2011). Most living systems are dynamic and complex, and consist of many positive and negative feedback loops that modify their behavior as time passes. Similarly, a learner's interaction with instructors, peers, and administrators is dynamic and complex, and consists of many feedback loops that change in time.

Key constructs in the TTD indicate the dynamic learning process of each individual learner at each moment in time. Consequently, methods of study that collect data at one point in time, such as test scores at the end of an academic term, do not reflect the evolving nature of teaching and learning. Living systems change in time, and data that are collected at one instance could change in the next interval. Researchers who collect one set of data that reflect a snapshot of the state of the learner or the instructor at one moment in time ignore the temporal nature of autonomy, dialogue, and structure, and consequently transactional distance.

In short, system dynamics is the preferable method of study for constructs in the TTD as it allows for:

* Accounting for the dynamic nature of teaching and learning;
* Analyzing the data for each individual learner; and
* Observing the effects of several variables on each other as they work together, for each individual learner, and over an extended duration of time.

Use of system dynamics as the method of study of the TTD is an essential requirement. It is not an elective method that could be simply ignored. (For a discussion of system dynamics method of research, see the Appendix.) This is an important issue as some scholars have attempted to analyze the TTD in a reductionist framework that may be appropriate for mechanical phenomena, but not for organic and living systems. Traditional physical sciences concentrated on the static interaction of discrete but similar objects under study (e.g. interaction of a drop of acid on a bar of a metal alloy). The TTD, at its core, is about the dynamic interaction of learners and instructors who have vast individual differences and are profoundly different from identical units of physical objects.

An example of the reductionist view of the TTD is a critique by Gorsky and Caspi (2005) that is often cited in scholarly articles and dissertations. They argued that the TTD could be reduced to a single tautological functional relationship: As the amount of dialogue increases, transactional distance decreases. Therefore, they concluded that the idea of transactional distance does not lend itself to articulating a full theory. This reductionist thinking highlights the fundamental misunderstanding of the authors in distinguishing between logical systems and living systems. Living systems are logical, but they are more than that. They operate based on a number of complex interrelated functions, all of which are necessary for the life of the system. Reducing them to a single or a few logical statements does not reflect the sufficient number of components and relationships among them that are necessary for any living system to function. For example, humans and other mammals require inhaling air to increase the amount of oxygen in their bloodstream and exhaling to reduce the amount of carbon dioxide. To argue that both of these functions can be reduced to one concept, i.e. that of breathing, although logically true, does not reflect the complexity of the respiratory system. Both processes are necessary. Similarly, in the TTD, all four statements originally set forward by Moore are necessary to provide a sufficient description of the TTD. Arguing that the statements "when we inhale, oxygen is increased" and "when we exhale, carbon dioxide is reduced" is a tautology and should be reduced to a single logical statement misses the importance of both of these subsystems for modeling and understanding the respiratory system as a whole. To fully explicate how the respiratory system works to sustain life in a living organism, both of these statements and many others explaining other subsystems are necessary.

The four statements posited by Moore are necessary and tentatively sufficient to explain the TTD at this time. As systems research takes shape in the future, additional subsystems related to Moore's four original system functions could emerge and would be added to the total paradigm of the TTD. Because of its native system dynamics method of inquiry, theorists of transactional distance can cast a wide net and incorporate new constructs to the TTD to further articulate a central comprehensive and paradigmatic theory. Moore (2013, p. 80) stated the following:

> Transactional distance theory provides the broad framework of the pedagogy of distance education. It allows the generation of almost infinite number of hypotheses for research into the interactions between course structures, dialog between teachers and learners and the student's propensity to exercise control of the learning process.

Following Dubin (1978) who presented a detailed process of theory building using dynamic systems, we have demonstrated how new hypotheses are formulated in further articulation of theory of transactional distance and presented the results in the hierarchical model of technology-based higher education systems. This model is introduced in Chapter 3 and each of its components is delineated in subsequent chapters. To fully articulate the relevant components of each of the eight system levels, we have drawn from a wide range of appropriate disciplines and have shown the critical influences that one system level has on the other levels. The comprehensive system model that has emerged would be applicable not only to further articulating the TTD but also to analyzing current institutional organizations. Because distance in education is not a function of the geographic separation of the learner and the instructor, this comprehensive system model applies both to when instructors and learners are teaching and learning in physical proximity in a classroom, as well as when they are not teaching and learning in the same space or at the same time.

In addition to its use for further development of the TTD, the hierarchical model of technology-based higher education systems could also be used for planning the future of each university in a comprehensive and purposeful approach that reflects the uniqueness of that institution. This systematic and systemic process would, hopefully, supplant the current ad hoc and piecemeal manner of planning and the organizational development in higher education that is partially responsible for the creation of seemingly irreconcilable dichotomies, paradoxes, and confounding problems. This planning process is explained in Chapter 13.

Transactional Distance Is a Postindustrial Concept

An important dimension of postindustrial systems of education is the degree of autonomy that is exercised by each learner. When thousands of young men and women flocked to universities after World War II, administrators strived to provide a standardized mass educational experience to all learners, practically disregarding their need for autonomy and assuming any responsibility for their own learning. In the system of mass education that emerged, the university governance, composed of both faculty and administrators, reserved the lion's share of power, control, and influence for the instructor and the administrator. Consequently, the control that learners could exert in their learning decreased substantially; transactional distance and structure increased, and autonomy decreased. Today, as social organizations transition into postindustrial forms, the primacy of the individual over the mass movement of the industrial era is a major point of friction among stakeholders in universities. When individual learners attempt to define their unique adult identity and distinguish their learning needs from those of the others, their efforts clash with institutions that are designed to provide uniform mass education both in their instructional programs and in their management practices. Higher education has become a primary arena in which the practices and policies of mass society are conflicting with postindustrial civilization. The result of such incongruity is evident in the lack of access to appropriate educational programs that meet the needs of individual learners, prolonged time for students to complete a program of study, and the inability of higher education institutions to reduce costs even by massive investment in acquiring information and communication technologies. A hallmark of the postindustrial society is personalization of products and services. The pragmatic American philosopher John Dewy imagined such a postindustrial society when he assigned taking some degree of personal responsibility to individuals for their learning if they were to flourish in a self-governing democratic society. Influenced by Dewy in conceptualizing transactional distance, Moore emphasized the theoretical and practical importance of individual differences among learners. This attention to the uniqueness of individual learners found its practical application in the concept of learner autonomy. Universities that recognize and respond to the needs of individual learners to exercise autonomy would transform from the industrial system of mass education to a postindustrial era. In the postindustrial university of the future, not only is instruction adaptive to the needs of each learner, but also his/her interaction with the entire system is flexible. Such flexibility includes participating in the establishment of a personal academic calendar, setting academic goals, and determining lifelong aspirations and career objectives.

Transactional Distance Is a Postmodern Idea

Postmodern systems of education are dynamic and nonlinear so that they can be responsive to learners with different profiles, as defined by personal learning preferences, prior knowledge, and future career and lifelong objectives and aspirations. This is in contrast to the modern systems of education that offer a preset curriculum to all students en masse with or without the use of information and communication technologies. In the TTD, there is provision for recognizing and responding to individual differences of the learner through learner-instructor and learner-learner communication. The TTD acknowledges "the otherness" of an individual learner. It affords systems (e.g. adaptive learning) to discover disparate variables in a wide net of systemic feedback loops in the learning space of each learner, and bring them together to provide a unique educational experience to each learner. For a detailed explanation of how learning management systems (LMSs) and adaptive learning systems (ALSs) perform these tasks, see Chapters 4 and 5. Also, see the discussion of postmodernism in the next section of this chapter.

Transactional Distance Represents a Paradigm Shift in Higher Education

The TTD implies a paradigm shift in research and development in the field of education in general and in open, flexible, and distance education in particular. Nowhere is this paradigm shift more apparent than in research methods in the fields of educational technology and distance education where one group of students is subjected to an instructional treatment (experimental treatment) and the average score of their learning is statistically compared to the average learning score of another group of students who do not receive the experimental treatment. These studies invariably return a familiar result: The experimental treatment shows "no statistically significant difference" between the two groups of students. In these studies, the aggregate data obscure the unique learning outcomes of individual learners when such outcomes are numerically averaged, and consequently do not shed any light on the effectiveness of experimental variables presented in instructional treatments to learners no matter what they are. This is also the case in an overwhelming number of studies about the principal concepts of transactional distance, a selected number of which are presented in the Appendix. In these studies, researchers also aggregated data that they collected from one group of students and compared the data to another group, effectively, obfuscating any significant difference in the behavior of each individual student in relation to the instructional treatment. By definition, an individual learner sets the flow of his or her autonomy by engaging in dialogue, thus controlling his/her autonomy, and establishing a value for transactional distance in relation to structure brought to bear by the instructor at each moment in time. The stock of transactional distance at each time interval, therefore, is unique to that learner. Analyzing autonomy, dialogue, or transactional distance by methods of study that aggregate the data collected from a group of students negates measuring the value of the flow or stock of these concepts as each learner determines the values of these variables dynamically. Regardless of the experimental variables involved, this discordance between the research method and the nature of constructs under study leads to the notorious "no statistically significant difference" result when the data from the experimental and control groups are compared.

Study of the principal concepts in the TTD requires collecting data from each individual learner in single-subject studies and analyzing the results separately from the data collected by other learners. Individual learners are unique and a "research methodology that uses rigid algorithms for filtering data into factors or applies multiple regression formulas for assessing how dependent and independent variables co-vary in an attempt to 'rigorously' quantify complexity, has only a limited problem solving capacity" in studying complex adaptive purposeful living systems such as learners (Hadjis & Papageorgiou, 2011, p. 1331). This methodological issue in studying the TTD is difficult to overcome as long as statistical procedures that were borrowed from physical sciences and applied to social sciences are taught in colleges throughout the United States and the world.

This procedural blinder has impeded researchers to realize that theoretically there is an unlimited combination of learner-treatment interactions, and it is virtually impossible and practically undesirable to find the "best" combination for all learners a priori. An artifact of the lack of realization that learners are unique, complex, adaptive, and self-organized individuals with vastly different learning histories is the dichotomous model that has emerged in instructional design literature. Objectivist learning vs. constructivist learning, content-based education vs. problem-based education, or teacher-centered instruction vs. learner-centered instruction are seen as discrete and contending models and not as two ends of the same spectrum that can be reconciled for each individual learner according to his or her profile. (For a discussion of instructional design models from the perspective of the TTD, see Chapter 8.) Instead of reconciling these variables through the use of ALSs for each individual learner at each moment in time, researchers have aimed to find their "best" combination for all learners! This theoretical and practical reconciliation is possible through radical empiricism as set forward by American philosophy of pragmatism. Described by Cornel West (1989), radical empiricism recognizes the limitation of theory as a static knowledge product, and offers it as a method (process) for knowledge acquisition (in the case of this book, theorizing about the relation between the learner and instructor or the learner and an administrator). In his analysis of William James's pragmatism, West (1989) stated the following: "The role of pragmatism is that of a 'happy harmonizer' and a 'mediator and reconciler.'" According to West, James's favorite example is to illustrate polar opposites, with which we have come to deal. Examples include the tender-minded vs. the tough-minded, or rationalistic (going by principles) vs. empiricist (going by facts), idealistic vs. materialistic, optimistic vs. pessimistic, and so on. As we will demonstrate in Chapter 8, analogs of these dichotomies in instructional design (e.g. instructor-centered vs. learner-centered) can be reconciled as a matter of degree in the education of an individual, depending on his/her prior learning, learning preferences, and educational objectives. While American postmodernism acknowledges the uniqueness of an individual learner as legitimate, it does not continue to deconstruct the instructional strategy assigned to a learner, or an educational institution in which the learner studies to oblivion in order to accommodate the diversity of students. A pragmatic approach to postmodernism discovers such diversity, and includes these newly recognized divergent categories in a wide net of systemic feedback loops as subcomponents of key constructs in the TTD. The pragmatic approach to the TTD and its application to solving practical problems of contemporary education are an important aspect of the paradigm shift from a static model of education to a dynamic, complex, adaptive, and self-organized system of teaching, learning, researching, developing, administering, and planning that has emergent properties. The profound ramification of the transformative nature of the TTD for the future of higher education is discussed in the remainder of this book.

Summary

In this chapter, we presented key concepts of the TTD and stated that the theory is best articulated in the language of systems dynamics from a postindustrial and a postmodern point of view. The TTD implies a paradigm shift in research and in education in general and in open, flexible, and distance education in particular. This shift is not only in the theoretical principles of the TTD but also in its native system dynamics methodology. Practitioners in each institution of higher education can also implement the TTD to develop system models that reflect their unique aspirations for the future of their distinguished university in a comprehensive and purposeful manner.

Chapter 13 is devoted to the presentation of how faculty, students, administrators, community leaders, and other stakeholders can participate in this planning process.

In the next chapter, we will discuss the broader context of the TTD in the contexts of:

- Hardware, software, and telecommunications systems that allow faculty, students, and administrators to communicate;
- Instructional and curriculum systems that provide the teaching and learning environment for faculty and students; and
- Management, societal, and global systems that influence how institutions are supported, funded, and managed.

References

Dubin, R. (1978). *Theory building* (Rev. ed.). New York: Free Press.

Hadjis, A., and Papageorgiou, G. (2011). Strategic management via system dynamics simulation models. *International Journal of Social, Behavioral, Educational, Economic, Business and Industrial Engineering, 5*(11), 1331–1336.

Kuhn, T. S. (1970). *The structure of scientific revolutions.* Chicago, IL: University of Chicago Press.

Moore, M. G. (1973). Toward a theory of independent learning and teaching. *Journal of Higher Education, 44*(9), 661–680.

Moore, M. G. (1983). The individual adult learner. In M. Tight (Ed.), *Adult learning and education* (pp. 153–168). London: Croom Helm.

Moore, M. G. (2013). The theory of transactional distance. In M. G. Moore (Ed.), *Handbook of distance education* (pp. 66–85). New York: Routledge.

Saba, F., and Shearer, R. L. (1994). Verifying key theoretical concepts in a dynamic model of distance education. *The American Journal of Distance Education, 8*(1), 36–59.

West, C. (1989). *The American evasion of philosophy: A genealogy of pragmatism.* Madison, WI: University of Wisconsin Press.

2

THE THEORY OF TRANSACTIONAL DISTANCE

The Broader Context

Introduction

In this chapter, we will expand on the basic concepts of the TTD, and demonstrate how these concepts influence the behavior of organizational components that are present in a university. To do so, we will offer a hierarchical model of technology-based institutions of higher education that represent these organizational components. The model illustrates how instructional systems, as defined by the principal constructs of the TTD, relate to other components that are active in any technology-based institution of higher education. The hierarchical model has eight levels representing hardware, software, telecommunications, instructional, curricular, management, societal, and global components. This model is the key to understanding the critical functions of the professionals who work at each system level in most institutions. It illustrates how what they do is intertwined in a wide network of influences that eventually sets the stock of transactional distance as the ultimate outcome of the system for each individual learner.

Pedagogical Foundations of TTD

The pedagogy of the TTD is rooted in the idea of individualized interaction between the instructor and the learner, as well as the autonomy that each learner brings to the learning situation, and the structure that the instructor or the instructional organization (e.g. a university) requires in each moment of instruction. This pedagogical framework defines the instructional system of a university. Because of its focus on the individual learner, the TTD shifts the orientation of the educational enterprise from providing standardized mass education to large groups of students to attending to the learning needs of each learner. This shift has ramifications for the entire system of a university, including its management practices, and how students with differing interests and traits are allowed to excel in an academic program. Currently, all students in a class start their learning at the same time and end it at the same time regardless of the progress they may have made during a course. Those who have some background in the subject of a course, or are able to respond to the learning situations presented to them quicker, may complete a sequence of instruction earlier than other students. Those who lag behind are simply given a lesser or even a failing grade. It is remarkable that the meaning of receiving a lesser grade is rarely discussed as a consequential issue in the academic progress of a learner. Does it mean that it is of no consequence that some students finish a course of study without mastering all of its requirements? Does it imply that these students are expected to perform poorer in other related courses? What about those who completely fail a course? Should they be given a chance to complete the parts of a course that they were not able to comprehend during the set period of time devoted to it? Should they receive tutoring, or be advised to change their program of study or even their declared major? What happens to those who perform quicker than others? Would they be given a chance to move ahead and start a new course of study? Would their program of study be dynamically revised to reflect their aptitude for completing specific learning tasks under certain conditions? Can they mentor other students who may be lagging behind in a systematic process for extra credit? Currently, the administrative system of most educational institutions is not designed to handle learning processes that respond to the individual differences of students. Therefore, all students suffer different setbacks and negative consequences in one form or another regardless of how well or poorly they have performed. Ultimately, this lack of attention to the individual performance of learners costs everyone who has a stake in students to succeed. These include parents who fund the education of students either directly by paying tuition or indirectly through state taxes, state governments which manage budget allocations to institutions of higher education, students who must delay their progress or compromise their learning altogether, and employers who are in search of qualified personnel.

Impact on Management

In the lock-step linear universe of most educational organizations, individualized learning will cause unanticipated problems in the general management of a university. How would an institution operate if classes of students were defined by their progress in acquiring certain knowledge and skills and not by when they were enrolled in a certain course? How would instructors interact with learners in these types of classes in which individual learners may leave when they have completed their learning objectives? How would instructors interact with others who remain for a longer period of time? How would students benefit from collaborative learning if they move in and out of certain classes without permanent cohorts who remain there for an entire semester? What would happen if there would be no semesters or quarters at all? How would department chairs and deans accommodate students in varying stages of their learning progress dynamically? How would colleges and universities be compensated when the unit of reimbursement is defined by learner achievement and not by sitting in a classroom during a set period of time? How can employers provide feedback to colleges and universities about what they expect from the alumni? How does a global system of economy and international relations impact the current static and linear system of teaching and learning? How can we analyze these complex and interrelated system variables and be ready to respond to these questions and other similar issues as they may arise in the future? Responding to these questions is not simple. Answering any one of the questions differs vastly among institutions. Our aim here is not to offer a dogmatic set of answers, but

1. Acknowledge and illustrate the complexity of higher education systems by offering a hierarchical model; and
2. Demonstrate how stakeholders can use this model in each institution to analyze the status of their organization and plan cooperatively to create a more academically desirable and dynamic future that would respond to the needs of individual learners.

Higher Education Systems

Colleges and universities are composed of administrative and academic units. The administrators are in charge of managing the day-to-day affairs of the institution as well as thinking ahead in terms of planning and budgeting for different organizational units. The faculty in academic units are in charge of teaching and research and upholding the academic standards of the institution. However, complexity arises when we realize that faculty in most institutions are also directly involved in setting policies for the institution through various bodies such as academic senates, or influencing such policies through faculty unions, thus playing a major role in the overall management of the university along with professional administrators. Decisions made by administrators also impact how faculty can acquire facilities to pursue their research, organize their teaching load, manage their tenure and promotion, and respond to an increasing array of government rules and regulations. In short, faculty decisions affect the policies and procedures the administrators must pursue, and what administrators do affect how faculty can fulfill their academic objectives in teaching, research, and providing service to the community.

Students are also becoming more involved in making decisions on how to structure their learning to maximize the benefit they receive relative to the investment that they make in time and effort as well as money, thus introducing another set of factors to an already complex system. Decisions that students make in selecting academic and career objectives affect administrative factors, such as instructional budgets. Students also affect the academic lives of faculty by influencing factors, such as faculty work load or time they may spend on research and development or providing service. In turn, the policies that faculty and administrators make affect students in various ways from the number of new prospects that a university may admit in each academic period to the quality of education students receive. These intricate networks of relations among stakeholders, through the decisions that they make and the influences that they set in motion, make any institution of higher education complex. Complex systems consist of a group of interacting parts that affect each other and are affected by each other in interrelated feedforward and feedback loops (Haines, 2000). In fact, complex systems are not necessarily things that we can touch and feel—they consist of interactions and interrelationships that are not tangible, and that is why they are difficult to visualize (Verma, 1998). Because of the interaction of its components as well as its relations with its environment, a system constantly changes; it "learns" from its behavior, anticipates the future, and responds to such anticipation. As a result, it dynamically self-organizes and adapts itself to interaction among its components internally, and adjusts to contingencies that are present in its environment externally (Byrne, 1998; Donahoe, Palmer, & Dorsel, 2004; Holland, 1995; Kauffman, 1993; Prigogine & Stengers, 1997; Waldrop, 1992) (Figure 2.1).

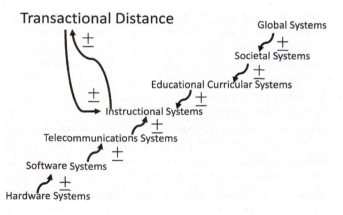

FIGURE 2.1 Causal loop diagram of a complex system representing the influence of system components on each other.

Analytic and Systemic Approaches

In recent years, administrators are paying increasing attention to studying the discrete components of colleges and universities through collecting and analyzing a massive amount of data on student behavior, the number of courses offered and taken, the time students spend in each course, and the completion rates for each course, as well as other similar information (Macfadyen, Dawson, Pardo, & Gaševic, 2014; MacNeill, Campbell, & Hawksey, 2014). While analytics sheds light on such discrete components and is necessary to bring to the fore important information for identifying and understanding the components of a complex system, decision-making also requires understanding how the behavior of each component is affecting all the others in a university. For example, if students begin to complete courses at a higher rate, what will that do to the demand for new courses in subsequent semesters or quarters? If more faculty decide to include instructional design principles in developing new courses and offer their courses through a learning management system augmented with social media, how will instructional design and technology services on a campus be able to respond to this increased demand for instructional designers and information technology support personnel?

In addition to analytical approaches for understanding the behavior of each organizational unit, a systems approach is necessary to understand the meaning of the data in terms of how professionals in different organizational components relate to each other and affect each other. Adopting a systems approach as well as an analytical method, however, requires investment in time and attention. One can see the conflict between the effort that should be put into collecting data to understand in depth each organizational unit of a university and the effort that educators, planners, and policymakers must put into creating comprehensive models of an institution in which they would illustrate the relations among various organizational units. Verma (1998) presented a thorough explanation of the characteristics of analytic and systemic approaches to planning and management and demonstrated that the analytic approach provides rigor to the process of decision-making, whereas the systemic approach offers the comprehensive vision that educators must have for the planning effort. He further asserted that the analytic approach is "strong in formal method but, it achieves this strength by discarding questions that cannot be answered rigorously" (p. 11). If taken to extreme, it leads to reducing the entire organization to a lifeless collection of departments and divisions that show up so many times in organization charts in the form of boxes that are connected with lines to each other, but they do not shed any light on how the organization functions, what its goals are, and how the community views its worth and importance. Verma went on to say: "Comprehensiveness is about recognizing the importance of preparedness, sharing, trust, loyalty, entrepreneurship, and risk-taking ability in decision-making. These are normative values that demand a theory of ethics, not criteria that can be feasibly optimized within an analytic calculus." (p. 54).

Ultimately, the solution is in striking the right balance between the rigor of analytics and the breadth of vision for being comprehensive. Verma, as well as the authors of this book, find the key to this dilemma in the American philosophy of postmodernism as conceptualized by William James (1981) (originally published in 1909). When James was composing his writings, the term post-modernism had not been coined yet. Nonetheless, we think that he showed the way to resolving multifaceted situations through the method of radical empiricism—the type of empiricism that is not dogmatic and allows for reconciliation of more than one approach for achieving useful ends. In understanding the complexity of universities, both analytical and systemic methods should be employed. These methods in combination offer a more thorough understanding of the operations of a university in its discrete organization units as well as the impact that the operation that one unit has on all the other units. System dynamics makes it possible to implement the postmodern vision of William James by combining analytical and systematic approaches to understanding the current status of universities. Also, system dynamics provides a powerful method for envisioning and planning the future of higher education. (For a detailed explanation of how system dynamics methodology and technology can be used for future planning, see Chapter 13.)

A Hierarchical Model for Technology-Based Higher Education Systems

In 1976,[1] Saba developed a hierarchical model of distance education to represent the different professionals who made up an educational television organization, as well as the subsystems and procedures that they must put in place in order to provide the necessary educational services to their students (Saba, 1976). The model consisted of eight nested levels as represented in Figure 2.2. Each of these system levels is complex in their own right, but relatively and cumulatively, they increase in complexity from the core of the model (Hardware Systems) to the outer layer (Global Systems). Over the years, the authors modified and revised this model several times to explain the idea of systems approach to distance education (Saba, 2007, 2013). The most significant changes in the model occurred in the early 1980s and throughout the 1990s when the authors were studying the theory of transactional distance and they realized that the TTD constitutes the core process of teaching and learning in the Instructional Systems Level of the hierarchical model of distance education. This was a transformative realization in our scholarship—one that led to a series of empirical experiments to verify key concepts in the TTD (Saba & Shearer, 1994). We used a dynamic systems method for conducting these studies that allowed us to understand the discrete components of the theory of transactional distance (i.e. structure, dialogue, and autonomy) as well as how each component affects the others and is affected by the others. Furthermore, the increasing use of digital media in instruction, and the growing number of students who receive their instruction via the Internet at the time convinced us that the hierarchical model of distance education could be generalized to model institutions of higher education for analyzing their current status and planning for the future.

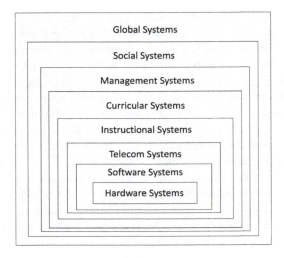

FIGURE 2.2 Components of technology-based higher education systems.

In this book, we have modified the hierarchical model of distance education to represent the components of technology-based higher education systems. These components include:

- Hardware, software, and telecommunication systems that information technology professionals put in place to connect faculty with students and enable students to communicate among each other;
- Instructional systems that faculty develop and present to students via hardware, software, and telecommunication systems;
- Curricular systems that faculty, department chairs, and deans organize to lead students to obtain a degree, a certificate, or other similar credentials;
- Management systems that faculty and administrators establish to achieve the vision and mission of their institution;
- Societal systems, such as laws and regulations that state or federal legislators enact to influence how institutions of higher education are managed; and
- Global systems that influence cultural and political conditions under which universities operate.

Elaborating on the structure and application of this model to higher education requires several preliminary explanations:

1. We understand that universities are more complex than the components and processes represented in this general model. More comprehensive representations will become necessary as educators use the proposed diagram here to design prototypes of their own institutions. Therefore, consider this model as a place to start for planning the future of your institution.

2. Each institution is unique and a general model cannot include specific academic programs and administrative structures that are in effect in each college or university. Educators should develop models that uniquely represent their organizational structure, workflows, and processes at the present time as well as those that they would like to plan for the future.

3. One may have many points of view for analyzing system levels in this model. We will introduce the professionals who make these systems work, and the ramification of the TTD for each system level in detail in the forthcoming chapters.

4. The system levels described in the model are for representational purposes, as described below:

   a. There are no clear-cut lines of demarcation between these levels as systems are not tangible entities in the mechanical sense where one component ends and the other begins. These levels consist of feedback and feedforward networks of influences and at times they overlap and may seem indivisible. In most organizations, faculty, administrators, and students play multiple roles that cross from one system level to one or more levels. This elaborate nature of human communication systems makes higher education complex and at times convoluted.

   b. The hierarchical nature of the model does not imply that one level is more important than the other. They all are equally important for the operation of an educational enterprise, as one cannot say that the lung is more important for sustaining life in the body than the heart. However, the hierarchy implies that while lower system levels influence higher levels, the higher levels influence and at times control the behavior of the lower system levels.

   c. One of the major characteristics of hierarchical complex systems is that each higher level subsumes the lower levels, and is directly or indirectly affected by all the other levels. For example, an increase in the production of digital cameras (hardware systems) in one country reduces the cost of ownership of video production equipment (management systems) and reduces the cost of production of instructional videos (software systems and instructional systems) in other countries (global systems).

   d. System levels are dynamic: they change in time. Therefore, the processes in them should be viewed as flows of influence that constantly change. Planners would be wise to collect data in regular intervals to learn about how each system level behaves in their organization to reflect the changing nature of processes in each system level.

   e. Open complex human systems consisting of faculty, students, and administrators are self-organizing and capable of unanticipated and unpredictable emergent behaviors. Because of the nonlinear property

TABLE 2.1 Summary of the Hierarchical Model of Complexity in Technology-Based Higher Education Institutions

Hardware Systems (Chapter 3)

- Operation managers, systems analysts, technicians, programmers, and administrative support personnel manage hardware systems for thousands of faculty and students in their respective institutions.
- Hardware for normal operations includes a vast number of computers and accessories including paper printers and the 3-D variety, video equipment, mobile devices, such as tablets, and smart phones, and a range of other tools, such as sensors that receive and transmit data to other hardware systems.
- All the other levels influence this system level. For example, decisions that are made at the management system level determine funding for acquisition and proper maintenance of hardware systems.
- This system level influences some of the higher order levels. For example, the hardware that is at the disposal of instructors and learners determines how instruction is created and presented to learners, thus influencing the level of transactional distance in on-campus as well as online courses.

Software Systems (Chapter 4)

- Software engineers and technicians are primarily responsible for the design, development, and operation of software systems. Professional textbook writers, including university faculty, instructional designers, graphic artists, photographers, and videographers, work at this system level as well.
- Software systems include simple email readers to sophisticated learning management, adaptive learning, and student information systems.
- All the other system levels influence this system level. For example, decisions that are made at the management and curricular system levels determine the types of software systems that are available for instructors and learners at the instructional system level. Inevitably, affordances of software systems are directly responsible for the potential rate of structure or the ability of students to engage in dialogue with the instructor. As such, software systems also directly influence other system levels in this model in many ways.

Telecommunications Systems (Chapter 6)

- Telecommunications engineers and technicians, as well as line personnel, are primarily responsible for the design, installation, maintenance, and operation of components of this system level.
- Telecommunication systems include local, regional, and global networks that link learners and instructors.
- Telecommunication systems influence what is possible to do at other system levels. For example, if learners have access to faster telecommunication services, then instructional designers can make use of richer media in their instructional projects.
- This system level is influenced by some of the others. For example, in the United States, the Federal Communications Commission at the societal system level sets the policies that govern availability and access to telecommunications services. Similarly, management of colleges and universities on each campus decides on access to and availability of telecommunication services for their students and staff.

Instructional Systems (Chapter 7)

- Faculty, instructional designers, subject matter experts, and a host of other professionals, such as programmers and graphic artists, work at this system level.

- These professionals create instructional systems that consist of courses and academic programs as well as processes and procedures that provide teaching and learning services to students.

- The theory of transactional distance explains the dynamic relationship between learner autonomy, as it is expressed by learner control, and structure, as it is expressed through instructor control during the process of teaching and learning at this system level.

- Instructional systems, in turn, influence other systems as well, such as decisions made about program offerings of a university at the curricular system level.

Curricular Systems (Chapter 9)

- Professionals who work at this system level include university deans, department chairs, and faculty.

- These professionals create and manage curricular systems that include academic courses and programs of study. They lead learners to acquire degrees, certificates, or other types of credentials, such as badges.

- Professionals who work at this system level make policy decisions that influence the program of studies for students and how these programs are sequenced, paced, and presented to learners. These decisions have a direct impact on how students shape their entire program of study and set life and employment objectives.

- Invariably, these decisions also influence some of the higher system levels, such as the expectations that employers may have from colleges and universities to fulfill their personnel requirements at the societal system level.

Management Systems (Chapter 10)

- Professionals who work at this system level make policy decisions that influence allocation of funds to instructional, telecommunications, hardware and software systems, and set the conditions under which faculty and students can use these systems.

- In consultation with university-wide governing bodies, such as academic senates, these professionals also manage the normal academic operations of a university. These operations range from assessing and modifying existing curriculum systems to implementing new curriculum systems, determining the rights and responsibilities of students, and administering faculty hiring, tenure, and promotion.

- In turn, systems operating at other levels influence the conditions under which administrators can set their policies and put them into effect. For example, societal support for higher education establishes the conditions under which levels of funding could be made available to institutions of higher education.

Societal Systems (Chapter 11)

- Legislators at the state and federal levels, government agency administrators, members of governing bodies of state boards of higher education and professional associations, as well as administrators and decision-makers of private foundations and NGOs work at this system level.

- Professionals working at this system level set policies for many functions, such as accreditation, telecommunications, copyright, and other similar functions that directly impact other system levels in this model.

(Continued)

TABLE 2.1 *continued*

- They also set policies for funding of educational systems either directly or indirectly through student loans, work-study programs, and scholarships. Decisions made at this system level influence the other system levels directly in many ways.

Global Systems (Chapter 12)

- Professionals at this level include policy- and decision-makers at the highest levels of governments throughout the world; managers and personnel of multinational corporations that publish books and develop and market hardware, and software systems; leaders and members of international organizations, professional associations, and key managers of private global educational corporations.
- International organizations, such as the United Nations and the World Bank, professional associations (e.g. International Council for Open and Distance Education) as well as a growing number of small private companies that have a global reach, such as those that offer massive open online courses (MOOCs) profoundly influence the operations of universities directly or indirectly at this system level.
- Some of the lower system levels have had a tremendous influence on global systems. For example, telecommunications systems have facilitated a rapid increase in availability of distance education programs worldwide during the last 20 years.
- World social, cultural, economic, and political conditions also influence many of the systems of this entire model. International professional organizations facilitate exchange of knowledge on how to promote technology-based education throughout the world positively, while depressed economic conditions in certain parts of the world have a negative impact on the availability of funds at the societal system level to support educational and instructional systems.

of creative human systems, certain decisions may have unexpected results. Therefore, it is necessary to periodically monitor and model the behavior of the organization as often as possible, keeping in mind that some behaviors would be surprising.

5.   Modeling your institution is a planning process as well. The process, as explained in Chapter 13, is as important as the product (i.e. the model) itself. Therefore, the value of the modeling exercise based on the system levels described below is to the extent that it involves as many stakeholders as possible. The more faculty, students, administrators, and other key players are involved in the modeling process, the model has a better chance to be actually accepted and implemented by everyone.

With these points in mind, we will begin to offer a summary of the basic structure of this model in Table 2.1, and then explain how it can be used for identifying important system components in your institution. Inevitably, you will realize that there are several components and relationships that exist in your organization that are not represented in this model. You can add them to your model as it develops.

Summary

In this chapter, we presented an overview of a hierarchical model of complexity in technology-based educational organizations, and we presented the rationale for analytic and systemic use of the model. You can use this generic model as a starting point to create a model for the levels of complexity that you observe in your university.

In the upcoming chapters, each of these system levels is examined and the implications of the TTD for each of them will be analyzed and explained.

Note

1   Dr. Gus Root, my professor and mentor at Syracuse University, greatly influenced my thinking in developing the hierarchical model of distance education.

References

Byrne, D. S. (1998). *Complexity theory and the social sciences: An introduction.* London: Routledge.

Donahoe, J. W., Palmer, D. C., and Dorsel, V. P. (2004). *Learning and complex behavior.* Richmond, MA: Ledgetop Pub.

Haines, S. G. (2000). *Systems thinking and learning.* Amherst, MA: HRD Press, Inc.

Holland, J. H. (1995). *Hidden order: How adaptation builds complexity.* Reading, MA: Addison-Wesley.

James, W. (1981). *Pragmatism.* Indianapolis, IN: Hackett.

Kauffman, S. A. (1993). *The origins of order: Self-organization and selection in evolution.* New York: Oxford University Press.

Macfadyen, L. P., Dawson, S., Pardo, A., and Gaševic, D. (2014). Embracing big data in complex educational systems: The learning analytics imperative and the policy challenge. *Research & Practice in Assessment, 9*(Winter) [EJ1062692].

MacNeill, S., Campbell, L. M., and Hawksey, M. (2014). Analytics for education. *Journal of Interactive Media in Education* (1), 7.

Prigogine, I., and Stengers, I. (1997). *The end of certainty: Time, chaos, and the new laws of nature* (1st Free Press ed.). New York: Free Press.

Saba, F. (1976). *The evolution of educational technology in Iranian education.* (PhD Unpublished Doctoral Dissertation), Syracuse University, Syracuse, NY.

Saba, F. (2007). A systems approach to theory building. In M. G. Moore (Ed.), *Handbook of distance education* (2nd ed., pp. 43–55). Mahwah, NJ: Lawrence Earlbaum.

Saba, F. (2013). Building the future: A theoretical perspective. In M. G. Moore (Ed.), *Handbook of distance education* (3rd ed., pp. 49–65). New York: Routledge.

Saba, F., and Shearer, R. L. (1994). Verifying key theoretical concepts in a dynamic model of distance education. *The American Journal of Distance Education,* 8(1), 36–59.

Verma, N. (1998). *Similarities, connections and systems: The search for a new rationality for planning and management.* Lanham, MD: Lexington Books.

Waldrop, M. M. (1992). *Complexity: The emerging science at the edge of order and chaos.* New York: Touchston.

3
HARDWARE SYSTEMS

Introduction

In the previous chapter, we presented an overview of a hierarchical model of levels of complexity in technology-based higher education organizations. The model consisted of eight system levels that are intertwined. Each level influences all the other levels and is influenced by them in varying degrees and for various reasons. These multiple and often simultaneous cause-effect relationships are numerous and specific to each institution of higher education at each moment in time. In this chapter, we will focus on the general effects of hardware systems on the academic and administrative affairs of an institution with the proviso that we cannot predict when they may occur, or what their specific effect may be on a particular institution. Faculty, administrators, students, and other stakeholders that are closely associated with an institution are best equipped to anticipate such effects, make a judgment if they are desirable or not in their particular situation, and devise methods, practices, and procedures to amplify or mitigate them. The case study in this chapter will further demonstrate how the acquisition of a hardware system impacted the operations and functions of a community college.

Professionals

Colleges and universities rely on the expertise of staff with advanced technical skills to manage their technology infrastructures. The complexity of these installations requires the expertise of operation managers, systems analysts, technicians, programmers, and administrative support personnel to keep them in working order. These professionals provide the variety of information and communication services that faculty, students, and administrators have come to expect throughout the academic year. Chief information officers are responsible for managing vast technology systems that consist of millions of dollars' worth of equipment ranging from advanced high-speed, super computers to video-conferencing facilities, smart classrooms, and specialized labs, each of which is configured for a different research, development, administrative, instructional, or community service purpose.

Implications of the TTD for Hardware Systems

Adding new equipment to the technology infrastructure of institutions of higher education is a multibillion-dollar market. IDC, an information technology market research firm, pegged the expenditures in 2015 to be $6.6 billion (IDC Government Insights, 2015). Despite billions of dollars of investment in information technology, neither the cost of education has decreased nor the quality of instruction has dramatically improved. Hardware systems have been deployed to support classroom instruction, but not to provide an optimal level of transactional distance for each individual learner through enabling instructors and administrators to dynamically respond to the academic needs of individual learners.

DeMillo (2012, p. 7) asserted that deployment of information technology in support of classroom instruction based on the current lecture model is doomed to fail. He said:

> The classroom is the handmaiden of a factory model of higher education, and the colleges that are truly strategically focused are already abandoning that model. Their technology investments will be aimed at reinventing education. Traditional universities are incumbents in an era of rapid change and new competitors, and the future is seldom bright for incumbents. Simply adopting the trappings of new technology has seldom been enough to save incumbents from marginalization and eventual extinction. Borders and Montgomery Ward were both technological innovators. But they were also incumbents. Their technology investments continued unabated until they shuttered their stores.

Although the authors do not share the pessimistic view of DeMillo in the case of all incumbents, his cautionary note must be heeded by all those who are involved in making strategic decisions for institutions of higher education. Adopting new hardware systems in support of the preindustrial model of teaching will not meet the needs of students who are preparing to live in the postindustrial era. Except in a few cases where universities use adaptive learning systems, instructional use of technology provides undifferentiated instruction to learners who have different academic backgrounds and learning preferences. Using hardware systems to mass produce and disseminate instruction limits the effectiveness of hardware systems. Mirriahi, Vaid, and Burns (2015, p. 1) pointed towards a general "lack of attention to the pedagogical affordances of technology when adoption decisions are made by instructors" and highlighted the need for leaders in universities to establish ways and means of promoting among faculty the "benefits technology-enabled teaching and learning can bring to advance educationally rich flexible learning opportunities."

Effective Use of Hardware Systems

There is nothing inherent in information technology to lead a university to achieve its academic and administrative goals. How educators design and implement instructional and management systems makes hardware technologies effective or useless. As we will show in the case study for this chapter, adopting hardware technologies in an institution could set in motion many causal effects. Only a clear and purposeful academic plan may result in maximizing desired consequences and minimizing unwanted outcomes. A remarkable example of effective application of hardware systems by educators is their academically purposeful use of smart phones and tablets to develop innovative learning and teaching strategies for students in and outside of the classroom (Berge & Muilenburg, 2013). These strategies have often involved novel means of inquiry that have enhanced learner engagement, promoted exploratory learning, and facilitated social interaction. Hamm, Saltsman, Jones, Baldridge, and Perkins (2013, p. 181) asserted that mobile learning affords more autonomy to the learner and seriously challenges the idea of classroom as the only place in which learning is maximized and the idea of the instructor as the sole source of authority for instructional information. Compton (2013, p. 12) posited six ways in which mobile learning strategies support students:

1. Contingent learning, allowing learners to respond and react to the environment and changing experiences;
2. Situated learning, in which learning takes place in the surroundings applicable to the subject at hand;
3. Authentic learning, with the task directly related to the immediate learning goals;
4. Context-aware learning, in which learning is informed by the history and the environment;
5. Personalized learning, customized for each unique learner in terms of abilities, interests, and preferences; and
6. Ubiquitous learning, in which the use of computers, as well as other communication and sensor devices are integrated into the daily life of a learner.

These instructional design factors are effective when they contribute to a learning environment in which each learner participates in:

• Setting his or her learning goals;
• Deciding on how to achieve them; and

- Determining if s/he has achieved her or his learning goals in a dynamic relationship with learning objectives and strategies that are structured by the instructor.

For learning to meet the criteria of the TTD, purposeful learner autonomy must be balanced with goal-oriented structure by the instructor to obtain an optimal level of transactional distance. Efforts similar to identifying pedagogical applications of mobile learning are needed when new technologies are adopted for teaching and learning.

Virtual reality (VR) and augmented reality (AR) are two examples of technologies that are increasingly deployed in university teaching and learning now. Research in VR/AR is still embryonic; however, recent scholarship has shown that they have specific applications in science, technology, engineering, and mathematics education (Delello, McWhorter, & Camp, 2015; Martín-Gutiérrez, Fabiani, Benesova, Meneses, & Mora, 2015; Rizov & Rizova, 2015).

Imagining the immersive learning environment of the future, Cavanaugh (2017) pictured Peter the student in year 2025:

> Peter is ready to attend class. He finds that the learning experience is equally immersive. Through state-of-the-art real presence, each student interacts with other learners and the faculty member. It's as if Peter's living room has turned into a holodeck. Course content is fully immersive, so he is virtually present during the building of the pyramids, or the Gettysburg battle, or Martin Luther King's "I Have a Dream" speech.

Immersive technologies could be enhanced with practical quantum computers that according to *MIT Technology Review* magazine are within reach in about five to ten years (Juskalian, 2017). What's more, with computing powers that are not practical today, quantum systems would provide for learning environments in which matching learner traits with instructional treatments become routine and easily accessible to instructors and learners. Learners would be able to exercise autonomy commensurate to their aptitude and optimize transactional distance in relation to the learning tasks seamlessly when ordinary computers are linked to quantum systems. Other applications of quantum computers to education will undoubtedly lead to practices that cannot even be envisaged today. What is certain, however, is that they will have profound effects on how knowledge is created, stored, retrieved, and used globally by millions of faculty, students, and administrators. The question will always be: How can educators get ahead of the growth curve in technology, and conceptualize its applications for teaching and learning?

Some contemporary examples could be replicated in the future for making use of high-end technological developments. By establishing cooperatives and consortia, universities have been able to bring together the expertise and specialties of several organizations, and access unique facilities as near as a homeland security lab next door or as satellite as far as outer space. These cooperative arrangements have made access to remote physical facilities available to students that are unique, expensive, or out of immediate geographic reach (Lahoud & Krichen, 2010). Learners are either manipulating instruments remotely or simulating certain experiments on a super computer in a safe mode before conducting the actual experiment in a real physical situation. NASA, for example, is assisting students in several universities to launch mini satellites dubbed as CubeSats to explore fundamental questions regarding the formation of the universe (NASA, 2015). Sharing such unique facilities not only provide access to a wide variety of hardware systems to students for learning purposes, it reduces the cost for each participating institution to establish highly specialized and expensive physical facilities of their own. A primary impact of the use of distributed learning environments and facilities by students and faculty is further decentralization of educational institutions. Institutions are less defined and recognized by their physical location and more by their brand, programs of study, and virtual learning environments.

Smaller, Cheaper, Faster, and Ubiquitous

At the consumer end of the spectrum, ordinary professional hardware systems are destined to become smaller, less expensive, and more widely available. Over 50 years ago, Gordon Moore, co-founder of Intel Corporation, predicated that the number of transistors in an integrated circuit would roughly double every two years. The professional and consumer electronic industries have demonstrated Moore's law in action by placing less expensive and more powerful devices in the hands of learners and educators every year. Meanwhile, Jonathan Koomey of Stanford University predicted that every year and a half devices would need less battery power by a factor of two to operate. In the years ahead, educators and learners will be able to afford more powerful personal information and communication devices at less cost. Before the turn of the century, universities maintained general-purpose computer labs for their students in many departments, including in-campus libraries. As communication devices have become portable, faculty, students, and administrators are increasingly using their own hardware on and off campus for academic and professional purposes. Ubiquity and mobility of information and communication devices decrease the need in universities to maintain general-purpose computer labs. Instead, they will be able to place new technologies in the hands of students that may not be affordable by individuals yet.

A current example of these devices is high-end industrial 3-D printers and robots. Students in several institutions of higher education are experimenting with additive manufacturing, developing art projects, and making objects for specific learning purposes using 3-D printers (Enis, 2015; Harris & Cooper, 2015; Martin, Bowden, & Merrill, 2014). They also design and build new robotic tools or experiment with advanced robots in disciplines related to science, technology, engineering, mathematics, industrial design, manufacturing, artificial intelligence, and linguistics, to name a few (Bianco, 2014; Bos & Smith, 2015).

Future consumer technologies will not only be cheaper, smaller, portable, ubiquitous, and distributed, they will be introduced to the market at a faster rate, too. Amirault (2015, p. 2) referred to this phenomenon as technology transience. He stated: "When technology transience is considered, we are looking at how specific incarnations of technology come and go, the length of time they are in existence, and their use within a given historical context." Because of the accelerating pace of development and marketization of new technologies, educational leaders will be facing difficult choices in selecting and deploying hardware systems in their institutions. Amirault (2015, p. 8) acknowledged the complexity of technology selection in the future and posed several strategic questions regarding procuring technology:

> More complex issues regarding technology transience apply to instructional design at the program and institutional level. How should programs be designed for resilience within a technology transient setting to minimize constant program revision? How should decisions be made on the choice of technologies to include both as the subject of instruction and as a delivery mechanism for instruction? How does an institution keep ahead of the technology curve, ensuring that the design of courses keeps students' skills current? How are costs kept under control during technological change? And how does an institution best predict if the next technology innovation (e.g., wearable computers) genuinely presages changes in how tomorrow's learners will learn and interact with subject matter content, or simply be a passing fad?

Responding to these questions will make the role of educational leaders in defining the future mission and vision of their institutions more crucial than ever before.

Summary

Information and communication technologies are smaller and cheaper, and are widely available with powerful features. However, billions of dollars of investment in hardware technology has neither brought down the cost of education nor helped students to reduce the time that it takes for them to achieve their academic goals and complete a degree program. In addition, the implementation of hardware technologies has had many unanticipated, and even undesirable effects when educators have installed systems without considering their impact on various levels of their organization. In the case study that follows, multiple impacts of adopting a hardware system in a community college are illustrated.

In the next chapter, we will discuss how software systems influence educational institutions and enable faculty and administrators to determine the level of transactional distance for each individual learner.

Case Study 3.1 Adoption of Video Capture Technology in Lake Community College

Lake Community College (LCC) is located in the heart of a mid-western state. In recent years, similar to many other community colleges, the demand for its courses increased tremendously. This was the result of many factors, one being increased tuition rates in four-year institutions in the state. Students by the droves looked towards LCC for taking their entry-level undergraduate courses. To respond to this rising demand, the provost in consultation with the college president decided to invest in a video capture hardware technology (cameras, lights, microphones, large screen projectors, and micro-processing systems) to stream some of the popular courses on the Web. He made this decision after seeing this system exhibited at a national conference and attending a presentation by one of his colleagues in a community college in California, whose faculty have been using the system for a year. However, neither the provost nor the president consulted the instructors who were the intended users of the system about their decision. The director of the information technology services (ITS) was informed about the decision, once it had already been made and the purchase order for acquiring the system had already been issued.

Once the system was installed, the provost reasoned, new students coming to LCC did not have to be on campus to attend a lecture, overloading classrooms. They could go on the Web and see lectures live, while the instructors were presenting them, or replay their recorded versions.

Eventually, the video capture system was installed in three experimental classrooms and the instructors were encouraged to use these "smart classrooms" to offer their courses for on–campus students while their lectures were streamed online to accommodate those students for whom there was no room on campus.

Case Analysis

The primary factor causing an increase in enrollment in LCC was the rising tuitions at four-year institutions that were geographically close to LCC. State legislators made this decision at the Societal Systems Level. However, their decision had a direct impact on LCC, an institution that was not even the subject of the decision of the state legislators!

Soon after the contractor installed the video capture system (Hardware Systems Level) in the smart classrooms, the campus technical staff of the

ITS realized that the decision to acquire the system at the Management Systems Level would increase their workload. They had to make sure that the system was in operational condition when the instructors wanted to use them, and they had to help the instructors to use its various features. Some early adopters among the faculty from different departments had already scheduled to use the smart classrooms, and the ITS staff had to provide them with technical support on a routine basis. The ITS staff was requested from their director to send a memo to the provost to inform him that they needed additional staff members to respond effectively to this new duty. The ITS director sent an email to the provost informing him of the lack of staff time to adequately support the video capture system. She also attached a memorandum to the email to the effect that the decision to offer courses via a video capture system had also increased the demand for additional software applications (Software Systems Level). Faculty from different departments decided to augment their courses with software applications that could be integrated into teaching their courses now that they had access to state-of-the-art equipment (Instructional Systems Level). Some of these software systems, such as Microsoft PowerPoint were readily available. However, the CAD-CAM application needed to teach one of the very popular engineering courses required more funds to be acquired. This software acquisition also had a long-term effect on the budget of ITS, as the license for the CAD-CAM software application needed to be renewed every year. The software company also informed the ITS that there would be semi-annual upgrades to the software for an additional fee. In a subsequent meeting with the provost, the director of ITS furthermore informed the provost that the use of the video streaming on an unprecedented level might eventually put additional pressure on the Internet bandwidth (Telecommunication Systems Level) that is available to the campus. The director of ITS asked the provost to consider adding more bandwidth to the LCC Internet backbone or joining the Internet2 consortium.

In the meantime, the instructional designer who was assigned to assist the instructors in the use of the smart classrooms informed her supervisor that none of the faculty who signed up for the use of the equipment knew how to effectively present their lecture in front of a live audience as well as for a live video camera. They did not know how to present in front of the classroom while attempting to have some eye contact with their online students. Some of the faculty looked clumsy on video and were in real need of training about how to handle the microphone and the multiple video cameras. In addition, some faculty brought their personal computers to the smart classroom on which they had loaded their slide presentations. However, when they wanted to use the slide presentations, they usually ran into considerable difficulty in connecting their PCs to the video capture system. The process was not intuitive, and software configurations needed to be manipulated to recognize their PCs and put their video signal through the system. More importantly, according to the instructional designer, the faculty suddenly became cognizant of the fact that presenting in the smart classroom while using the video capture system required them to be much more prepared and organized compared to presenting in a standard classroom. This required additional preparation time on their part, as well as coordinating with the technical staff and conferring with the instructional designer about how to improve the design of their courses. Some faculty already had stated learning objectives for their individual lessons, but the instructional designer observed that not all the learning objectives were supported by the content of the courses. She also noticed that there were test items for which there were no learning objectives nor was there adequate coverage in the course content. The course on the CAD–CAM also required students to complete specific lab work, but the rubric by which students were graded for the lab session was not shared with them. The instructional designer asked her supervisor for time to provide further training to faculty about how to redesign their courses and streamline lesson objectives with the content of each lesson and the test items in the course mid–term and final exams (Instructional Systems Level).

Another issue at the Instructional Systems Level had direct influence on the Management Systems and Societal Systems in which LCC operated. Since students could preview the captured lectures more than once, the faculty also became concerned about copyright issues (Societal Systems Level). They demanded from their department chairs additional pay not only for the royalty on multiple Web streaming of their class presentations but also for the additional time that it required each faculty to prepare for the video capture technology (Curricular Systems Level). Some instructors were also advocating a discussion of the reuse of their lectures with the faculty union representative on campus in an effort to revise their contract in the upcoming salary negotiations with the chancellor of the community college system (Societal Systems Level).

While these events were transpiring, the president of LCC became the host of a group of higher education administrators from the People's Republic of China. The Chinese guests were particularly interested in the engineering course that taught students how to use CAD–CAM software and were wondering if students in China could also attend this course because it was available on the Web (Global Systems Level). After the visit of the guests from China, the president of LCC organized a committee consisting of the provost, the chair of the engineering department, and the faculty member who taught the course on the use of the CAD-CAM software application. The meeting grew to be longer than the president had expected. In addition to the obvious issue of the language of the course, the committee members were concerned about the support from LCC that students could receive who were literally halfway across the world. A major question was how ITS personnel would provide learner support in Mandarin to students in China. Thus, a relatively simple decision by the provost to acquire and install a video capture technology, a decision that should have been limited to the Hardware Systems Level in the proposed model here, had direct impact on all of the other system levels.

This case shows how a decision at the Societal Systems Level to increase tuition in four-year colleges impacted enrollments at a community college and how the decision to acquire a video capture system to accommodate new incoming students had a cascading effect on other system levels of the college. It also illustrated how the professional lives of faculty, as well as staff technicians, and the instructional designer involved in the project were directly influenced by such a decision. The network of influences presented in this case indicated the complexity of institutions of higher education and how various system levels in such complex systems affect each other and are affected by each other. A change at one system level can have profound and enduring effects on other system levels.

References

Amirault, R. (2015). Technology transience and the challenges it poses to higher education. *The Quarterly Review of Distance Education, 16*(2), 1–17.

Berge, Z. L., and Muilenburg, L. Y. (Eds.). (2013). *Handbook of mobile learning.* New York: Routledge.

Bianco, A. (2014). Basic robotics in the classroom. *Technology & Engineering Teacher, 73*(7), 32–38.

Bos, B., and Smith, S. (2015). The power of educational robotics as an integrated STEM learning experience in teacher preparation programs. *Journal of College Science Teaching, 44*(5), 42–47.

Cavanaugh, J. (2017). Alchemy, innovation, and learning in 2025. *EDUCAUSE Review.* Retrieved from http://er.educause.edu/articles/2017/1/alchemy-innovation-and-learning-in-2025.

Compton, H. (2013). A historical overview of m-learning: Toward learner-centered education. In Z. L. Berge and L. Y. Muilenburg (Eds.), *Handbook of mobile learning* (pp. 3–14). New York: Routledge.

Delello, J. A., McWhorter, R. R., and Camp, K. M. (2015). Integrating augmented reality in higher education: A multidisciplinary study of student perceptions. *Journal of Educational Multimedia and Hypermedia, 24*(3), 209–233.

DeMillo, R. A. (2011). *Abelard to Apple: The fate of American colleges and universities.* Cambridge, MA: MIT Press

Enis, M. (2015, May 1). UMass Amherst opens 3-D print center. *Library Journal, 140,* 18–18, 12/13p.

Hamm, S., Saltsman, G., Jones, B., Baldridge, S., and Perkins, S. (2013). A mobile pedagogy approach for transforming learners and faculty. In Z. L. Berge and L. Y. Muilenburg (Eds.), *Handbook of mobile learning* (pp. 176–186). New York: Routledge.

Harris, H., and Cooper, C. (2015). Make room for makerspace. *Computers in Libraries, 35*(2), 5–9.

IDC Government Insights. (2015). U.S. higher education institutions expected to spend $6.6 billion on it in 2015, according to IDC government insights [Press release]. Retrieved from www.idc.com/getdoc.jsp?containerId=prUS25608415.

Juskalian, R. (2017). Practical quantum computers advances at Google, Intel, and several research groups indicate that computers with previously unimaginable power are finally within reach. Retrieved from www.technologyreview.com/s/603495/10-breakthrough-technologies-2017-practical-quantum-computers/.

Lahoud, H. A., and Krichen, J. P. (2010). Networking labs in the online environment: Indicators for success. *The Journal of Technology Studies, 36*(2), 31–40.

Martin, R. L., Bowden, N. S., and Merrill, C. (2014). 3D printing. *Technology & Engineering Teacher, 73*(8), 30–35.

Martín-Gutiérrez, J., Fabiani, P., Benesova, W., Meneses, M. D., and Mora, C. E. (2015). Augmented reality to promote collaborative and autonomous learning in higher education. *Computers in Human Behavior, 51*(2015), 752–761.

Mirriahi, N., Vaid, B. S., and Burns, D. P. (2015). Meeting the challenge of providing flexible learning opportunities: Considerations for technology adoption amongst academic staff. *Canadian Journal of Learning and Technology, 41*(1), 1–16.

NASA. (2015). NASA announces university CubeSat space mission candidates. Retrieved from www.nasa.gov/content/nasa-announces-sixth-round-of-cubesat-space-mission-candidates.

Rizov, T., and Rizova, E. (2015). Augmented reality as a teaching tool in higher education. *International Journal of Cognitive Research in Science, Engineering and Education, 3*(1), 7–16.

4

SOFTWARE SYSTEMS

Introduction

In the last chapter, we focused on hardware systems and how they potentially affect the performance of the other system levels. This chapter is about the revolution in software systems from analog to digital communication that ushered in the era of direct communication with each individual learner and made personalizing instruction potentially possible. In the last five years, more elaborate learning management systems, powerful adaptive learning systems, use of social media for instructional purposes, and application of videoconferencing tools for teaching and learning increased the potential for interaction between the instructor and the learner. These software technologies afforded the possibility for faculty to structure their courses better and respond in creative ways to learner autonomy. Administrators also have been using various types of databases and social media to communicate with students regarding the requirements for administrative structure. The ability of administrators to increase the frequency and improve the quality of communicating with learners is an important aspect of the TTD. The concept of administrative structure is presented in Chapter 8.

The case study for this chapter indicates the challenges that educators face in implementing software systems that support learners and instructors.

Professionals

Numerous professionals contribute to the design, development, production, evaluation, and distribution of software systems worldwide. Among them are software engineers, designers, and programmers who collaborate with writers, graphic designers, and videographers to provide a plethora of platforms and applications. Smaller and more affordable hardware systems have also enabled the faculty to create their own instructional materials and share them with students and peers. Students also have joined the ranks of educational software creators who publish their materials on the Internet.

Implications of the TTD for Software Systems

Many classes of software systems have had a profound impact on responding to the needs of individual learners in recent years. While the primary focus in this chapter will be on learning management systems (LMSs) and adaptive learning systems (ALSs), the impact of digital media on textbooks cannot be overlooked, as it has been transformative. In an article titled *The Object Formerly Known as Textbook*, Jeffrey Young (2013) wrote in the *Chronicle of Higher Education*:

> Textbook publishers argue that their newest digital products shouldn't even be called "textbooks." They're really software programs built to deliver a mix of text, videos, and homework assignments. But delivering them is just the beginning. No old-school textbook was able to be customized for each student in the classroom. The books never graded the homework. And while they contain sample exam questions, they couldn't administer the test themselves.

The ever-increasing type and variety of interactive learning materials have had a profound effect on enabling learners to take an active role in their education. Even in highly structured faculty-centered, lecture-oriented class sessions, learners conduct searches online about concepts and ideas that are set forward by the instructor or they communicate with each other via social media while the lecture is in progress. Classroom response systems in some large lecture halls have also made the instructors' presentations more interactive and open to learner participation. Nevertheless, learning management systems and adaptive learning systems have had the most potential impact on institutions of higher education to move their instructional activities to a technology-based practice.

Learning Management Systems

Learning management systems in their original versions were faculty-centered and primarily mimicked instructional activities that were possible in the confines of a classroom. They offered high structure and low autonomy. However, LMSs have evolved to provide "configurability" by instructors so that they can regulate instructor control and provide more control to learners to exercise autonomy. Wang, Doll, Deng, Park, and Yang (2013) conducted a study of the effects of the perception of configurability of LMSs on teaching practices of faculty. Configurability was defined as the extent to which faculty could:

1. Change the feel and look of the LMS in the course website;
2. Establish communicative mechanisms among students or between students and faculty; and
3. Load or modify course materials on the system.

Their study supported its primary hypothesis that the greater the LMS's configurability, the more the LMS is used by faculty to help implement the following seven principles of effective teaching:

1. Encourage contacts between students and faculty;
2. Develop reciprocity and cooperation among students;
3. Use active learning techniques;
4. Give prompt feedback to students;
5. Emphasize the importance of the time students spend on learning tasks;
6. Communicate high expectations from learners; and
7. Respect diverse talents and ways of learning among learners.

LMSs have also included videoconferencing, social media, text messaging, interface with mobile devices, and other similar capabilities that enhance interactivity among learners and between faculty and students. Hill, Domizi, Kim, and Kim (2013) presented a framework for negotiated distance learning environments (NDLE), which "are designed to facilitate the negotiation of leaning goals and promote learner autonomy" (p. 372). Based on constructivist pedagogy, an NDLE offers a variety of tools and resources to:

> (a) store, locate, and share information and resources, (b) engage in higher-order and critical thinking by providing a problem-solving context or virtual world, and (c) communicate and network with peers, instructors, and other members in a community of practice.
>
> *(p. 376)*

Discussing modes of interaction, Friesen and Kuskis (2013) provided a comprehensive analysis in which the concept of interaction, particularly in technology-based educational systems, included:

• Student–institution interaction in which students use a variety of Web 2.0 affordances to interact with the university administration (e.g. the office of the registrar), the campus bookstore, the library, as well as technology and academic help–desk services.

- Learner-teacher interaction in which, in addition to the usual class maintenance communication, various technologies provide the means for enhancing dialogue through social, teaching, and cognitive presence.
- Student-student interaction in which the potential for collaboration and
  cooperative learning is enhanced beyond what is possible in the confines of
  the classroom. These interactions are facilitated by the idea of social constructivism for deep learning when the learner is enabled to see as "another
  would see" a situation.
- Student-content interaction in which students in various types of software environments can interact with the system to pursue a topic through
  hyperlinks, or set the conceptual or language difficulty level for a particular content area. In highly interactive environments, learners can take
  an active role by manipulating, rewriting, redesigning, and redeveloping
  content or becoming engaged in a simulation, a game; or being immersed
  in a virtual world.
- Teacher-content interaction in which, depending on the legal limitations,
  instructors can adapt or modify content for their learners, or contextualize
  the content for a particular learning scenario. This would also include using LMSs more creatively as tools become more powerful yet increasingly
  cumbersome to use.
- Teacher-teacher interaction in which instructors rely on knowledgeable
  peers—not necessarily experts—to receive timely suggestions and information as well as discuss outstanding issues online by forming active communities of practice.

Despite the fact that progress in software development has added tremendous
potential for these types of interactions in the recent past, Friesen and Kuskis
(2013) concluded that "In the 21st century, we are doubly challenged to identify
myriad forms and potentialities of interaction, and to understand the equally
complex possibilities for their effective combination" (p. 366). While the authors
acknowledged that the quest for simple solution in finding the right combination
is not possible since each "institution, discipline, region, and user group is certain
to continue to develop unique cultural practices and expectations related to their
needs for and use of interaction in its myriad forms," they still called for researchers to "get the mixture right" between interaction and independence.

As we have presented in previous chapters, however, transactional distance
is different for each individual learner, at each moment of learning during the
course of an educational program while instruction is in progress in real time.
While there may be a "right mix" for the learning of some predetermined
objectives for a group of learners, from the perspective of the TTD, the "right
mix" for interaction is negotiated dynamically in real time as the teaching
and learning process continues for each individual learner at each moment of

instruction/learning. Theoretically, there is an unlimited potential number of combinations for the types of interactions described in the analysis by Friesen and Kuskis (2013) during the course of an instructional session (see the discussion on aptitude treatment interaction analysis in Chapter 5). Such combinations cannot be determined prior to the moment of learning. In a complex adaptive and self-organized system of learning, the right combination is determined progressively through the emerging behavior of the learner when it is matched dynamically with the relevant properties of a software system at the moment that prehension becomes comprehension. This is while several types of interactions (e.g. instructor–learner interaction, learner–content interaction, or instructor–instructor interaction) might be in effect at the moment of transition from prehension to comprehension. (See Instructional Systems Level in Chapter 7 for a more extensive explanation of the concept of prehension and its transition into comprehension as an emergent property of learning.)

Because of this complex and dynamic nature of learning, LMSs have evolved over the years to include an increasingly sophisticated number of features. Perhaps the most important feature for the TTD is technologies that make learning systems adaptive to the profile of the learner.

Adaptive Learning Systems

Because of the centrality and importance of adaptive learning systems in the implementation of the TTD, the next chapter is devoted to a detailed discussion of their pedagogical and technological underpinnings. It is sufficient here to say that creating learning environments that respond to individual learner characteristics is becoming increasingly possible through the use of ALSs. These software systems use one or a combination of statistical analytics, and artificial intelligence with principles of neuroscience, and cognitive science to present instruction in multimedia and hypermedia for personalizing instruction. Because these core technologies enable ALSs to respond to the individual differences of learners, they could pave the way for the implementation of the TTD in institutions of higher education. However, their true impact is mitigated by the traditional management system prevalent in most institutions (see Chapters 9 and 10 for these mitigation factors). These dynamic software systems sit in contrast to the first generation of LMSs that were developed to mimic static traditional lecture-based classroom instruction. In most first-generation LMSs, the flow of information was unidirectional from the instructor to the learner and the chance for influencing the process of learning and teaching through the ebb and flow of learner dialogue in real time was at a minimum or entirely nonexistent. Currently, either stand-alone ALSs or their implementation in tandem with an LMS augmented with social media software and built-in videoconferencing capabilities have made it possible to put the principles of the TTD into practice for thousands of students.

Summary

Software systems have moved from simple email readers and Web browsers in the 1990s to more advanced applications with multiple features and affordances. They have placed a plethora of information at the disposal of learners both in open access and proprietary repositories. Through the use of advanced LMSs and ALSs, it is becoming increasingly possible to respond to individual learner characteristics and optimize transactional distance for each student. However, similar to hardware systems, software systems do not live in a vacuum. How educators implement and use them affect other system levels of a university in multiple ways.

In the case study for this chapter, it will be demonstrated how software systems affect the lives of professionals and systems they use at various levels of a technology-based institution of higher education.

In the next chapter, we will present a detailed discussion of the technology and pedagogy of ALSs.

Case Study 4.1 Centralizing Learning Management Systems in Middle State University

Since the advent of LMSs, Middle State University took a decentralized approach to their selection, adoption, and use. Departments at the vanguard of the use of information technology for teaching and learning selected their own LMSs and, in certain cases, more than two or three LMSs were in use in some academic programs.

This approach was exciting during the early years of the emergence of LMSs. Early adopters among the faculty were able to examine the LMS of their choice, receive help from the embryonic campus information technology unit to load it on a server, and work with students to ensure they could use it properly. However, with the passage of time, many of the original 200+ LMS companies went out of business; some of the more successful companies in the marketplace bought the smaller ones and took their software out of the market. Also, new LMS companies emerged that had more advanced software applications. These cutting-edge LMSs were available in a software distribution model in which the applications were hosted by a vendor or service provider (software as a service or SaaS). Also, they had capabilities for configuring the application for a variety of users ranging from system administrators to faculty, students, instructional designers, and even course reviewers from accreditation agencies. They also offered more sophisticated course development features with multimedia capabilities; imbedded discussion forums and email servers; evaluation and grading options; and a host of other affordances, such as intelligent agents.

In the meantime, a greater number of faculty had become interested in using an LMS and were asking their colleagues, who already had some experience with these types of applications, about which one to select for their courses. Invariably, they were finding out that although there were several open source software applications that could be downloaded and used for free, the cost of using a commercial LMS in an SaaS model had increased tremendously and had gone beyond the means of a single department to purchase and sustain. Some software applications required interoperability with third-party applications for guarding against plagiarism and grading student assignments that put them beyond the ability of a faculty to program and use. New issues, such as keeping servers secure on campus and meeting regulations, such as the provisions of the Family Educational Rights and Privacy Act (FERPA) and Americans with Disabilities Act (ADA), had also emerged. These considerations made configuring, managing, and sustaining an LMS a full-time job. Gone were the days that a few enthusiasts could sustain an LMS as a side job!

Issues related to the use of LMSs were also percolating up to the deans and through them to the office of the vice president for academic affairs (VPAA). The VPAA had supported the decentralized approach to adopt and use LMSs from the outset, and had backed the ad hoc efforts of faculty to acquire the necessary servers to put them to use. He also was proactive in extending telecommunication services to faculty offices and assigning information technology and instructional design assistance to them to develop and present as many courses online as possible. But now the director of the campus instructional development and technology (IDT) services was increasingly complaining to the VPAA about the variety of LMSs on campus and the need for coordinating and streamlining unless more resources were put into supporting so many different servers, platforms, and formats that were in use across the campus. In a word, the IDT director intimated to the VPAA that the situation had become "crazy!"

The administrative staff members of the university were not the only ones who were becoming concerned about the increasing popularity, variety, and use of LMSs on campus. A few members of the campus Academic Senate (AS) had also requested time from the president of the AS to discuss the issue of the selection, maintenance, and use of LMSs in a full meeting of the Senate and develop new policies and procedures for their use on campus. In fact, in a previous meeting of the AS a few months ago, one of the senators put a motion on the floor to establish a subcommittee to study the issue and report the results back to the full membership. The motion was carried by an overwhelming majority of the senators. Once the result of the work of the subcommittee on LMSs was ready, the AS devoted a full session to this issue and invited the VPAA to participate in the special session on LMSs. Realizing that this issue touches several campus-wide divisions, the VPAA invited directors of the instructional development and technology services, the information technology division, the head campus librarian, as well as the associate vice president for security and risk management to participate in this meeting.

Rarely the rosters in an AS meeting were so long for senators to speak on an issue. There were at least five senators who were not in favor of using any LMSs. The senate president called on one of them to present the views of the group. Senator Luddite took the floor and accused the attending administrators of caving to corporate interests in adopting LMSs. Having read an earlier draft of the subcommittee report on LMSs that called for centralizing their use, Dr. Luddite also alleged that centralizing the use of LMSs would drastically reduce academic freedom of the faculty. In fact, she said, "it is best to stay away from these technological gimmicks that take power away from instructors and allow faculty to be faculty. Hell no, we won't be replaced by a robot called an LMS. Down with LMSs, long-live faculty!" Her presentation was followed by the applause of at least half of the senate members present. However, it was difficult for the VPAA to ascertain if the ovation was for the powerful oratorical style of Professor Luddite or the merits of her argument. The vice president was neither interested in caving to the "corporate interest" nor in usurping power of the faculty and replacing them with robots, he thought. After a few other short and long speeches in favor of and against LMSs in which senators either praised or condemned their use, finally the chair of the subcommittee on LMSs had a chance to present her report.

Dr. Amiable, chair of the subcommittee on LMSs, was a rare individual. She was trusted by most of the senators. Also, although her academic area was English literature, she had taken the time to earn a Master's degree in instructional design and educational technology as well.

She reported that the subcommittee had worked diligently over the last two months. Their efforts included:

- Speaking to faculty in several departments who had and had not used an LMS;
- Discussing the issue with a broad spectrum of stakeholders consisting of the head librarian, director and staff of the information technology division, director and staff of the instructional development and

technology services, deans of the colleges of education, and computer science as well as extended and professional studies, and the staff of the office of distance education;

- Taking a field trip to a nearby community college, which had implemented a centralized LMS for the entire campus; and
- Attending a professional conference and speaking with several vendors representing the leading LMSs in the market.

After completing these activities, the committee had spent several hours deliberating about their observations and findings and had concluded that given:

- The increasing complexity of LMSs;
- The increasing frequency of upgrades of LMSs by vendors;
- The need for interoperability with central campus databases, for data, such as student enrollments in specific classes, student grades, and daily attendance;
- The obligation of the university for keeping student data secure and observing regulations regarding FERPA, ADA, and Copyright Law of the United States;
- The necessity for providing a uniform training for faculty and students;
- The requirement for offering help to faculty and students on a 24/7 basis;
- The necessity of observing standardized instructional design elements in all courses, such as specific sections in a syllabus, stating course and lesson objectives, specifying instructional and learning activities that would enable the learners to achieve course and lesson objectives, and evaluation practices to ascertain that learners have achieved the course objectives; and
- The need to maximize collaborative learning among faculty regarding how to use an LMS in their respective disciplines; and whether it is best to adopt a single LMS for the entire campus.

Furthermore, the subcommittee recommended that the information technology division and the instructional development and technology services, as well as the campus library, collaborate to complete the selection phase and the implementation phase for a new campus-wide LMS.

The selection phase should bring in the input of a wide group of users, including deans, department chairs, faculty members, and students to ensure that a broad buy-in occurs during the implementation phase and the entire project would not be derailed because of lack of interest.

The subcommittee also indicated that during the implementation phase, in cooperation with deans and department chairs, a strategic plan should be developed for migrating courses from the old LMSs to the new one. The plan should specify the priority for transferring courses and the time that is needed for such migration to take place. Porting courses to the new LMS would be a major consideration for faculty who teach general education courses. The students in these courses would be faced with yet another new interface and may complain to the faculty about the confusion that launching a new LMS would create. It is important that the migration plan would include a public information campaign to keep the undergraduate students informed about the impending changes.

In summary, the strategic plan should also include the following:

- A thorough review of third-party software applications that some departments have been using in conjunction with their old LMSs to decide which must be retained or discarded;
- A review of learning tools interoperability (LTI) standards and their integration with the new LMS;
- Establishment of a training program for faculty, staff, and help desk personnel to become proficient in the use of the new LMS;
- Launching of a public information campaign to keep faculty, students, library staff, deans, department chairs, and other stakeholders abreast of the progress in implementation of the LMS and the changeover of specific courses from the old systems to the new one.

After Dr. Amiable presented her report, Dr. Luddite yelled "down with robots," the chair of the senate called for adjournment, the 250+ attendees shouted "I," and the senate meeting ended.

Case Analysis

Similar to the previous case, this situation also indicated that a change in one system level (Software Systems) has a ripple effect on other system levels. If the subcommittee report is implemented and the use of the LMS is centralized, it would directly impact Instructional Systems. Most faculty would realize that some of their course materials must be revised to conform to the format of the new LMS to make use of its new affordances. Also, the faculty will notice that entering and keeping data on student grades and attendance might become easier because those functions are now incorporated in the new LMS (Management Systems). Furthermore, administrators must allocate resources for staff training, as well as for maintaining and upgrading the system.

A change that affects professionals in most if not all of the system levels would inevitably bring some chaos in the lives of faculty. Some faculty may convey the disorder in the language of complaints to their union and their state representatives at the Societal Systems Level. Certainly, such complaints would be fed back to the university president and the VPAA. But perhaps more importantly, the vice president of academic affairs must resolve the political issues raised by Dr. Luddite. Faculty have always been weary of collaboration with large corporations. They often assigned motives to the companies other than the interest to sell a product to the university for its intended use and accused them of wanting to infiltrate the university, impose a business model on the institution, and change its culture from a public service institution to one that was primarily interested in making a profit. The VPAA had to deal with these societal issues and made sure that the faculty realized that accepting a campus-wide LMS was not tantamount to "selling out" to the corporate interest—that the interest of the university would be the most important issue for him.

References

Friesen, N., and Kuskis, A. (2013). Modes of interaction. In M. G. Moore (Ed.), *Handbook of distance education* (3rd ed., pp. 351–366). New York: Routledge.

Hill, J. R., Domizi, D. P., Kim, M. C., and Kim, H. (2013). Teaching and learning in negotiated online learning environments. In M. G. Moore (Ed.), *Handbook of distance education* (3rd ed., pp. 372–389). New York: Routledge.

Wang, J., Doll, W. J., Deng, X., Park, K., and Yang, M. G. M. (2013). The impact of faculty perceived reconfigurability of learning management systems on effective teaching practices. *Computers & Education, 61*, 146–157.

Young, J. R. (2013). The object formerly known as the textbook. *The Chronicle of Higher Education.* Retrieved from http://chronicle.com/article/Dont-Call-Them-Textbooks/136835/.

5

INTRODUCTION TO ADAPTIVE LEARNING SYSTEMS

Adaptive learning systems (ALSs) allow learners to match their personal traits with instructional treatments. Figure 5.1 shows that some learner traits correspond with some instructional treatments. Such correspondence, however, is personal for each learner and not all of the affordances of an ALS respond to the traits that a learner brings to the learning environment. The interaction of a learner with an ALS is personal and, as such, a learner could master predetermined objectives according to his or her learning style, preferences, and aptitude. Furthermore, ALSs allow for manifestation of a learner's emergent behavior: a learning outcome that cannot be determined a priori. ALSs are conducive to nascent behavior of the learner that appears spontaneously and can best be characterized as, ingenuity, creativity, and inventiveness under varied conditions. These conditions are obtained when the design of the educational environment allows for:

- Requisite structure to guide the learner towards what s/he must learn to become competent in a knowledge domain and acquire specific skills;
- Desired dialogue to accommodate the learner's need for learner control; and
- Adequate autonomy to keep the learner engaged and motivated towards achieving academic and lifelong goals.

Boticario and Santos (2007, p. 2) summarized definitions of adaptation offered by seminal authors in the field as follows:

> adaptation is about creating a learner experience that purposely adjusts to various conditions (personal characteristics, pedagogical knowledge, the learner interactions, the outcome of the actual learning processes) over a period of time with the intention to increase pre-defined success criteria (effectiveness of eLearning: score, time, economical costs, user satisfaction).

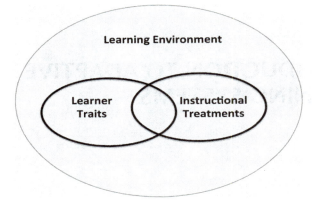

FIGURE 5.1 Learning environments.

Emphasizing the dynamic and just-in-time nature of ALSs, the U.S. Department of Education, Office of Educational Technology (2013, p. 27) presented the following description:

> Digital learning systems are considered adaptive when they can dynamically change to better suit the learning in response to information collected during the course of learning rather than on the basis of preexisting information such as a learner's gender, age, or achievement test score. Adaptive learning systems use information gained as the learner works with them to vary such features as the way a concept is represented, its difficulty, the sequencing of problems or tasks, and the nature of hints and feedback provided.

Paramythis (2004) referred to Vasilyeva, Pechenizkiy, and Puuronen (2005, p. 113) who provided a process-oriented definition of adaptive learning systems:

> an e-learning system is considered to be adaptive if it is capable of: monitoring the activities of its users; interpreting these on the basis of domain-specific models; inferring user requirements and preferences out of the interpreted activities, appropriately representing these in associated models; and, finally, acting upon the available knowledge on its users and the subject matter at hand, to dynamically facilitate the learning process.

They continued: "We want to add to this definition that an adaptive e-learning system is acting according the meta-knowledge that specifies the context of adaptation, i.e. how, where, and when the system could be adapted."

Individualizing instruction by matching learner traits to mediated instructional treatments is not a new idea. In the 1960s, the concept of adapting instruction to learner differences became the subject of much theoretical speculation and practical application (Saettler, 1990). An example was Programmed Logic for Automated Teaching Operations (PLATO) that was designed and implemented at the University of Illinois and was commercialized by Control Data Corporation (Magidson, 1974; Shearer, 2017). Thousands of students throughout the country used this early example of an individualized learning system in K-12 as well as in college courses (Shearer, 2017). However, studies in the 1970s, dubbed as trait-treatment interaction analysis (later called aptitude interaction analysis), revealed that individualizing instruction by prescribing predefined interactions between learner traits and media attributes was not an easy task. Learner attributes included a wide range of cognitive, affective, and behavioral states. Media variables were also numerous and could range from the size of the typeface in the text of a paragraph of instruction to the quality or speed of audio or the ability of the learner to decode visual symbols in a video clip. Potentially, there were unlimited combinations of learner states that could be aligned with media variables. Also, neither the learner states nor the media variables were static: They changed in real time as a teaching-learning session progressed. Static analog media systems of the 1970s could not assess learner traits in real time and adapt media variables to them dynamically. In addition, analog technologies did not include today's social media that give learners the possibility to interact with their instructors and peers on demand and regardless of time and space. Even in computer-based instruction systems, such as PLATO, learner interaction was limited to preprogrammed learning materials and predetermined objectives, although there was rudimentary learner-instructor interaction when both were working at their computer terminals at the same time (Shacham & Cutlip, 1981). In this period, experiments that were designed to match learner traits with media attributes became perplexing and resulted in a phenomenon that became known in the research literature of the time as confounding variables (Clark & Salomon, 1985).

Perplexing Research Results

A major source of the puzzle was early studies that the U.S. military conducted to assess the effectiveness of media for training service members during World War II (Saettler, 1990). This was a time when trainers were in short supply and researchers in these early studies focused on comparing various media, such as motion pictures and filmstrips, with a live instructor to see if any of these media were as good as a trainer. During this period, various media were also compared with each other. For example, filmstrips that contained a collection of static frames were compared to motion pictures in research studies to see if there were any differences between static and moving images in their effectiveness for teaching a particular task or concept. These initial studies invariably showed no statistically significant difference between a teacher and a particular medium. Nor was there any statistically significant difference in learning when one medium was compared with another. Comparative research continued throughout the 1960s when Schramm (1962) compared instructional television with classroom instruction only to find no statistically significant difference between the two.

Researchers continued to be puzzled by the "statistically no significant difference" results in these comparative studies. This development shifted their attention to consider learner traits in relation to media attributes. In order to differentially respond to learners with varied learning histories and personal backgrounds and determine the optimal instructional blend for them, researchers in the 1970s and 1980s conducted a series of experiments that came to be known as aptitude-treatment interaction analyses (ATI) (Cronbach, 2002; Snow, 1987; Snow & Farr, 1987; Snow, Federico, & Montague, 1980a, 1980b). The idea was that a learner's aptitude could be paired with appropriate instructional treatments to achieve optimal results for the learner. In the words of Snow et al. (1980a, p. 9),

> It appears that if instruction is to be successfully accommodated to individual differences among learners, then mediation mechanisms of their correlates must be measured and employed to prescribe particular teaching. Intervening processes used by distinct students to learn, retain, and retrieve a specific subject matter must be analyzed before the most appropriate instructional technique can be selected. Ascertaining the nature of this mediating cognitive activity will allow the selection of alternative teaching strategies and tactics that will increase the effectiveness and efficiency of instruction.

Focusing on the learner, Cronbach (2002, pp. 3–4) defined aptitude as

> the degree of readiness to learn and to perform well in a particular situation or in a fixed domain. That is, aptitude aids in goal attainment (whether the goal is that of the performer or that of a teacher, employer, or other leader).

With continued research and theory building on the subject of aptitude, the researchers began to use the term in plural. It became evident that preparedness for learning any knowledge or skill requires several aptitudes divided into at least two classes:

- Cognitive preparedness for information processing, developing schemas, retaining and retrieving knowledge, problem solving and decision-making; and
- Conative preparedness for meta-cognition or self-regulation of the learning process, which includes attentiveness to the demands of the task at hand, understanding the nature of the materials to be learned, awareness of one's own capabilities to complete the learning task, and desiring or being motivated to finish the learning task (Gitomer & Glaser, 1987).

Initially, ATI researchers were not as clear about defining the terms "treatment" or "instructional treatment" as they were about aptitude. It was not until Salomon (1979) suggested focusing on symbol systems representing content in a medium, instead of considering a medium as a whole, that the idea of treatment became clearer. In other words, researchers focused on how information is represented in words in a book or images in a television program instead of considering the medium of television as a whole for research purposes. Symbol systems, however, were not limited to the media and learning did not take place only when a learner was reading a book, or viewing a television program. Instructional treatments were also presented to learners when they were attending a laboratory session where learners conducted an experiment for a chemistry or physics course. Laboratory sessions, field trips, or sociological data collection, however, presented an "ecological" dimension to the term "treatment". This environmental connotation of the term was emphasized in Cronbach's (2002, p. 216) account of Snow's more advanced thinking about aptitude in which the term "treatment" was supplanted with "situation." At this point, the discussion had advanced to the transaction between a person and a situation. Also, of importance here was that Snow's concept of aptitude evolved to be a dynamic trait of the learner and not a static attribute that is predisposed and predetermined in an individual learner. Cronbach explained:

> He [Snow] would, however, urge that language move away from aptitude-in-person toward aptitude-in-person-in-situation. For example, replacing the idea of individual 'strengths' and 'weaknesses' with 'attunements' or 'matches' and 'mismatches' would be consistent with Snow's reasoning. Note that even a situation-conscious reference to 'aptitude *for* a situation' does not fit Snow's thinking. Aptitude emerges in the course of person-situation transaction.

Thus, aptitude was not conceived as a static, preordained trait of the learner. A person's aptitude was deemed to be dynamic. It would emerge and change depending on the context in which s/he performed. Cronbach presented an example of an expert who had thorough knowledge of a domain but was not a good teacher when it came to presenting such knowledge to novices. While this expert would be in his elements in a consulting situation, a teaching situation would not evoke his best aptitude and as a result his best performance.

In fact, as the original ATI research progressed, it became increasingly evident that interaction or "interface" between aptitude and a performance situation is complex. In addition to emergence, which is a characteristic of complex adaptive learning systems, ATI research accentuated the potentially unlimited combinations of cognitive and conative states with instructional treatments and other ecological factors in the learning or performing situation (e.g. watching the news on television, solving an environmental contamination problem, or repairing a jet engine). This realization defied parsimony and closure in explaining the impact of instructional treatments on learners. Clark and Salomon (1985) presented a comprehensive review of research in media and teaching and called this phenomenon confounding variables.

At an advanced stage of his research, Snow and his colleagues (1987) came to the following conclusions:

- In education, ATIs are common and occur as learning takes place.
- Most ATI combinations are complex and include myriad stimuli in the learning spaces that are afforded to the learner daily with aptitudes they evoke.
- ATIs are not static outcomes as revealed in a test at a particular moment in time; they change as the process of learning continues.
- ATI is a process of interaction between the individual learner's traits and a performance situation at each moment in time.
- Aptitudes are potential (emergent) attributes of the learner. They are evoked in the course of learning when the learner encounters a particular situation and decides to respond to it (or withhold a particular response) at each moment in time.

Although Snow and his colleagues arrived at these clearly systemic and dynamic conclusions, their method of research remained reductionist. The general program of their research was to pair certain treatments with a particular construct comprising learners' aptitude. They used conventional statistical procedures to analyze their results. Applying traditional reductionist research methods to phenomena that turned out to be holistic, complex, and dynamic in nature led to the puzzling phenomenon of "confounding variables" that the researchers could not explain. In real life and outside of the confines of the laboratory, countless learners could potentially encounter unlimited affordances in their environments during the course of their daily lives. Each learner could evoke a different set of aptitudes in varying degrees in such interfaces or transactions, in a particular situation. This would make accounting for the interaction of each affordance with each learner's aptitude set in each situation at each moment in time practically impossible with traditional scientific methods. Isolating and measuring these variables and examining their interactions one by one by conducting statistical regression analyses would not and did not resolve the puzzle. Too many changing pieces were involved here, and they did not lend themselves to research methods that were primarily suitable for understanding static mechanical phenomena as discrete and isolated variables.

This realization has far-reaching and unfulfilled ramifications for the contemporary practice of instructional design as it relates to the theory of transactional distance. It suggests allowing the instructor and the learner to assess the needs of the learner at each interval of the learning-teaching session and offering the learner the treatment that would optimize his/her performance at each moment in time depending on the learner's aptitude, that is, how the learner interacts with a learning/performing situation. Such combinations are too numerous and potentially infinite. If researchers approach them with conventional scientific reductionist methods of interminable combinations, it would lead to confounding results that Clark and Solomon indicated more than 30 years ago. Contemporary practice in needs assessment, performance analysis, and other similar techniques reveal the requirements for learning or performing situations at one point in time only. Almost as soon as the analysis is completed, the learner as well as the situation changes for many reasons including the mere fact of conducting the analysis itself. Therefore, to fully realize the benefits of ATI research, instructional systems must:

- Offer an ongoing (dynamic) process of needs assessment (how the learner is performing in a situation in a particular moment in time);
- Inform the instructional system of the learner's aptitude at a certain moment in time; and
- Move the learner to the next level of attainment in the next moment in time by providing the learner an appropriate learning/performing situation that corresponds with his/her aptitude.

The static approach of ATI researchers did not offer them the opportunity to move their research agenda further. Nevertheless, through many experiments, Snow and his colleagues made tremendous progress in defining aptitude as a complex psychological construct and revealing its role in learning. More importantly, ATI researchers:

1. Opened the way for subjecting ATI analysis to the dynamic systems method of inquiry by highlighting the complex and emergent properties of learner-situation interaction;

2. Defined the idea of aptitude as the interaction of the learner in a particular situation while performing a specific task; and

3. Led future researchers to think about the grand question in education: How would you design educational (teaching and learning) environments in which the learners can interact dynamically with the instructors and with instructional media stimuli depending on their aptitude? This was in sharp contrast to the previous grand question: How would you statically pair learner attributes with instructional materials?

Today, software applications can receive data from learners, and provide them with differential responses based on their traits. However, despite decades of research on learner traits, there is no universal approach to identifying and classifying these attributes (Cooper, 2010).

Identifying and Classifying Learner Traits and Individual Differences

Researchers have developed different approaches to understanding learner characteristics for well over a century. These include assessing learning styles, identifying multiple intelligences, and distinguishing cultural differences. Although these approaches have developed independently, there are similar categories among them, as the following brief introduction to each category will show. However, there are also vast differences and there is no agreement among scholars on a set of learner traits that influence how each person learns and chooses to control his or her learning process. More than two decades ago, Jonassen and Grabowski (1993, p. 4) presented a detailed explanation of indicators of individual differences based on the available research at the time. Their inventory of individual traits included the following:

- General mental abilities;
- Primary mental abilities;
- Cognitive controls;
- Cognitive styles: information gathering;
- Cognitive styles: information organizing;
- Learning styles;
- Personality: attentional and engagement styles;
- Personality: expectancy and incentive styles; and
- Prior knowledge.

Since then, research in the above categories has continued. However, the picture has become more complex. New areas of theory and research, such as the theory of cognitive load, point to the fact that these categories are not discrete, that there is a dynamic interplay between them; they inform each other, and their influence in determining individual differences varies over time. What is certain, however, is that each individual brings a unique aptitude to the learning process. To highlight learner differences and traits, three categories of learning styles, multiple intelligences, and cultural differences are discussed below. This brief explanation, however, demonstrates the complexity of categorizing individual differences.

Learning Styles—The concept is based on the assumption that different learners have idiosyncratic cognitive, emotional, and behavioral characteristics that habitually influence them to select different ways and means to learn. Learning styles have been studied since the turn of the last century, and many inventories for classifying them have been developed in this long period of time. Wilson (2012) identified 71 different inventories of learning styles that were suggested by various researchers in a span of 100 years between 1902 and 2002. Despite this long history, the concept has remained perplexing as the variety of inventories and the diversity among the concepts that they include indicate. What makes the study of the learning styles more confounding is that they are not static, as learners mature and change over time. Also, individuals may combine various learning styles in different degrees of intensity at each moment in time.

Rita and Kenneth Dunn pioneered the contemporary study of learning styles since the 1960s. They developed an assessment tool for adult learners titled The Building Excellence Survey ("The Dunn & Dunn Model," 2014). The survey includes the following styles:

- Perceptual Domain: auditory, visual word, visual picture, tactual and/or kinesthetic, verbal;
- Psychological Domain: analytic/global, impulsive/reflective;
- Environmental Domain: sound, light, temperature, seating design;
- Physiological Domain: time of day, intake, mobility;
- Emotional Domain: motivation, task persistence, conformity, structure; and
- Sociological Domain: alone, pairs, small group, large group, authority, variety.

Other researchers have proposed classifications that point to different ways that individual learners process perception, information, and cognition and decide to engage in specific learning strategies and activities. Papp (2001, pp. 17–18) listed five instruments that different scholars developed to ascertain the variables that determine a learner's learning style. These included:

1. Kolb's Learning Style Inventory (LSI). Variables in this scale comprise the following:

    a. Concrete experience;
    b. Reflective observation;

    c. Abstract conceptualization; and

    d. Active experimentation.

2. The ASIST (Approaches and Study Skills Inventory for Students) instrument developed by Tait and Entwistle

    a. Deep: Intention to understand, relation of ideas, active learning;

    b. Surface: Intention to reproduce, unrelated memorizing, passive learning;

    c. Strategic: Study organization, time management, intention to excel; and

    d. Apathetic: Lack of direction, and interest.

3. Solomon and Felder's Index of Learning Style (ILS)

    a. Active: Trying things and working with others vs. reflective: Thinking things through and working alone;

    b. Sensing: Oriented towards facts and procedures vs. intuitive: Oriented towards concepts, theories, meaning, and innovation;

    c. Visual: Prefer visual learning materials vs. verbal: Prefer written or spoken instruction; and

    d. Sequential: Linear, orderly in thinking, learn in small increments vs. global: holistic thinkers, learn in large steps.

4. The Learning Styles Questionnaire (LSQ) developed by Honey and Mumford

    a. Activists: Enjoy new experience, make intuitive decisions, dislike structure;

    b. Theorists: focus on ideas, logic, and systemic planning, mistrust intuition;

    c. Pragmatists: Favor practical approaches, group work, debate, risk-taking; and

    d. Reflectors: Observe and describe, try to predict outcomes, try to understand meaning.

5. Academic Self-Efficacy Scale

    a. To what extent a learner's self-efficacy positions him/her for distance learning.

Wilson (2012) presented a general criticism about the desirability of matching learner traits with instructional treatments suggesting that such matching would deprive learners from experiencing certain learning activities that do not match their traits. Such analysis, however, does not take into consideration the complex and dynamic nature of the matching process. In static predetermined systems, such criticism is apt. However, complex systems allow for theoretically unlimited matching of traits and treatments with emergent results that can be anticipated but not predicted in advance. Also, matching does not take place only one time; it is iterative and ongoing. Therefore, certain traits may not match with particular instructional treatments initially when a learner has just started to learn about a field of study. However, as learners move from being novices to experts, their aptitudes (how they perform certain tasks under certain conditions) evolve and they may engage in learning activities that has not been previously matched with their traits. In fact, when they have a chance in small classrooms, highly skilled teachers constantly try to match instructional treatments with learner's aptitudes.

Multiple Intelligences—Gardner (1993) proposed the concept of multiple intelligences in his groundbreaking book titled *Frames of Mind: The Theory of Multiple Intelligences*. Originally, Gardner asserted that individuals are endowed with seven traits in varying degrees and later, he updated his model to include the following categories:

- Naturalist Intelligence—The human ability to discriminate among living things. This trait led to the development of agricultural and industrial societies in which consumers were capable of discriminating among the many goods and services that humans have created and benefit from them.
- Musical Intelligence—The capacity to distinguish among pitch, rhythm, timber, and tone. This trait leads to the creation of music, development of mathematical ability, and discernment of various human emotions.
- Existential Intelligence—The capability to puzzle regarding human existence. Ask what the nature and purpose of life is, and why we are here, and pose questions about the nature of death and dying.
- Interpersonal Intelligence—The skill to interact with others, i.e. understand their perspectives, judgments, moods, and social and political tendencies.
- Bodily Kinesthetic Intelligence—Sense of timing in mind-body coordination and the ability to manipulate physical objects.
- Linguistic Intelligence—The most widely shared human competence to think in words, communicate ideas, and reflect on the nature of language.
- Spatial Intelligence—Mental imagery, thinking in three dimensions, spatial reasoning.

Since Gardner proposed these categories, many scholars have conducted several studies on validating and measuring multiple intelligences and showing how they can be applied to instruction (McClellan & Conti, 2008). In several recent studies, developing instruments for measuring multiple intelligences resulted in proposing new categories. Tirri, Nokelainen, and Komulainen (2013) suggested five "sensitivities." These included: spiritual sensitivity, environmental sensitivity, ethical sensitivity, emotional sensitivity, and intercultural and interreligious sensitivities (p. 455). As the list of human intelligences has grown, the question has remained whether the concept is one construct with various dimensions, or as Gardner has implied, whether humans have distinct intelligences. Almeida et al. (2010, p. 299) defined intelligence as a

> complex aptitude that involves important aspects of problem solving, as well as the ability to infer relationships and to think in an abstract manner. This definition reveals the multiple dimensions of intelligence and highlights that cognitive skill measures are positively correlated with each other depending on the cognitive processes involved and on the tasks' content.

Even in seemingly simple tasks, such as walking, several aptitudes are involved when human behavior is purposeful, suggesting that research in this field needs to continue. Hopefully, future researchers would acknowledge the complex adaptive nature of learning styles and select research methods that lend themselves to the holistic and dynamic nature of the phenomenon.

Cultural Differences—Cultural traits of learners are another set of complex variables in determining the appropriate level of transactional distance for each individual learner. Gunawardena (2014) and Jung and Gunawardena (2014) presented a summary of studies about cultural characteristics in relation to learning in years past and emphasized the emergence of new concepts and categories in recent scholarship. They highlighted the work of Hofstede and Hall, as summarized in the following.

1. *Hall's Dimensions of Culture*—Another set of classification of cultural traits analyzed by Jung and Gunawardena was high context communication vs. low context communication set forward by Hall in the 1950s. Hall's cultural dimensions were based on the social background of communication taking place in different societies. High context communication was generally attributed to Eastern societies in which body language, silence, and other similar nonverbal cues are as important as the verbal communication. Low context communication is generally attributed to Western societies where verbal and written communication is direct and explicit, and the context of the conversation is not as important as in Eastern societies.

Hofstede's Dimensions of Culture—In the 1980s, Hofstede set six bipolar categories for cultural traits of individuals within the structure of an organization, as shown in Table 5.1.

Jung and Gunawardena continued their analysis of cultural factors beyond dimensional models of Hofstede and Hall to include holistic models set forward by Shaw, Barter-Power, and Levy.

TABLE 5.1 Hofstede's Dimensions of Culture

High power distance (hierarchical organizations and societies)	Low power distance (democratic organizations and societies)
Individualism (reliance on one's personal abilities)	Collectivism (reliance on social connections, integration in a group)
Masculinity (assertive, competitive)	Femininity (collaborative, emphasizing quality of life)
Uncertainty avoidance (high tolerance for ambiguity and uncertainty)	Uncertainty avoidance (low tolerance for ambiguity and uncertainty
Long-term orientation (orientation towards the future for planning, persistence, achievement of goals)	Short-term orientation (respect for tradition, steadiness, preservation of one's face, fulfilling social obligations)
Indulgence (gratification of needs and desires)	Restraint (controlling desires and impulses)

1. *Shaw and Barter-Power* suggested a set of 29 cultural characteristics in learners. Their model differentiated between two sources of cultural differences: readily detectable attributes and underlying attributes. Readily detectable attributes were those that can easily be recognized in a person, such as gender or nationality/ethnic origin. Underlying attributes are divided into two categories. The first category (Underlying Attributes I) represents cultural values, perspectives, attitudes, beliefs, and other conflict resolution styles, which are closely correlated with readily detectable attributes. The second group of attributes (Underlying Attributes II) includes socioeconomic and personal status, education, functional specialization, human capital assets, past work experiences, and personal expectations. These attributes are less strongly connected to nationality/ethnic origin, age, or gender of individuals.

2. *Levy's Model*, as distilled by Jung and Gunawardena, included five categories:

    a. Culture as elemental—We are deeply embedded in our own culture and have to learn about it first to better understand our frame of reference.

    b. Culture as relative—Culture is, fundamentally, a relative concept. One culture is understood in relation to the others.

    c. Culture as group membership—Humans are members of several groups with corresponding values and traditions: family, school cohort, work groups.

    d. Culture as contested—Culture is contested from within and without at many levels: international, national, societal, organizational.

    e. Culture as individual—Culture varies among individuals as it is personally constructed. Understanding of seemingly the same culture differs for each person.

Cognitive Load

Another area of research that adds to the complexity of learning styles, multiple intelligences, and cultural differences is the theory of cognitive load. It addresses how individuals process new information in their working memory (WM) and encode it to store it in the long-term memory (LTM). An expert has the ability to take more new information in the WM and readily integrate it with existing schema or episodic events in the LTM. This is because an expert has already developed a larger schema for the knowledge domain in the LTM, whereas a novice's ability to encode information in the LTM is limited to the small schema s/he has for a knowledge domain.

A central issue in designing ALSs from the perspective of cognitive load theory is to provide information to the learner that s/he can process easily at each moment in time that the learning process is in progress (Kalyuga & Singh, 2016; Morrison & Anglin, 2005; Ozcelik & Yildirim, 2005; Reedy, 2015; Schweppe & Rummer, 2014; Sweller, 2006; van Merrienboer & Ayers, 2005). Cognitive load theorists base their current research and development on the original study of Baddley (1992) who posited that individuals have a limited capacity for the amount and duration that information is held in the WM. New information, therefore, must be encoded into the LTM if it is going to be retained. Otherwise, it dissipates from the WM altogether in a matter of seconds. The ability for each learner to encode new information to the LTM is based on several individual factors, including cognitive skills, such as reasoning. Therefore, the structure of the information and how it is presented to the learner determines its efficacy for learning. Structure of the information, in turn, is a function of its element-interactivity. Information that is presented to the learner could have relatively low element-interactivity if the elements comprising the learning material could be learned individually. An example is the function keys on a computer keyboard. In this case, element-interactivity is low because the function of each element (each function key on the keyboard) can be learned individually without reference to any other item.

In contrast, learning a photo editing software on a computer in its entirety consists of many learning elements, some of which are related to each other. Element-interactivity for the novice learner, in this case, is high because s/he must process many elements in combination to succeed in successfully editing a photo. In the parlance of the cognitive load theory, the demands on WM capacity imposed by element-interactivity are intrinsic to the material being learned.

- Intrinsic cognitive load refers to the difficulty associated with the nature of the learning problem and the context in which it is presented to the learner. Intrinsic cognitive load, in other words, is a function of the element-interactivity of the learning space.

- Extraneous or ineffective cognitive load is increased and learning is decreased when element-interactivity is high, and the nature of the learning task is too complicated.
- Germane or effective cognitive load is increased when element-interactivity is optimized for the learner, and learning is increased.

Pass, Renkl, and Sweller (2003, p. 2) observed the following:

> Intrinsic, extraneous and germane cognitive loads are additive in that, together, the total load cannot exceed the working memory resources available if learning is to occur. The relations between the three types of cognitive loads are asymmetric. Intrinsic cognitive load provides a base load that is irreducible other than by constructing additional schemas in LTM and automating previously acquired schemas. Any available working memory capacity remaining after resources have been allocated to deal with intrinsic cognitive load can be allocated to deal with extraneous and germane loads. These can work in tandem in that, for example, a reduction in extraneous cognitive load by using a more effective instructional design can free capacity for an increase in germane cognitive load.

Research in this area is new, and researchers continue to revise the application of cognitive load theory in instructional design as new evidence becomes available.

Referring to new research results, Kalyuga and Singh (2016, p. 849) said:

> According to the traditional view of cognitive load theory, novice learners benefit most from fully guided explicit instruction (the worked example effect), while more knowledgeable learners may learn most effectively from instructional materials with reduced or minimal levels of instructional support. However, studies within the above alternative frameworks seemingly oppose this view by demonstrating that minimally guided learning tasks provided prior to explicit instruction could be more effective for achieving better and longer-lasting learning outcomes with novice learners than providing explicit instruction first.

Other individual factors that may affect WM span include motivation, attention, and emotional response of the learner to the learning materials. These original principles and more recent exploratory hypotheses have become the bases for developing a new breed of learning environments that dynamically adapt to a learner's cognitive load. The process of adaptation has been made possible by computer programs dubbed as software agents are computer programs that:

- Interact with the user;
- Learn how the user behaves in searching for information or learning certain concepts and tasks;
- Suggest solutions to the user that s/he might find useful; or
- Do certain things on behalf of the user to decrease his or her extraneous cognitive load.

Pedagogical and learning agents are written in a variety of languages, ranging from those that are used in the field of artificial intelligence to markup languages, such as XML (Arif & Hussain, 2015; Govindasamy, 2014; Rani, Nayak, & Vyas, 2015). Today, rudimentary software agents assist learners in a variety of disciplines ranging from language learning to engineering and computer science. The application of software agents to instruction and learning, however, is in an embryonic stage. Currently, the following three types of adaptive learning systems are widely used by thousands of university students:

- Adaptive hypermedia systems (AHS);
- Intelligent tutoring systems, (ITS); and
- Adaptive simulations and serious games (ASSG).

In the next section, we will focus on these platforms.

Approaches to Developing Adaptive Learning Systems

Advances in computer technology coupled with developments in hypermedia, cognitive science, and artificial intelligence have provided the basic ingredients for researchers to create software platforms that can respond individually and differentially to learners. The literature on this subject is vast and is growing every day. Also, new systems are developed and put on line at a quicker pace than ever before. Examples of systems provided here are to highlight major features that are shared by most applications. Each system consists of many detailed components and how they interact with each learner as well as with each other. This brief high-level introduction offers a general overview of the key features of adaptive applications as gleaned from seminal studies (Beal, 2004; Beck, Stern, & Haugsjaa, 2004; Bouchet, Azevedo, Kinnebrew, & Biswas, 2012; Cruces & Arriaga, 2000; Essa, 2016; Huong, 2016; Meshref & Noor Mohamed, 2012; Phillips & Johnson, 2011; Trausan-Matu, Boyer, Crosby, & Panourgia, 2014; Tsiriga & Virvou, 2004; Virvou & Tsiriga, 2001; Wijekumar, Meyer, & Lei, 2013; Yang, 2010).

The proceedings of the annual International Conference on Intelligent Tutoring Systems, *ACM Transactions on Interactive Intelligent Systems,* a periodical of the Association for Computing Machinery, and the proceedings of the annual European Conference on Games Based Learning provide current information about recent developments in this field. Current information about ALSs is regularly posted on http://Distance-Educator.com/.

Developing adaptive learning application software is a flourishing area of scientific work, software development, and entrepreneurship. Researchers, developers, and designers have taken several innovative approaches to making instructional/learning environments more interactive and adaptable (*Proceedings of the 22nd International Conference on Computers in Education ICCE,* 2014). These technologies provide various approaches to differentially present learning experiences and instructional content to the learner (Desmarais and Baker, 2011). In most cases, the designers and developers have focused on making the content, navigation, or presentation of instructional materials adaptable. These include:

- Presenting instruction to learners based on real-time assessment results;
- Varying pacing of learning;
- Offering scaffolding and progressive prompts to learners;
- Providing feedback to learners based on their metacognitive characteristics; and
- Placing learners in learning communities depending on their objectives, needs, and interests.

Most current adaptive systems share a general architecture to perform certain necessary processes (Figure 5.2). These include the following:

1. Collect data from the learner;
2. Develop a learner model;
3. Collect information about a knowledge domain (declarative and procedural knowledge, rules, theories, hypothesis, research results, examples, applications, cases, etc.);
4. Acquire and develop a knowledge model;
5. Acquire and develop an expert model;
6. Acquire and construct instructional models;
7. Match learner model with instructional model;
8. Generate adapted instructional model;
9. Make statistical predictions about the learner;
10. Generate adapted content/suggestions/information for the learner;
11. Present adapted content/suggestions/information to the learner;
12. Collect new data from the learner; and
13. Revise learner model, knowledge model, and instructional model.

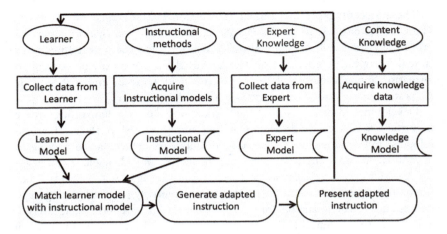

FIGURE 5.2 Diagram of functions performed by adaptive learning systems in a simplified prototype.

The iterative process presented above not only includes revision of the learner model but also revision of the content and instructional models as new content and instructional methods become available to the system. Furthermore, the system may acquire a substantial amount of information to enrich its content model. This information can range from simple documents to multimedia learning objects, ontologies, knowledge schemas, or entire expert models. Because of their dynamic and expansive architecture, one can imagine that these models can quickly become complex.

Specht and Burgos (2007) provided a classification scheme for developing adaptive learning systems in hypermedia. They based their model on questions regarding what is actually adapted in a system. We have adopted these questions and expanded them to apply not only to hypermedia but to intelligent tutoring systems (ITSs) and serious simulation and games as well.

What is adapted in a learning system? This question relates to identifying one or more elements that are present in a learning system would be adapted to a learner's characteristics. Examples of these elements include:

- Differential presentation of content to each individual learner based on his/her prior knowledge of the subject matter, or other characteristics, such as learning styles or meta-cognitive skills;
- Pacing of the presentation of the learning materials according to a learner's preference;
- Configuring hardware and software systems based on ergonomic requirements of individual or groups of learners; and
- Referring a learner to join a collaborative group working on a specific problem or subject matter.

Why does the system adapt? This question primarily focuses on the pedagogical model(s) that are a good fit for a particular learner depending on:

- Variables, such as his or her learning style and preferences; and
- The discrepancy between what a learner knows about a subject and standards for achieving mastery of that knowledge domain.

How does the system gather the information for the adaption process? This question relates to a variety of methods by which a system collects information from the learner to model the learning behavior and preferences of that learner, as well as his or her level of knowledge of a particular domain. These include:

- Tracking learner interface with the system (information ranging from what time the learner has logged in to the system and how long s/he has stayed logged in to data about more complex tasks that the learner has completed); and
- Assessing learner's knowledge of the subject matter through a variety of means including offering quizzes or other forms of testing.

Depending on the design, complexity, and sophistication of the system, it may also collect information to develop a content model in ontologies or other forms of content information about a subject matter, and an instructional model that includes strategies that guide the learner's progress.

How does the system perform these tasks? This question relates to core technologies in a system that allows it to dynamically adapt to the learner. These technologies offer the following components to a system:

- A learner model that provides the ability to statistically infer how well a learner may perform certain tasks under specific conditions based on:
  - Current information that the system can collect about the learner in real time; or
  - Information about the learner's past performance (e.g. previous test scores, grades, preferred times of study).

    This information includes learner's current, and past behavioral, cognitive, and affective states, such as his or her motivation levels, cognitive style(s), and behavioral patterns in responding to certain situations. Such responses include processing information, committing to actual performance, and performing a task.

- A content model includes primary concepts, definitions, theories, hypotheses, rules, research results examples, and applications of a knowledge domain. To the extent that knowledge domains are dynamic, such models would include statements of relationships among its primary concepts as well as rules governing such relationships. In some systems, content models include expert models in which information is stored about how one or a group of experts may solve a problem or deal with a particular performance scenario, such as a specific case in law or a particular patient's condition in an emergency room of a hospital.

• An instructional model includes the structure of the pedagogy, as well as the methods and technologies by which instruction is provided to the learner. The instructional model matches the data from the learner with the best available content (as well as other variables, such as pacing or scaffolding) in the system and provides the optimal instructional path for each individual learner to perform a certain task under specific performance conditions.

Core technologies that can implement the processes described above are fast evolving. There are several experimental systems at various stages of research and development in institutions of higher education that specialize on the application of artificial intelligence, cognitive science, and hypermedia in developing instructional and learning systems. Entrepreneurs are also either facilitating the developments of these applications or developing new ones from the ground up, and investing in their adoption by the publishing and software industries. Three classes of these applications are discussed below.

Current ALS Applications

The current experimental and commercial applications in use by most learners worldwide can generally be placed in the following three categories:

• Adaptive hypermedia systems (AHS);
• Intelligent tutoring systems (ITS); and
• Adaptive simulations and serious games (ASSG).

As the field is rapidly growing, these categories are bound to increase. Also, one cannot find a sharp line of demarcation between these categories. Scientific principles and core technologies in these three types of systems have been in place for decades. Inevitably, researchers, designers, and developers who have originally started working on one approach have learned from each other and have adopted different techniques from each other. There are adaptive hypermedia systems that use concepts and technologies of artificial intelligence, and intelligent tutoring systems that use hypermedia to lead students to the most suitable content for them. Both of these systems may also involve students in an adaptive simulation or a serious game either directly or indirectly through integration with an LMS or another similar platform. Pavlik Jr. and Toth (2010) highlighted the difficulty in categorizing multiple approaches even within the confines of ITSs. Various solutions in place today are inspired by at least one of the subfields including computer interface design; perceptual, cognitive, affective, and behavioral psychology; statistics; artificial intelligence; and cognitive neuroscience. Pavlik Jr. and Toth offered three methods of combination, integration, and resolution to align these subfields for synthesizing disparate concepts and finding a common language for defining and describing ITSs and their components. Despite their call for action, considerable divergence exists. Nevertheless, in the following, we will present examples of AHS, ITS, and ASSG for the purpose of clarity, with the proviso that actual systems in place today in universities are not pure, and combine these three approaches.

Intelligent Tutoring Systems (ITS)

ITSs provide expert knowledge to students as they model the learner's understanding of a subject matter. They also contain a pedagogical model that offers the learner instructional strategies, as well as a communication model that displays the learning information. These systems offer feedback to learners about the accuracy of their responses to assessment options, such as test items, or the process by which a learner arrived at a particular response. In ITSs:

- The student module tracks information about how an individual learner is performing and provides information to the pedagogical module. An important function of student module is to identify learner misconceptions about a subject matter.
- The pedagogical module offers instructional strategies to the learner (e.g. sequence of topics to be presented, suggestions for reviewing certain information) based on the information received from the individual learner.
- The domain knowledge module represents the content of a field that the system has acquired for the purpose of presenting it to the learner.
- The expert model module contains the knowledge domain of a field as represented by an expert. It is similar to the domain knowledge module, but includes heuristics and expert pinpointing of processes that usually is not included in the domain knowledge data.
- The communication module provides user interface and controls the learner needs for interacting with ITSs.

Examples of systems that perform these operations are numerous. The following highlights different approaches to ITSs.

Phillips and Johnson (2011, p. 90) developed an intelligent tutoring system for accounting students. The main feature of the system or the transactional analysis tutor allowed:

> a range of interactions similar to what could occur with a human tutor. For example, if a student does not know how to start a problem, he can ask the

tutor to analyze each step of the problem for him using conversational-style natural language. On the other hand, if a student wishes, he can analyze the transaction without seeking help or feedback from the tutor. If errors arise in his analyses, the tutor will provide corrective feedback when he proceeds from one sub goal (e.g., analyzing accounting equation effects) to the next (preparing a journal entry). The student can ask the transaction analysis tutor to check his work, explain how the tutor would think through a particular part of the problem, or provide instruction on specific topics (e.g., Why is contributed capital categorized as equity?). An important feature of the tutor is that it dynamically generates its explanations and instructional points for each individual student, based on the specific part of the particular problem on which each student is working and the particular responses the student has previously given. After each explanation or instruction, the tutor allows the student to ask as many follow-up questions as the student feels is necessary.

Pedrazzoli (2009) introduced OPUS One, an ITS that could be added to a learning management system for making Web-based learning adaptable. The system:

- Diagnosed student subject matter understanding;
- Recommended target oriented, optimized "learning approach adaptations";
- Tailored tutorial actions accordingly;
- Supported collaboration activities, such as recommending suitable collaborators and actions;
- Adapted the interface to facilitate collaborative activities;
- Advised students how to interact efficiently;
- Specified/proposed techniques to acquire additional knowledge materials about a subject matter; and
- Used the knowledge base to solve problems in that domain or subject matter.

Latham, Crockett, McLean, and Edmonds (2012) proposed a conversational ITS in which students could interact with the computer using natural language. In such systems, either a semantic Web or a mapping technology is used to allow learners to interface in written or oral natural language with the computer. Their proposed system dubbed Oscar aimed to:

> mimic a human tutor by implicitly modeling the learning style during tutoring, and personalizing the tutorial to boost confidence and improve the effectiveness of the learning experience.
>
> *(p. 1)*

The system allowed learners to intuitively explore and discuss topics in natural language that helped to establish a deeper understanding of the subject.

Rus, D'Mello, Hu, and Graesser (2013) presented recent advances in conversational adaptive systems; a class of ITSs that use explanation-based constructivist theories of learning and the collaborative constructive activities that occur during human tutoring. They posited that conversational ITSs have several advantages compared to systems with less anthropomorphic interactions with learners. Conversational systems:

- Require learners to explain their reasoning for their approach to problem solving, therefore increasing understanding of their cognitive and meta-cognitive processes;
- Encourage learners to use scientific concepts and terms instead of more informal language in discussing scientific subjects;
- Provide animated agents that can hold a conversation with learners and suggest to them modeling pedagogy; and
- Offer learning environments in which:

> Both single agents and ensembles of agents can be carefully choreographed to mimic virtually any activity or social situation: curiosity, inquiry learning, negotiation, interrogation, arguments, empathetic support, helping, and so on. Agents not only enact these strategies, individually or in groups, but can also think aloud while they do so.
>
> *(p. 43)*

Examples of conversational ITSs include:

1. AutoTutor—Developed at the University of Memphis, the system allows students to form a deep understanding of concepts of Newtonian physics by composing their explanation of difficult concepts in natural language and receive adaptive tutoring from the system (D'mello & Graesser, 2012).
2. DeepTutor—This system is based on the concept of learning progression in which successful learning paths of learners are monitored and used by the system to identify:
   a. Current student thinking;
   b. Likely antecedent understandings of the learner; and
   c. His or her next steps to move the student towards more sophisticated understandings (Rus, Stefanescu, Niraula, & Graesser, 2014).

Self-regulated ITS monitor the content that learners select to learn, as well as their ability to respond to a learning situation. They detect learner's metacognitive performance regarding selection of learning objectives, and take steps to achieve those objectives. In self-regulated systems, scaffolding provides successive prompts to the learner that would lead her/him to a better understanding of the subject at hand by using the results of the learner's interaction with the system in comprehending the subject matter, as well as accomplishing metacognitive tasks.

Poitras and Lajoie (2014) developed an agent-based system for adapting learning about history in which successive instruction provided to the learner was refined by real-time assessment of skills that were acquired by him/her. The self-regulated user modeling technique in this system monitored goal-setting behavior of the learner, as well as when learners selected inappropriate content or applied unsuitable strategies to the learning situation. Refinement in the learner model allowed for better predicting learner performance and guiding the learner in acquiring new knowledge and skills about history as the learning process continued in the system.

A burgeoning area of research and development in artificial intelligence is affective computing in which human emotional expressions are captured and analyzed. Lin, Wang, Chao, and Chien (2012) developed an ITS to provide feedback to learners based on their emotional states. A webcam captured the facial expressions of individual learners. The data were analyzed by the Detected Emotion based on Active Shape Model (DEASM) algorithm developed by the authors to match data points in the captured video with one of the six "fundamental" human emotions. Learners received feedback based on their facial expressions, as well as other data collected and analyzed by the system to provide them with a more enjoyable learning experience.

Adaptive Hypermedia Systems (AHS)

AHSs make the wealth of information that is available on the World Wide Web or a propriety system, such as an encyclopedia on an intranet, adaptive to one or more of a learner's characteristics, learning styles, or prior knowledge of the learner about a particular subject matter.

Brusilovsky (1996, p. 88) who conceptualized the basic building blocks of adaptive systems on which the contemporary applications are built posited that:

> by adaptive hypermedia systems we mean all hypertext and hypermedia systems which reflect some features of the user in the user model and apply this model to adapt various visible aspects of the system to the user.

Using extended markup language (XML) technology, Tarpin–Bernard and Habieb–Mammar (2005) developed an adaptable hypertext learning environment to model the cognitive characteristics of the learner called Cognitive User Modeling for Adaptive Presentation of Hyper-Documents (CUMAPH). This elaborate system used a series of tests to evaluate the cognitive profile of each learner for visual and auditory information. Using XML in a Web environment, the users then adapt the presentation of information by selecting certain elements on the screen that best fit their cognitive profile.

Mampadi, Chen, Ghinea, and Chen (2011) used an XML-based adaptive hypermedia system for comparing learning between two groups of learners with different cognitive styles dubbed as holists and serialists. In short, the holists made great use of concept maps in learning a subject matter while the serialists used keyword indexes to learn the same knowledge. Their research study was in the tradition of earlier studies in adaptive hypermedia systems, some of which showed cognitive style as a determining factor in learning while other studies did not show a significant improvement in learning by differentiating learners based on their cognitive style. This study did not resolve the contradictory results about effectiveness of adaptive hypermedia systems. Nonetheless, it highlighted the limitation of comparing two groups of learners when the important factor is the difference among unique individuals and not where one individual fits statistically in a group of learners.

Somyürek (2015) reviewed recent literature in adaptive hypermedia systems in which she presented current trends in the field. She identified standardization as the most important albeit unresolved issue. Standardization of meta-data becomes of crucial importance in sharing content information across different platforms and systems because hypermedia systems depend on standard metadata models to adapt available content to the profile of individual learners. Considering the fact that the body of multimedia resources available on the World Wide Web is growing exponentially, metadata that are standardized across information system platforms become of crucial necessity and importance. Somyürek further elaborated that semantic Web technologies are used to standardize sharing of knowledge resources through developing:

- Ontologies that construct the following:
  - Knowledge domains;
  - Learner models;
  - Tasks; and
  - Teaching strategies in a shared language and query language that are used to conduct searches across ontologies in a standard format.

Other major recent trends identified by Somyürek included:

- Developing data mining filtering technologies through which researchers can query instructional materials that match the learning needs and profiles of specific learners with learning resources;
- Using neural networks, fuzzy logic, and Bayesian probability computation to analyze learner behaviors for developing learner models;

- Employing features of social media, such as tags for peer recommendation and adaption of learning content; and
- Adapting learning materials across different mobile devices, such as tablets, and smartphones.

Adaptive Simulations and Serious Games (ASSG)

Perhaps the most attractive and promising adaptive learning systems are educational simulations and games (Lavieri Jr., 2014). These learning systems have proven to be effective in a variety of subject matters ranging from management studies and political science to medical education and military training. Computer-based simulations and games offer realistic situations, such as flight simulators, by using 3-D animation or video footage shot in real life or both. Aldrich (2006, p. 52) indicated:

> Things that seem simple, narrow, and isolated when 'taught' through traditional linear means are deep, complex, and extendable when practiced in simulations.

In addition, simulation and serious games offer many desirable features that can be controlled in advance by designers, instructors, or learners as they engage in a game, or a problem-solving or decision-making simulation. Dickey (2005, p. 70) proposed the elements of engaged-learning for designing educational games and simulations, which would provide cognitive-constructivist framework for their development and evaluation. These elements were:

- Focused goals,
- Challenging tasks,
- Clear and compelling standards,
- Protection from adverse consequences for initial failures,
- Affirmation of performance,
- Affiliation with others,
- Novelty and variety,
- Choice, and
- Authenticity.

Students frequently use games and simulations for entertainment purposes and engage in formal and informal role-playing while learning. This blending of playing and learning indicates their very high level of motivation for using simulations and games. If played in groups, games also provide an element of competition or collaboration to the learning environment (Yu, Chang, Liu, & Chan, 2002). Focusing on social and emotional aspects of serious educational games, Kim and Ho (2014, p. 597) stated: "Central to this interplay between play and learning are learners' emotions. Learners constantly appraise what is presented in the game and act accordingly." Furthermore, they continued: "Learners' emotional engagement truly become their resources for playful learning: when learners find personal meanings of their activities, their emotions could direct their attention toward them." Simulations and games also offer nonthreatening learning environments for students to experiment with objects and events on the screen and see the consequences of their actions, while implementing the same experiments in a real-life situation may have catastrophic results (Simpson, 2005).

Zarraonandia, Ruíz, Díaz, and Aedo (2012) introduced a set of reusable rules for adaptive educational games in which several layers of the game ranging from its initial state to its storyline and scenario could be adapted to the profile of the learner. Using these rules, two games with similar educational purposes that have been designed for different types of learners could share the same scoring mechanism to provide a measure of the player's success during the game.

Obikwelu and Read (2013) summarized prior research by Ismailovic, Haladjian, Kohler, Pagano, and Brugge (2011) who described characteristics of an adaptive game in the following:

- Learns from learner's behavior by:
  - Intelligent monitoring, and
  - Interpreting learner's actions in the game's world.
- Intervenes in the game's world by:
  - Automatically adjusting the learning content, and
  - Adjusting the game elements according to:
    - Students' individual knowledge of a learning domain and his or her other characteristics.

Obikwelu and Read (2013) continued their summary of the literature in the field by presenting a detailed taxonomy and description of four stages in which the system monitors the players, collects information about them, generates adaptive responses, and intervenes in the game environment.

Adaptive Learning Systems in the Market

Leading textbook publishers and LMS companies have adopted core technologies from adaptive system providers, such as Assessment and Learning in Knowledge Spaces (ALEKS), Knewton, Snapwiz, and others, to make learning more personal for students. Adaptive system providers, such as Realizeit, have also taken the initiative to offer their technologies directly to institutions of higher education.

McGraw-Hill offers adaptive learning through ALEKS, a system developed at the University of California, Irvine. The system is based on knowledge space theory that was originally developed for psychometric studies. ALEKS assess the knowledge state of learners and provide learning options by constructing discipline-specific knowledge structures to learners.

Pearson and Macmillan use Knewton data mining technology to analyze instructional materials based on numerous data points in their contents including concepts, structure, and difficulty level. Knewton then correlates learner profiles with recommended content.

Wiley has partnered with Quantum Adaptive Learning Assessment Software to use Quantum's expert system technology for offering two self-assessment tools, *Targeted Practice* and *How Am I Doing?*, tools that make learning more personalized for students. Wiley has also adopted Snapwiz technology that tracks individual learner performance to allow instructors to gain an overview of problem areas and assist learners to overcome them.

Elsevier, a major publisher of books in medical sciences, uses Cerego, an adaptive learning system that is based on principles of neuroscience. The system is particularly useful when a large amount of information must be committed to LTM for an extended period of time.

Desire2Learn (D2L), a leading provider of learning management systems, acquired LeaP adaptive algorithm and semantic analytics engine. LeaP consists of three engines: mapping, ranking, and recommending.

D2L described the workflow of LeaP in the following:

First, LeaP takes the Learning Objectives, Content, and Questions and curates these data inputs until LeaP has a pure text version of all inputs.

Then, using semantic (sometimes known as search) algorithms, LeaP determines how related each of the Learning Objectives, Content Items, and Questions are to each other and everything else in the content repository.

These relationships are then made available to D2L LeaP so it can make intelligent recommendations as to what:

- **Content** should be presented to a learner when they are in the process of learning a particular Learning Objective
- **Questions** should be used to determine if a learner has met the Learning Objective
- **Recommending Reading** content items the learner should be offered if they get a particular question wrong
- **Quizzes and Practice Questions** should be offered to students as they learn and expand their understanding and knowledge development of a given set of Learning Objectives

(Desire2Learn)

Smart Sparrow adaptive learning platform grew out of the doctoral dissertation of Dror Ben-Naim at the University of New South Wales, Australia. Aimed at increasing the "pedagogical ownership" of instructors over instructional content, the research project was inspired by new developments in data mining, authoring tools, cognitive load theory, and instructional design. In this system, instructors as action researchers can affirm or disprove their hypotheses regarding the effectiveness of their content on learners and move to revise their content (Ben-Naim, Bain, & Marcus, 2009).

Realizeit offers a content agnostic intelligent learning engine consisting of mathematical models that improve and refine themselves. The system can take any domain and provide an adaptive learning experience for an individual. The system provides a new way to create and organize courses by introducing the concept of a learning map (network) and allowing content to be authored or ingested to enrich the map. Courses can be created from subsets of maps (crossing knowledge domains) and the system will automatically personalize these to match each learner's standard of knowledge, ability level, and learning styles/preferences. The system uses its own analytics to improve itself. Faculty can also access these data to gain insights into the learning patterns and standard of knowledge of students. These analytics, in turn, support the course development process by providing real feedback on weak areas of content materials, such as concept definitions, examples of concepts, applications of concepts, and formative test questions.

Current Use and Effectiveness of Adaptive Learning Systems

Despite the progress in the development of adaptive learning technologies and their adoption by software and textbook publishing industry, their use in institutions of higher education is very low.

In a survey of faculty and chief information officers at four-year and two-year colleges, 96 percent of respondents agreed that: "adaptive learning technology has great potential to improve learning outcomes for students." However, only four percent of courses use ALSs. Green (2015, p. 1). Several issues impede deployment of ALSs:

- Current applications, including commercially available programs, are complicated and most faculty require technical support to use them.
- There are no intuitive authoring tools with graphical user interface for faculty to make their own instructional materials adaptable to the learning profiles of their students.
- Because most ALS technology development projects are still in an experimental phase, integrating them with LMSs in use in universities is not an easy task and requires high-level technical expertise.

- There is a dearth of evaluation studies to demonstrate to what extent ALSs have been effective, or how faculty can integrate ALSs in their teaching practice.
- Ethical issues, such as student privacy and access to learner data collected by ALSs, have not been resolved (Barb, 2016; Verhagen, Dalibert, Lucivero, Timan, & Co, 2016; Yarnall, Means, & Wetzel, 2016).

Consequently, faculty and other decision-makers do not have the necessary information they need in order to integrate adaptive learning to their courses and programs. Ironically, the few studies that have been conducted on the effectiveness of adaptive learning systems have compared the statistical significance of aggregated scores of students who were divided into two groups: experimental students who have been subjected to the use of an ALS and control students who learned the same curriculum without the benefit of an ALS. For example, Yarnall et al. (2016) conducted comparative studies of aggregated data for students who participated in courses characterized as blended adaptive vs. lecture, online adaptive vs. online, and blended adaptive vs. blended. As we have indicated, such comparative studies invariably show no statistically significant results between the two groups that are compared. We present details on two additional examples here to illustrate the point. Griff and Matter (2013) evaluated the effectiveness of LearnSmart, an ALS developed by McGraw-Hill Higher Education, that was used in physiology courses across six institutions of higher education. They concluded that there were no statistically significant differences between "improvement on post-tests relative to pre-tests, grade distributions and retention between treatment sections using LearnSmart, an adaptive learning system developed by McGraw-Hill Higher Education (MHHE), and control sections given questions online from an MHHE test bank" (p. 1). However, the researchers indicated that both experimental and control sections showed increased performance on post-tests relative to pre-tests. We contend that had the researchers chosen system dynamics as their research method and had they focused on data collected from each individual learner over a period of time, a different pattern of learning achievement by each learner would have been observed. In another study with a similar research design, Aslan, Özturk, and Inceoglu (2014, p. 1165) compared a middleware designed to provide a tutoring environment responsive to the learning style of a group of university students with a "traditional" Web-based tutoring program without adaptive capability. The researchers indicated that:

> For the within-group analysis, both the experimental and control groups achieved higher scores on the post-test. The difference between pre- and post-test scores was statistically significant. When the two groups' pre- and post-test results were compared, there was a non-significant difference.

Again, had the researchers stayed away from comparative studies that invariably have shown no statistically significant results in the study of mediated educational programs, their hypothesis probably would have been confirmed.

To measure the effectiveness of ALSs, it is imperative to collect data on each single-subject and analyze such data over a period of time for each individual learner. By definition, ALSs are made to respond to individual differences of each student and not to characteristics of a group of students. Ideally, the data collected from each individual learner should be analyzed using system dynamics method of analysis to reveal patterns of learning for each learner. Looking at a group of learners to measure the effectiveness of an ALS in response to individual differences among learners is logically as well as methodologically flawed.

Nonetheless, in a meta-analysis of 50 research projects assessing the effectiveness of intelligent tutoring systems, Kulik and Fletcher (2015, p. 53) concluded the following:

> Students who received intelligent tutoring outperformed control students on pre-tests in 46 (or 92%) of the 50 studies. In 39 (or 78%) of the 50 studies, tutoring gains were larger than 0.25 standard deviations, or large enough to be considered of substantive importance by the standards of the What Works Clearinghouse .... Thus, the vast majority of studies found ITS effects that were not only positive but also large enough to be important for instruction.

In an earlier meta-analysis of intelligent tutoring systems, Ma and Adesope (2014, p. 219) showed similar results:

> The overall result of our meta-analysis is that ITS outperformed, in aggregate, the other modes of instruction to which it was compared in evaluative studies. Moderator analysis found that using ITS was associated with significantly higher achievement outcomes than using each of the other modes of instruction except small-group human tutoring and individual human tutoring, and the difference in learning outcomes between ITS and these two forms of human tutoring was not statistically significant. ITS was also associated with greater achievement regardless of whether it was used as the principal means of instruction, as an integral part of classroom instruction, to support in-class activities such as laboratory exercises, for supplementary after-class instruction, or as part of assigned homework. In analyzing 18 other moderator variables related to characteristics of the ITS, students, research setting, outcome assessments, and research methods, we found no substantive, significant differences among levels of the moderators under a random-effects model.

Conclusion

Technical, methodological, and organizational issues notwithstanding, the use of ALSs in universities are increasing (The New Media Consortium, 2017). Bryant (2016) commented: "Over the past three years, adaptive learning has gone from an ill-defined concept in higher education to an important category of teaching and learning technology." To the extent that educators are recognizing a need to personalize learning for students, attend to at-risk students more closely through the use of analytics, and make instruction more relevant to competencies learners require, the use of ALSs will increase in the future.

Today, in software development laboratories as well as in experimental, and regular online courses throughout the world, there are in place many prototypes and commercial applications of adaptive intelligent tutoring systems, adaptive hypermedia systems, and adaptive simulation and serious games. These systems are used by hundreds of thousands of students to personalize their learning experience. This is while students generate and provide an unprecedented amount of valuable data to researchers, designers, and developers about how to improve these learning systems. Yet, this is just the beginning. As reflected in the literature of the field, refinement of current core technologies and applications are to continue while the cadre of researchers, designers, and developers working in the field are bound to devise new systems and novel approaches to the adaptive learning systems in the foreseeable future. These research and development efforts, along with the increased availability of commercial adaptive system technologies, provide an unprecedented opportunity to educators to implement the theory of transactional distance in their institutions and evaluate their effectiveness with appropriate research designs as suggested in this chapter.

Summary

Adaptive learning systems (ALSs) allow learners to match their personal traits with instructional treatments. Different systems in use today take into consideration a wide range of personal affective, cognitive, behavioral, and cultural characteristics to match instructional treatments for each learner. The interaction of a learner with an ALS is personal and as such, a learner could master predetermined objectives according to his or her learning style, preferences, and aptitude. Furthermore, ALSs are dynamic open systems and allow for the emergent behavior of the learner in addition to predetermined learning objectives. Most adaptive learning systems in use fit one of the three categories below:

- Adaptive hypermedia systems (AHS),
- Intelligent tutoring systems (ITS), and
- Adaptive simulations and serious games (ASSG).

However, some systems are combinations of these categories, making a strict classification difficult. The art and science of developing ALSs is still young and new systems will emerge in the future that would use these and newly developed approaches to make instruction adaptable to the profiles of individual learners.

In the next chapter, we will continue our extensive explanation of the hierarchical model of technology-based institutions of higher education by turning our attention to the Telecommunication Systems level and how they support optimization of transactional distance.

References

Aldrich, C. (2006). 9 paradoxes of educational simulations. *Training and Development, 60*, 49–52.

Almeida, L. S., Prieto, M. D., Ferreira, A. I., Bermejo, M. R., Ferrando, M., and Ferrándiz, C. (2010). Intelligence assessment: Gardner multiple intelligence theory as an alternative. *Learning and Individual Differences, 20*, 225–230.

Arif, M., and Hussain, M. (2015). Intelligent agent based architectures for e-learning system: Survey. *International Journal of u-and e-Service, Science and Technology, 8*(6), 9–24.

Aslan, B. G., Özturk, Ö., and Inceoglu, M. M. (2014). Effect of Bayesian student modeling on academic achievement in foreign language teaching (university level English preparatory school example). *Educational Sciences: Theory & Practice, 14*(3), 1160–1168.

Baddley, A. (1992). Working memory. *Science, 255*(5040), 556–569.

Barb, F. (2016). Clearing the hurdles to adaptive learning: Overcoming six challenges encountered in adopting adaptive learning. Retrieved from www.universitybusiness.com/article/adaptive-learning-clearing-hurdles-higher-ed/.

Beal, C. R. (2004). Adaptive user displays for intelligent tutoring software. *CyberPsychology & Behavior, 7*(6), 689–693.

Beck, J., Stern, M., and Haugsjaa, E. (2004). Applications of AI in education. www1.acm.org/crossroads/xrds3-1/aied.html.

Ben-Naim D., Bain, M., and Marcus, N. (2009). *A user-driven and data-driven approach for supporting teachers in reflection and adaptation of adaptive tutorials.* Paper presented at the the International Conference on Educational Data Mining Cordoba, Spain.

Boticario, J. G., and Santos, O. C. (2007). An open IMS-based user modelling approach for developing adaptive learning management systems. *Journal of Interactive Media in Education, 1*. http://jime.open.ac.uk/article/view/2007-2.

Bouchet, F., Azevedo, R., Kinnebrew, J. S., and Biswas, G. (2012). *Identifying students' characteristic learning behavior in an intelligent tutoring system fostering self-regulated learning.* Paper presented at the 5th International Conference on Educational Data Mining, Chania, Greece.

Brusilovsky, P. (1996). Methods and techniques of adaptive hypermedia. *User Modeling and User Adapted Interaction*, *6*(2–3), 87–129.

Bryant, G. (2016). *Learning to adapt 2.0: The evolution of adaptive learning in higher education.* Retrieved from http://tytonpartners.com/library/learning-to-adapt-2-0-the-evolution-of-adaptive-learning-in-higher-education/.

Clark, R. E., and Salomon, G. (1985). Media in teaching. In M. Wittich (Ed.), *The handbook of research on teaching*. Washington, DC: American Educational Research Association.

Cooper, C. (2010). *Individual differences and personality*. London: Hodder Education.

Cronbach, L. J. (Ed.). (2002). *Remaking the concept of aptitude: Extending the legacy of Richard E. Snow*. Mahwah, NJ: Lawrence Erlbaum Associates.

Cruces, A. L. L., and Arriaga, F. D. (2000). Reactive agent design for intelligent tutoring systems. *Cybernetics and Systems: An International Journal*, *31*, 1–47.

Desire2Learn (2015). How does the LeaP adaptive algorithm and semantic analytics engine work? Retrieved from http://content.brightspace.com/wp-content/uploads/LeaP_How_Does_It_Work3.pdf/.

Desmarais, M. C., and Baker, R. S. J. D. (2011). A review of recent advances in learner and skill modeling in intelligent learning environments. *User Modeling and User-Adapted Interaction: The Journal of Personalizaiton Research*, *22*(1–2), 9–38.

Dickey, M. (2005). Engaging by design: How engagement strategies in popular computer and video games can inform instructional design. *Educational Technology Research & Development*, *53*(2), 67–83.

D'mello, S., and Graesser, A. C. (2012). Autotutor and affective Autotutor: Learning by talking with cognitively and emotionally intelligent computers that talk back. *ACM Transactions on Interactive Intelligent Systems*, *2*(4), 1–39.

The Dunn and Dunn Model. (2014). Retrieved from www.learningstyles.net/en/about-us.

Essa, A. (2016). A possible future for next generation adaptive learning systems. *Smart Learning Environments*, *3*(3–16).

Gardner, H. (1993). *Frames of mind: The theory of multiple intelligences* (10th anniversary ed.). New York: BasicBooks.

Gitomer, D. H., and Glaser, R. (1987). If you don't know it work on it: Knowledge, self-regulation and instruction. In R. E. Snow and M. J. Farr (Eds.), *Aptitude, learning, and instruction: Volume 3: Conative and affective process analyses*. Hillsdale, NJ: Lawrence Erlbaum Associates.

Govindasamy, M. (2014). Animated pedagogical agents: A review of agent technology software in electronic learning environments. *Journal of Educational Multimedia and Hypermedia*, *23*(3), 163–188.

Green, K. (2015). The 2015 national survey of eLearning and information technology in US higher education. https://www.campuscomputing.net/content/2015/10/29/the-2015-campus-computing-survey.

Griff, E. R., and Matter, S. F. (2013). Evaluation of an adaptive online learning system. *British Journal of Educational Technology*, *44*(1), 170–176.

Gunawardena, C. N. (2014). Online identity and interaction. In I. Jung and C. N. Gunawardena (Eds.), *Culture and online learning* (pp. 34–44). Sterling, VA: Stylus.

Huong, M. T. (2016). Integrating learning styles and adaptive e-learning system: Current developments, problems and opportunities. *Computer in Human Behavior*, *55*, 1185–1193.

Ismailovic, D., Haladjian, J., Kohler, B., Pagano, D., and Brugge, B. (2011). *Adaptive serious game development*. Paper presented at the IADIS International Conference-Game and Entertainment, Rome, Italy.

Jonassen, D. H., and Grabowski, B. L. H. (1993). *Handbook of individual differences, learning, and instruction*. Hillsdale, NJ: Lawrence Erlbaum Associates.

Jung, I., and Gunawardena, C. N. (Eds.). (2014). *Culture and online learning: Global perspective and research*. Sterling, VA: Stylus.

Kalyuga, S., and Singh, A. (2016). Rethinking the boundaries of cognitive load theory in complex learning. *Educational Psychology Review, 28*, 831–852.

Kim, B., and Ho, W. (2014). Emergent practices and distributed emotions in educational game play. In C.-C. Liu, H. Ogata, S. C. Kong, and A. Kashihara (Eds.), *Proceedings of the 22nd International Conference on Computers in Education. Japan: Asia-Pacific Society for Computers in Education*. (578–587). Nara, Japan: Asia-Pacific Society for Computers in Education.

Kulik, J. A., and Fletcher, J. D. (2015). Effectiveness of intelligent tutoring systems: A meta-analytic review. *Review of Educational Research, 86*(1), 42–78.

Latham, A., Crockett, K., McLean, D., and Edmonds, B. (2012). A conversational intelligent tutoring system to automatically predict learning styles. *Computers & Education, 59*, 95–109.

Lavieri Jr., E. D. (2014). *A study of adaptive learning for educational game design*. Colorado Technical University. ProQuest database.

Lin, H.-C. K., Wang, C.-H., Chao, C.-J., and Chien, M.-K. (2012). Employing textual and facial emotion recognition to designing an affective tutoring system. *Turkish Online Journal of Educational Technology, 11*(4), 418–426.

Ma, W., and Adesope, O. O. (2014). Intelligent tutoring systems and learning outcomes: A meta-analysis. *Journal of Educaitonal Psychology, 106*(4), 901–918.

Magidson, R. (1974). *Mastery learning and PLATO*. Retrieved from ERIC database [ED 100 435].

Mampadi, F., Chen, S. Y, Ghinea, G., and Chen, M.-P. (2011). Design of adaptive hypermedia learning systems: A cognitive style approach. *Computers & Education, 56*, 1003–1011.

McClellan, J. A., and Conti, G. J. (2008). Identifying the multiple intelligences for your students. *Journal of Adult Education, 37*(1), 13–38.

Meshref, H., and Noor Mohamed, I. (2012). *Intelligent tutoring systems: A new proposed structure*. Paper presented at the International Conference on Advances in Computing, Communications and Informatics, Chennai, Tamil Nadu, India.

Morrison, G. R., and Anglin, G. J. (2005). Research on cognitive load theory: Application to e-learning. *Educational Technology Research and Development Journal, 53*(3), 94–104.

The New Media Consortium. (2017). NMC Horizon Report > 2017 higher education edition. Retrieved from www.nmc.org/publication/nmc-horizon-report-2017-higher-education-edition/.

Obikwelu, C., and Read, J. (2013). *Serious game adaptive learning systems*. Paper presented at the European Conference on Games Based Learning, United Kingdom.

Ozcelik, E., and Yildirim, S. (2005). Factors influencing the use of cognitive tools in web-based learning environments: A case study. *Quarterly Review of Distance Education, 6*(4), 295–308.

Papp, R. (2001). *Student learning styles & distance learning*. International Conference on Informatics Education & Research (ICIER). Retrieved from ERIC Database [ED474077].

Paramythis, S. L.-R. (2004). Adaptive learning environments and e-learning standards. *Electronic Journal of e-Learning, 2*(1), 181–194.

Pass, F., Renkl, A., and Sweller, J. (2003). Cognitive load theory and instructional design: Recent developments. *Educational Psychologist, 38*(1), 1–4.

Pavlik Jr., P., and Toth, J. (2010). *How to build bridges between intelligent tutoring system subfields of research.* Paper presented at the 10th International Conference on Intelligent Tutoring Systems, Pittsburgh, PA.

Pedrazzoli, A. (2009). *Opus One: An intelligent adaptive learning environment using artificial intelligence support.* Paper presented at the American Institute of Physics, San Francisco, CA. http://dx.doi.org/10.1063/1.3460231.

Phillips, F., and Johnson, B. G. (2011). Online homework versus intelligent tutoring systems: Pedagogical support for transaction analysis and recording. *Issues in Accounting Education, 26*(1), 87–97.

Poitras, E. G., and Lajoie, S. P. (2014). Developing an agent-based adaptive system for scaffolding self-regulated inquiry learning in history education. *Educational Technology Research and Development Journal, 62,* 335–366.

Proceedings of the 22nd International Conference on Computers in Education, ICCE 2014. (2014). Paper presented at the International Conference on Computers in Education, Nara, Japan.

Rani, M., Nayak, R., and Vyas, O. P. (2015). An ontology-based adaptive personalized e-learning system, assisted by software agents on cloud storage. *Knowledge-Based Systems, 90,* 33–48.

Reedy, G. B. (2015). Using cognitive load theory to inform simulation design and practice. *Clinical Simulation in Nursing, 11,* 355–360.

Rus, V., D'Mello, S., Hu, X., and Graesser, A. C. (2013). Recent advances in conversational intelligent tutoring systems. *A I Magazine, 34*(3), 42–54.

Rus, V., Stefanescu, D., Niraula, N., and Graesser, A. C. (2014). Deeptutor: Towards macro- and micro-adaptive conversational intelligent tutoring at scale. *Proceedings of the First ACM Conference on Learning @ Scale Conference (4 March 2014),* 209–210.

Saettler, P. (1990). *The evolution of American educational technology.* Englewood, CO: Libraries Unlimited.

Salomon, G. (1979). *Interaction of media, cognition, and learning.* San Francisco, CA: Jossey Bass.

Schramm, W. (1962). What we know about learning from instructional television. In W. Schramm (Ed.), *Educational television: The next ten years.* Stanford, CA: The Institute for Communication Research.

Schweppe, J., and Rummer, R. (2014). Attention, working memory, and long-term memory in multimedia learning: An integrated perspective based on process models of working memory. *Educational Psychology Review, 26,* 285–306.

Shacham, M., and Cutlip, M. B. (1981). Computer-based instruction: Is there a future in ChE education? *Chemical Engineering Journal, XV*(2), 78–84.

Shearer, R. L. (2017). Adaptive learning, competency-based education, and personalization: Implications for distance education and adult learners. *Journal of Lifelong Learning Society, 2*(28), 49–71.

Simpson, E. S. (2005). What teachers need to know about the video game generation. *TechTrends, 49*(5), 17–22.

Snow, R. E. (1987). Aptitude complexes. In R. E. Snow and M. J. Farr (Eds.), *Aptitude, learning, and instruction: Volume 3: Conative and affective process analyses*. Hillsdale, NJ: Lawrence Erlbaum Associates.

Snow, R. E., and Farr, M. J. (Eds.). (1987). *Aptitude, learning, and instruction: Volume 3: Conative and affective process analyses*. Hillsdale, NJ: Lawrence Erlbaum Associates.

Snow, R. E., Federico, P.-A., and Montague, W. E. (Eds.). (1980a). *Aptitude, learning and instruction: Volume 1: Cognitive process analysis of aptitude*. Mahwah, NJ: Lawrence Erlbaum Associates.

Snow, R. E., Federico, P.-A., and Montague, W. E. (Eds.). (1980b). *Aptitude, learning, and instruction: Volume 2: Cognitive process analyses of learning and problem solving*. Mahwah, NJ: Lawrence Erlbaum Associates.

Somyürek, S. (2015). The new trends in adaptive educational hypermedia systems. *International Review of Research in Open and Distributed Learning, 16*(1), 221–241.

Specht, M., and Burgos, D. (2007). Modeling adaptive educational methods with IMS learning design. *Journal of Interactive Media in Education, 2007*(1), 1–13.

Sweller, J. (2006). Discussion of emerging topics in cognitive load research: Using learner and information characteristics in the design of powerful learning environments. *Applied Cognitive Psychology, 20*(3), 353–357.

Tarpin-Bernard, F., and Habieb-Mammar, H. (2005). Modeling elementary cognitive abilities for adaptive hypermedia presentation. *User Modeling and User-Adapted Interaction, 15*(5), 459–495.

Tirri, K., Nokelainen, P., and Komulainen, E. (2013). Multiple intelligences: Can they be measured? *Psychological Test and Assessment Modeling, 55*(4), 438–461.

Trausan-Matu, S., Boyer, K., Crosby, M., and Panourgia, K. (Eds.). (2014). *Proceedings of the 12th International Conference on Intelligent Tutoring Systems ITS 2014, Honolulu, HI, USA, June 5–9, 2014: Proceedings*: Springer.

Tsiriga, V., and Virvou, M. (2004). A framework for the initialization of student models in web-based intelligent tutoring systems. *User Modeling and User-Adapted Interaction, 14*(4), 289–316.

van Merrienboer, J. J. G., and Ayers, P. (2005). Research on cognitive load theory and its design implications for e-learning. *Educational Technology Research and Development Journal, 53*(3), 5–13.

Vasilyeva, E., Pechenizkiy, M., and Puuronen, S. (2005). Knowledge management challenges in web-based adaptive e-learning systems. *Proceedings of I-KNOW '05*. Retrieved from http://www.win.tue.nl/~mpechen/publications/pubs/VasilyevaIKNOW05.pdf/.

Verhagen, J., Dalibert, L., Lucivero, F., Timan, T., and Co, L. (2016). Designing values in an adaptive learning platform. Retrieved from http://www.laceproject.eu/wp-content/uploads/2015/12/ep4la2016_paper_1.pdf/.

Virvou, M., and Tsiriga, V. (2001). An object oriented software life cycle of an intelligent tutoring system. *Computer Assisted Learning, 17*(2), 200–205.

Wijekumar, K. K., Meyer, B. J. F., and Lei, P. (2013). High-fidelity implementation of Web-based intelligent tutoring system improves fourth and fifth graders content area reading comprehension. *Computers & Education, 68*, 366–379.

Wilson, M. L. (2012). Learning styles, instructional strategies, and the question of matching: A literature review. *International Journal of Education, 4*(3), 67–87.

Yang, F.-J. (2010). The ideology of intelligent tutoring systems. *ACM Inroads, 1*(4), 63–65.

Yarnall, L., Means, B., and Wetzel, T. (2016). Lessons learned from early imple-
mentations of adaptive courseware. Retrieved from www.sri.com/sites/default/
files/brochures/almap_final_report.pdf/.

Yu, F. Y., Chang, L. J., Liu, Y. H., and Chan, T. W. (2002). Learning preferences toward computerized competitive modes. *Journal of Computer Assisted Learning, 18*(3),
341–350.

Zarraonandia, T., Ruíz, M. R., Díaz, P., and Aedo, I. (2012). *Combining game designs
for creating adaptive and personalized educational games.* Paper presented at the European
Conference on Games Based Learning, Cork, Ireland.

6

TELECOMMUNICATIONS SYSTEMS

Introduction

In the last three chapters, we discussed how hardware and software systems could affect minimizing or optimizing transactional distance for each student. This chapter focuses on how factors related to telecommunications systems, such as adequate bandwidth affect maintaining instructor-learner, learner-learner, and learner-instructional materials interaction, thus setting the conditions for increasing or decreasing structure and autonomy. The case study in this chapter highlights the evolving role of telecommunications systems in universities; illustrates how networks have been established and grown; and describes the opportunities and challenges that educators face in making efficient use of them now and in the future as they inevitably change.

Professionals

Professional engineers, system administrators and analysts, technicians, line service members, and their support staff are responsible for the telecommunication infrastructures and services that students, faculty, and administrators have come to rely on in the last few decades. Usually under the auspices of the campus chief information officer (CIO), a complex network of wired (i.e. coaxial, twisted pair and fiber-optic lines) as well as wireless systems ranging from radio and television transmitters, telecommunication satellites, and terrestrial microwave transmitters to Wi-Fi and Bluetooth make such connections possible on campuses and beyond.

Implications of the TTD for Telecommunications Systems

Provision of access to educational services is the most important implication of telecommunications systems in enabling learners to exercise autonomy in their learning environment and instructors to structure the learning space. Educators and students need to have access to at least 10 Mbps of download speed to maintain academic interactions that would lead to desired flow of dialogue by learners, as well as social, teaching, and cognitive presence by educators, thus establishing the flow of structure at each moment of instruction as an instructional session proceeds. Higher levels of bandwidth provide unprecedented capabilities to educators and students for engaging in immersive learning experiences. Music departments in universities around the country are already experimenting with multi-site performances where orchestra members are distributed in various locations. Low latency telecommunication systems that transport audio and video via Internet2, at speeds close to what a musician may experience sitting across the stage from other orchestra members, allow performers across the country to hold concerts in real time. Similarly, other arts and humanities programs are experimenting with collaborative efforts, such as rehearsing for dance sessions and dramatic performances, holding multi-venue recordings, and performing live distributed events in real time.

At these levels of telecommunication services, few interactions that are possible in the classroom environment cannot be replicated online, thus removing any barrier in distance or time for achieving the desired level of transactional distance. Additional technologies could also augment interaction. Examples include augmented reality in which learners are provided supplementary information when an instructor is demonstrating a science laboratory procedure. With additional bandwidth, access to observational and experimental environments, such as faraway terrestrial telescopes and laboratories located in another continent, becomes a reality. Similarly, students can access platforms that are in space hundreds of miles away. The Hubble Telescope, the International Space Station, and the many CubeSats that are in orbit are some examples. While these learning experiences are available to few students on rare occasions now, expansion of telecommunication services would enhance the capabilities of more institutions of higher education to make such learning mainstream and an ordinary occurrence. Therein lays another instance of the complexity of technology-based higher education systems. Extending additional bandwidth to students requires focused attention, coordination, and collaboration among professionals at hardware, software, and telecommunications levels who are in charge of network services, as well as those who regulate telecommunication services at the societal (e.g. FCC) and global (e.g. ITU) system levels. In recent years, professionals at these system levels have had to address issues arising from new technological developments, as well as regulating the provision of bandwidth to educational institutions. These issues include:

1. Providing cloud computing services to universities;
2. Keeping networks safe from cyber attacks and intrusions;
3. Regulating telecommunications networks and services to ensure access to students and educators;
4. Conceptualizing and implementing services and programs using Internet2; and
5. Connecting hardware systems together via Internet of Everything (IoE).

As shown below, we will discuss the characteristics of these factors and their effect on how telecommunication professionals are able to provide services to faculty, students, and administrators. However, telecommunication technologies are fast developing. While the current issues may not be a problem in five to ten years, new ones will emerge that will need the particular attention of educators.

1. Cloud computing—Arguably, cloud computing has made the most impact on how faculty, students, and administrators access and use networks, computing platforms, and software applications; and store, use, and share data. Through cloud computing, expensive software applications and platforms as well as storage and basic computing services can be shared with many users in one university or among several institutions. Thus, universities can provide applications that enhance learner autonomy and enable the instructor to structure the learning space on demand at an affordable cost. There are many examples of such cloud-based services, ranging from video conferencing systems (e.g. BlueJeans, Adobe Connect) to Google Apps for Education that are used by thousands of students for collaborating work, sharing resources and exchanging data. According to Bedrossian et al. (2014), for higher education institutions, cloud computing provides:

    - Increased computing power on demand. Institutions are able to provision and deprovision hardware, telecommunications, and software capacity dynamically as they need them.
    - Improved resiliency and reliability of computing services. Universities have access to geographically distributed systems that increase their control of disaster mitigation and recovery.
    - Enhanced agility and speed in deployment of software upgrades. Universities have access to the most recent software systems in minutes compared to days or months when applications were hosted in-house.

Because of access to these more powerful and versatile services, institutions are capable of designing, developing, and implementing unique learning spaces that include a plethora of tools and resources that go beyond the limitations of using a single learning management or adaptive learning platform. Ding (2014, p. 1267) presented a detailed description of the architecture of such a learning space in which:

> learners can choose learning tasks and determine learning contents, learning objectives and learning time. Meanwhile, they can customize their own personalized learning tasks according to their own cognitive styles, learning ability and personality characteristics. Besides, learning feedback can be obtained through network examination, assignment submission, group evaluation or teacher evaluation.

Manca, Waters, and Sandi (2016) designed, developed, and implemented an example of such a cloud-based learning environment by combining a variety of network and application solutions for teaching Geo Information Sciences (GIS). These included the following:

- Software-as-a-Service (SaaS) that enabled the educators to provide access to the learning environment for virtually an unlimited number of students;
- On-Demand Application Delivery that provided access to multiple users;
- Virtual Private Network (VPN) that offered a secure connection when it was needed;
- A variety of plugins for the different operating systems, such as Android, iOS, Windows, MacOS, and Linux that made the GIS instructional environment available to students using different devices;
- Video conferencing and online discussion applications that offered collaborative and information sharing capabilities to students; and
- The Virtual GIS Environment where students and faculty using multiple devices could either access the servers via a virtual private network (VPN) or on a local area network (LAN).

Relying on cloud computing for basic academic and administrative services or implementing a more complex learning environment as described above, however, has increased vulnerability to network intrusion and has compromised the reliability and security of telecommunication services.

2. Cybersecurity has become paramount as institutions of higher education increase their dependence in telecommunication networks for academic and administrative purposes. The primary challenge for network administrators is to keep the lines of communication open without compromising students' personal data, proprietary faculty research results, as well as university financial and administrative data. Campus network managers and cybersecurity professionals strive to:

- Keep the campus infrastructure secure;
- Provide safe access to cloud computing services; and
- Keep faculty, students, and administrators informed about how to securely use network services.

Established by EDUCAUSE in 2000, the Higher Education Information Security Council (www.educause.edu/heisc) aims to support higher education institutions with assessing risk, protecting data, implementing privacy programs, and educating faculty, students, and administrators to keep personal and professional data secure. Due to the lack of training, students, faculty, and administrators unwittingly compromise personal and professional data as they interface routinely with a plethora of online resources. Providing instruction about how to keep data secure in student orientation sessions, faculty development workshops, and staff training programs will be necessary on an ongoing basis in the foreseeable future.

3. Regulating networks—In 2015, the Federal Communications Commission updated its broadband benchmark speeds from 4 Mbps download/1 Mbps upload standard set in 2010 to 25 Mbps for download and 3 Mbps for upload. A report issued in the same year stated that users require more than 10 Mbps to participate in an online class, download files, and stream video (The Federal Communications Commission, 2015b). Depending on the geographic location (rural vs. urban), speeds that U.S. consumers can expect currently range from 3 Mbps to 24 Mbps for download while citizens in other countries, such as South Korea, enjoy faster rates. As students, faculty, and administrators begin to rely more on mobile devices that use wireless telecommunication, they should not be content with slower download speeds of 5 Mbps to 11 Mbps. According to Gary Shapiro (2013), President of Consumer Electronics Association, the increasing use of such devices has put pressure on the availability of wireless bandwidth throughout the country, especially in major urban areas. Shapiro stated that the key in increasing wireless bandwidth in the United States lies in the regulatory powers of the Federal Communications Commission (FCC) by opening new spectrum for this purpose. As of January 2014, nearly all of the U.S. population who lived in a census block was covered by at least one of the four major wireless service providers. Download speed for the best major provider was estimated at 100 Mbps while other major providers served their customers at rates ranging from 10 Mbps to 35 Mbps download. The estimate for the poorest provider was set at 3 Mbps (The Federal Communications Commission, 2015a, 2015b). These standards are bound to change in the near future, as the ISPs elevate the bandwidth available to their customers, and the FCC set new rules in place to regulate commercial service providers.

A recent development in the regulatory regime that affects the availability of bandwidth for institutions of higher education is net neutrality. It is perhaps the most important contemporary regulatory issue for universities to continue having unfettered access to the Internet. After the Department of Defense and the National Science Foundation, institutions of higher education were the first organizations to benefit from the availability of the Internet, but now many commercial content providers are on the Internet challenging the availability of services to institutions of higher education and other nonprofit organizations. Originally, the Internet was designed for all traffic to receive equal treatment (Frieden, 2008). As the Internet grew exponentially and became the primary network for news, information, and entertainment, new protocols developed that would require more bandwidth and may be offered to customers based on a differential pricing model. An example of this is Internet Protocol Television (IPTV) that allows storage of television programs on a server for users to view on demand. For such a new service that required additional investment in technology infrastructure, commercial Internet Service Providers (ISPs) sought to exact a higher price on the consumer. As diversity in users and types of services, such as IPTV, becomes available, it is conceivable that a differential model for provision of Internet services for different sources of information (e.g. sports, movies, live concerts) may emerge and challenge the unencumbered access of educators and students to the Internet at a reasonable level of speed and price. In other words, ISPs may choose to favor higher paying content providers over universities in their traffic, particularly during peak prime time programming and special events. In a declaration of net neutrality principles, the American Council on Education (2014, p. 1) on behalf of several national higher education associations stated:

> an open Internet is essential to our nation's freedom of speech, educational achievement, and economic growth. The Internet now serves as a primary, open platform for information exchange, intellectual discourse, civic engagement, creativity, research, innovation, teaching, and learning. We are deeply concerned that public broadband providers have financial incentives to interfere with the openness of the Internet and may act on these incentives in ways that could be harmful to the Internet content and services provided by libraries and educational institutions. Preserving the unimpeded flow of information over the public Internet and ensuring equitable access for all people is critical to our nation's social, cultural, educational, and economic well-being.

In clarifying its position, the American Council on Education stated that their position does not:

> object to paying for higher-capacity connections to the Internet; once connected, however, users should not have to pay additional fees to

receive prioritized transmission and their Internet messages or services should not be blocked or degraded. Such discrimination or degradation could jeopardize education, research, learning, and the unimpeded flow of information. As the FCC set the rules for net neutrality, Internet content and service providers may contest them and try to change them in ways that would not be advantageous to institutions of higher education. This issue requires continued and long-term attention and engagement of the university administrators to make sure that educators are not shortchanged. While at the current time students, faculty, and administrators must compete with other users for telecommunication services, new technology developments have already ushered in an era of abundant and perhaps even unlimited bandwidth.

4. Internet2—A consortium of national and international organizations has been experimenting with a very high-speed telecommunication system dubbed Internet2 (https://www.internet2.edu) to provide wider bandwidth, as well as secure and reliable network services to colleges and universities. The consortium consists of 220 U.S. universities along with 60 leading corporations, 70 government agencies, 38 regional and state education networks, as well as more than 65 national research and education networking partners representing over 100 countries. This state-of-the-art network offers customized high-capacity network capabilities to participating higher education institutions at very high speeds ranging from 10 gigabits to 100 gigabits, or even 400 gigabits, eventually expanding to one terabit!

   Except in a few demonstration markets, Internet2 level telecommunication capacity is not available to consumers in the United States. Thus, educators are limited in their use of high-end instructional systems, simulations, and serious games with rich media, high-definition video, high-resolution graphics, and multichannel audio, particularly in synchronous sessions in which multiple students and faculty in different locations are involved. Nonetheless, similar to the development of quantum computers that would put unlimited computing power at the disposal of users, next-generation optical networks may usher in the age of unlimited bandwidth.

5. Internet of Everything—Telecommunication systems have also made it possible to connect various devices. This complex network of hardware systems, known as Internet of Everything (IoE), has already enabled students to conduct a variety of projects ranging from harvesting energy to conducting experiments using sensors in multiple locations, and other similar projects in courses related to science, technology, engineering, and math (STEM).

Thus, the confluence of technical, regulatory, administrative, and academic factors has a dramatic impact on the frequency, intensity, and quality of interaction between students and instructors and among students. In essence, the quality and quantity of access to telecommunication services that educators and learners have influences the stock of transactional distance, as well as flows of dialogue and structure, as they become more dependent on using the Internet.

Summary

A thorough understanding of technical, regulatory, and security issues related to telecommunication technologies becomes of utmost importance for planners and policymakers in higher education to ensure that adequate bandwidth is made available to learners and instructors. Telecommunication services are crucial to opening the door for enriched teaching and learning experiences. However, decision-makers in higher education must balance the instructional needs of the learners with the cost of increased bandwidth and connectivity. As commercial use of the Internet increases, Internet service providers may offer a tiered pricing structure, thus changing the current equitable treatment that educational institutions receive. New technologies, such as advanced optical networks, promise an era of unmitigated access to network services in the next ten years.

The following case study clarifies the role of telecommunication systems by illustrating the intricate relationships it has with other system levels in a university.

In the next chapter, we will move the discussion to the Instructional Systems level where hardware and software technologies provide instructor and learner control through telecommunications systems.

Case Study 6.1 Establishing a Telecommunications Policy Committee at Middle State University

Middle State University is a land-grant institution. It was established 125 years ago. Its campus telecommunication infrastructure reflects the growth and development of the telecommuncations industry in the past century. This history has also been concomitant with a lot of internal turf wars and bureaucratic rivalries as different administrative and academic departments gained ownership of parts of the campus network infrastructure. Although these conflicts died down considerably when the university president consolidated the management of the campus network under the leadership of a single chief information officer, the organizational memory of the history of the development of the infrastructure has been hard to forget, even among the younger generation faculty and staff who were not present when such conflicts developed many decades ago. The campus set up a telephone switchboard and created a campus-wide twisted pair wire network for voice communication in the late 1800s. The university business services division supervised the phone system since its inception until 1984 when deregulation of the telephone industry compelled it to outsource the management of the voice network to a local private telecommunication service company.

There is also a widespread coaxial cable network that was put in place by a local cable company in the late 1970s. The company provided free cable service to administrative, academic, and student housing buildings. In return, the university allowed the cable company to use the television studios in the radio and television department (RTD) for local access programming. In addition to supervising the management of the coaxial cable network of the campus, RTD, an academic unit of the university educating future broadcasters, has been in charge of a student radio station broadcasting on an AM band since the 1920s. The Department has also been the home for the local PBS affiliate television station since the late 1960s, when the university received a TV broadcasting license from the Federal Communications Commission (FCC). During the last decades, the local cable company also provided RTD with satellite up-link and downlink capabilities and supported the university administration in the early days of video conferencing via its satellite dishes. As such, two networks developed on campus, one for voice communication supervised by the university administration and managed by a private phone company, and another for video communication supervised by an academic department and managed in collaboration with the local cable company.

In the meantime, since the 1980s, the university computing services put in place an expanding fiber-optic network for Internet connection throughout the university campus, adding a third network infrastructure, managed by yet another division of the university. In the 1990s, computing services also started making use of the campus coaxial cable network as well as the twisted pair network for offering various digital voice, video, and data services as the distinction among networks had disappeared because of the slow but growing analog to digital technology conversion. In 2000, After a few years of pitched battle between RTD, the university business services, and computing services for hanging on to their network turfs, all networks and telecommunication services were consolidated in one unit, and were put in the hands of a newly appointed chief information officer. Since then, things seemed to be working well. The infighting among different campus units for safeguarding their respective fiefdom nearly disappeared, and a new spirit of cooperation gradually evolved. However, in the last few years, the vice president for business services, as well as the vice president for academic affairs, have been receiving an increasing number of memos, email messages, and reports that all was not well in the telecommunication wonderland again. Several issues had surfaced that required the immediate attention of the university leadership. These included:

- An increasing number of attacks on the campus network. Although no major breaches had occurred, at least one intruder was able to access a server on campus holding proprietary research data and possibly stealing the content of the entire database. A report from the computing services indicated that it was just a matter of time for sensitive student data to be compromised if network security should remain at the level that it is now.
- An unprecedented level of network usage by the university library. This was due to the expansion of the digital holdings of the library beyond text that now included high-definition video, high-resolution graphics, and an ongoing streaming of course-related materials in video webcasts and audio podcasts on a 24/7 basis.
- A growing level of network usage by the geography department. The department had received a grant from the U.S. Department of Homeland Security to monitor and analyze satellite images of the Earth. The geography department was scolded by faculty of the engineering department for having become a "bandwidth hog"; a dubious status that, ironically, was held by the engineering faculty until then!
- A dramatic rise in the use of campus wireless networks. Many undergraduate and nearly all graduate students, as well as some faculty and administrators, brought at least two and at times three or more mobile devices to campus ranging from phones to laptops, tablets, and wireless video cameras. This growth in bring-your-own-device (BYOD) usage was putting unprecedented stress on several of the wireless networks that were not originally designed for the BYOD lifestyle.
- An overwhelming number of calls to the campus help desk. Students needed assistance on a variety of issues ranging from managing their credentials to accessing various servers, as well as knowing how to use software applications required by faculty in a wide range of disciplines in on-campus and online courses.

- New training needs among the technical staff. Both students and professional staff of the computing services that managed the campus information and communication networks required ongoing training to learn about new processes and techniques for making the campus infrastructure more secure and efficient while responding optimally to the growing needs of the faculty and students.
- The need for studying and responding to state and federal legislative initiatives, as well as complying with regulations. Issues ranging from net neutrality, extension of wireless services to rural areas, and participating in statewide telecommunication networks could no longer be ignored or relegated solely to the campus attorney. These issues had become front and center for the day-to-day operation of the campus network, as they affected compliance and efficiency.
- Responding to the increasing need of the faculty on setting up proprietary research servers. Special research laboratories with high-performance image, and video processing, robotics, and various levels of 3-D printing had been installed on campus through state, federal, and private foundation grants. These laboratories each had specific needs for network configuration, at times challenging network managers to keep them secure and efficient.
- Facilitating an increasing number of faculty using smart classrooms, video conferencing rooms, and desktop webcasting for on-campus and online teaching purposes.
- Responding to the needs of students and faculty involved in various forms of mobile learning. An increasing variety of mobile devices for learning in courses related to social sciences, as well as in STEM courses, were present on campus every day. Some faculty had placed sensors to communicate with mobile devices that collected data ranging from chemicals in the soil to weather-related information.

These recent developments have put the campus computing service in touch with almost all the academic and administrative units of the university, including the campus security and fire departments that were making wide use of the campus network for keeping buildings secure, managing access to them, and ensuring that fire drills and evacuation procedures took place as scheduled. A recent memo from the chief information officer of the university to the Vice President for academic Affairs, and copied to the VP of business services stated that the Middle State University has moved to a new level of complexity in its use of telecommunication services. With fast emerging technologies, such as IoE, its daily operations are going to be even more complex in a few months. The CIO requested establishing a standing telecommunication policy committee consisting of as many stakeholders as necessary to put in place procedures for the growth and use of the campus telecommunication system on an ongoing basis. More specifically, the CIO stated in the memo that a new mission statement is needed for the computing services division to include the new realities with which it must deal on an ongoing basis. These include provision of a secure network that is ubiquitous and capable of performing at a high level of throughput and efficiency on a 24/7 basis.

After consultation with the university president, the two VPs of academic affairs and business services drafted a joint memo to all campus units to select a delegate to the plenary session of the standing telecommunication policy committee. The first order of business for the plenary session was for the delegates to elect a steering committee to draft a mission statement for the consideration and ratification of the full telecommunication policy committee. The VPs were aware that some of the old issues from the "good old days" when each unit managed the telecommunication network most relevant to its need would surface again. However, they both took a deep breath, the VP of academic affairs clicked on the "Send" icon on his email software and transmitted the invitation to all on his distribution list.

Case Analysis

In this case, the growth and development of telecommunication services since the inauguration of the Middle State University show that information and communication technology is a fast-evolving field. In addition to everyday changes, roughly, every ten years, a major shift in basic technology occurs that is disruptive to the normal operation of the university and requires an overarching review of policies and procedures that are in place. In short, although the Telecommunications Systems Level is at a lower tier of the hierarchical model presented here, it influences all the other system levels of the model. Also, as we have shown in this chapter as well as in Chapter 7 on Instructional Systems Level, telecommunication services affect what students can do in receiving instruction, keeping in touch with instructors, and collaborating with their peers. Similarly, educational innovations (Curricular Systems), such as distributed mobile learning, and offering MOOCs has put unprecedented pressure on the available services. These developments ultimately reach the university administrators (Management Systems). Administrators in collaboration with high-level decision-making bodies, such as the academic senate, must work through a variety of conditions and concerns ranging from legal requirements (Societal Systems) to budgetary constraints (Management Systems) and reconcile them with the realities of new telecommunication technologies to respond to the needs and demands of faculty and students. These efforts are necessary to keep a university competitive not only within the borders of the United States but also with international institutions that are growing in academic strength and sophistication every year (Global Systems).

References

American Council on Education. (2014). Net neutrality principles from the higher education community. Retrieved from http://www.acenet.edu/news-room/Documents/Net-Neutrality-Principles.pdf/.

Bedrossian, A., et al. (2014). Cloud strategy for higher education: Building a common solution. *American Journal of Distance Education*. Retrieved from https://library.educause.edu/~/media/files/library/2014/11/erb1413-pdf/.

Ding, J. (2014). Construction of a digital learning environment based on cloud computing. *British Journal of Educational Technology, 46*, 1367–1377.

Frieden, R. (2008). A primer on network neutrality. *Intereconomics, 43*(1), 4–15. doi:10.1007/s10272-008-0237-z.

Manca, G., Waters, N., and Sandi, G. (2016). Using cloud computing to develop an integrated virtual system for online GIScience programs. *Knowledge Management & E-Learning, 8*(4), 514–527.

Shapiro, G. (2013). CEA President Gary Shapiro talks network and innovation. Retrieved from www.tianow.org/videos/cea-president-gary-shapiro-talks-network-and-innovation/10664.

The Federal Communications Commission. (2015a). *2015 measuring broadband America fixed report*. Washington, DC. Retrieved from www.fcc.gov/reports-research/reports/measuring-broadband-america/measuring-broadband-america-2015.

The Federal Communications Commission. (2015b). *Broadband availability in America*. Washington, DC. Retrieved from https://apps.fcc.gov/edocs_public/attachmatch/DOC-331734A1.pdf/.

7

INSTRUCTIONAL SYSTEMS

Introduction

In chapters 3, 4, and 6, we focused on hardware, software, and telecommunications systems that support academic and management functions of a university and explored how such systems can potentially influence administrative and academic affairs of a university to optimize transactional distance for each learner. In this chapter, we focus on instructional systems.

Instructional designers represent instructional systems in highly articulated models to indicate learning objectives, activities, and outcomes. These models embody the non-tangible but all-important shape of the teaching-learning space, or the design of the teaching-learning environment that defines the form of a course or other types of instructional offerings. The theory of transactional distance describes how the format of a course or a similar learning program would optimize transactional distance for each individual learner. As such, instructional design models that instructional designers embed in a course or a similar instructional-learning offering enhance or inhibit the ability of the instructor to structure a course commensurate to the aptitude of the learner for autonomy. Similarly, such designs assist or hinder the learner to exercise autonomy in relation to a course's structure. In this chapter, we will examine current instructional design models that are widely used in universities. Each of these models, depending on its characteristics, set the conditions for learner dialogue and autonomy, as they determine learner-instructor and learner-learner interactions. We put forward the proposition that models such as learner-centered design vs. instructor-centered design, constructivist vs. behaviorist, or individualized vs. collaborative learning are not mutually exclusive, and in actual practice, they represent two ends of a spectrum. Their stocks in formatting a course, or other instructional offerings, depend on the individual profile of a learner. A detailed analysis of instructional design models from the perspective of the theory of transactional distance is presented in the next chapter.

The case study for this chapter highlights the relationship of decisions made at the Instructional System Level about a particular course with the expectations and performance of faculty, administrators, and students.

Professionals

Instructional designers, course developers, and evaluators support faculty in many tasks related to conceptualizing and implementing a course at this system level. Course teams rely on other professionals who work at the hardware, software, and telecommunication system levels to create and present instructional programs. Faculty whose work culture can best be described as postindustrial and are willing and able to establish a cybernetic bond with their learners benefit the most from the efforts of these professionals. Those faculty who are in a preindustrial work culture receive the least amount of benefit from course teams, while those faculty, who teach in an industrial culture of mass education can benefit from a course team to the extent that the one-size-fits-all course format, typical of industrial mass production, would accommodate implementing principles of instructional design.

Implications of the TTD for Instructional Systems

The concept of transactional distance is a serious challenge to the lecture-based classroom format of teaching and learning. A presupposition of the concept of autonomy in the theory of transactional distance is that in a program of study, each learner can exercise autonomy by having a direct input in setting learning objectives, deciding learning activities, and determining when s/he has met instructional objectives. Transactional distance for each individual learner is regulated when learner autonomy is balanced with structure that is required by the instructor, the design of a course—or other forms of instructional offerings—the discipline of the subject matter taught in a course, and the conditions imposed by the university administration. This dynamic process is fundamentally different in comparison to the static format of classroom instruction in which the learner, particularly in large undergraduate classes, is a passive observer and has very limited or no input in how a course is taught and how s/he can engage in learning activities that match her or his individual profile.

In dynamic systems of instruction, design of a course affords the learner autonomy and provides the instructor the necessary support to structure a course. In such a system, learner-centered vs. instructor-centered, constructivist vs. behaviorist, or individualized vs. collaborative approaches to teaching and learning are not mutually exclusive; these forms of instructional design represent two ends of a spectrum. Each of these bifurcated choices optimizes transactional distance for each individual learner by enhancing/limiting autonomy as desired by the learner and adjusting structure as determined by the instructor through learner-instructor interaction during an instructional/learning period.

In a learner-centered course, autonomy is maximized and structure and transactional distance are minimized. In contrast, in an instructor-centered course, structure and transactional distance are maximized, and autonomy is minimized. However, as depicted in Figure 7.1, since no course is purely instructor-centered or learner-centered, a dynamic balance is achieved between autonomy and structure when the course format affords control to learners and instructors to optimize transactional distance for each individual learner.

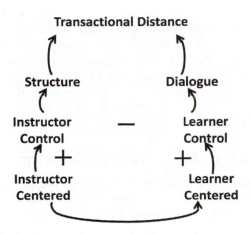

FIGURE 7.1 Causal loop diagram of an instructor-centered, learner-centered subsystem in relation to the level of transactional distance.

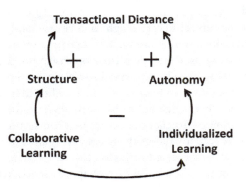

FIGURE 7.2 Transactional distance as determined by collaborative and individualized learning.

In a totally collaborative learning environment, the group superimposes a certain amount of structure on the learning environment, which decreases autonomy and transactional distance. Figure 7.2 shows how the values of collaborative learning and individualized learning determine the rates of structure and autonomy, which in turn set the stock of transactional distance.

Similarly, Figure 7.3 shows how constructivist learning increases autonomy and decreases structure and transactional distance.

Ultimately, these choices impact other system components, such as cost of developing courses and programs as well as expenditure on hardware, software, and telecommunications technologies that contribute to maintaining an optimal stock of transactional distance for each individual learner.

A Dichotomous World

If we look at the literature of instructional design without the benefit of the dynamic systems theory and the theory of transactional distance, we find a bipolar universe. Very often, ideas such as synchronous vs. asynchronous learning or content-based instruction vs. problem-based instruction have been presented as mutually exclusive choices. In theory and practice, these modes of design are not addressed as a range of possibilities between two extremes of processes that are in effect in varying degrees in an educational session, depending on the needs of each learner and the requirements of an instructor. From the viewpoint of dynamic systems, the degree of the variance in any of these continua depends on the requirement for structure and the need for dialogue and autonomy as determined by an instructor in relation to one learner. (See the next chapter for a detailed discussion of instructional design models from the perspective of the TTD and system dynamics.)

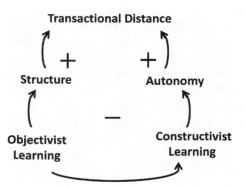

FIGURE 7.3 Transactional distance as determined by objectivist and constructivist learning.

If, however, we do not take a dynamic systems approach to the design of instruction, we come to unsatisfactory conclusions. This is when we live in a bipolar universe of online vs. classroom learning or synchronous vs. asynchronous distance education, or we see the world of the instructor and the learner in discrete and unrelated terms and not in a dynamic balance between autonomy and structure. Bernard, Abrami, Wade, Borokhovski, and Lou (2004) conducted a meta-analysis of comparative studies of distance education with classroom instruction in order to develop a theory of equivalency for synchronous distance education. In discussing their study, they posed several questions and responded to them with an unsatisfactory conclusion as presented here:

> Why do effect sizes vary so widely, even after they are categorized as synchronous or asynchronous? What should be included in synchronous DE to make it as effective as (equivalent to) classroom instruction, or at least the best it can be? What practices should be avoided? What are the ranges of instructional practices and learning strategies that best support achievement and satisfaction in asynchronous DE? Answers to these kinds of questions did not emerge as clearly as they could have if the literature were more complete.
>
> *(p. 107)*

From the perspectives of the TTD, synchronicity or asynchronicity, as well as classroom instruction vs. online learning in any educational program is a matter of degree as a program of study evolves for a single learner. A more complete research literature in a reductionist paradigm that conceptualizes synchronicity and asynchronicity discretely cannot resolve the complex nature of learning and demonstrate that in real life there is rarely a purely synchronous or an asynchronous course! The degree to which students communicate synchronously or asynchronously is determined by the needs of the learner and the requirements of the instructor for such forms of communication and instruction and not as an a priori research or design decision. In such a dynamic system, variance in individual learners and responses by instructors are theoretically unlimited. The optimal level of transactional distance for each individual learner is, therefore, an emergent characteristic of the system that cannot be designed or determined in advance. Learners select to engage in different modes of communication as their need for autonomy requires, albeit if provision for interaction in a course is not provided, such a need is left unsatisfied and leads to lack of progress in a course of study. The design of the instructional/learning environment allows learners to use synchronous communication or asynchronous communication depending on their learning needs. The flows of these two types of communication in varying frequencies, durations, and qualities, ultimately, contribute to the stock of transactional distance. Learners may also choose to meet with an instructor in person, if they think that would further their learning. Similarly, when learners require more structure, objectivist teaching becomes necessary. When their level of expertise increases, they may require more constructivist approaches and less objectivist learning strategies.

As we have seen over the years, comparing distance education and classroom instruction, or synchronous learning vs. asynchronous learning, invariably has shown the unsatisfactory "no statistically significant difference" outcome. Research designs that are not based on systems thinking do not allow for exploring the complexity of learning for each individual learner, the dynamic nature of the learning process, and the emergent behavior of the learner when meaningful learning occurs. Invariably, researchers who are not engaged in system dynamics research and single-subject research aggregate data sets collected from a group of learners together, which obscure individual differences among learners. When differences are obscured, no statistically significant difference can be detected! But, perhaps more importantly, comparative studies of classroom vs. online learning do not consider that classroom instruction and online learning are two different phenomena and are not comparable. Classroom instruction in its traditional form is a craft-oriented premodern practice of a single instructor who addresses learners in mass. Technology-based learning, particularly in advanced dynamic adaptive environments, is a postmodern collaborative practice of many professionals who address learners individually. Trying to find a theory of equivalency between these two vastly dissimilar phenomena does not obtain useful or satisfactory results either for theoretical and research purposes or for practice in the field.

Teaching and Learning as a Complex, Dynamic, Adaptive, Self-Organized System with Emergent Properties

It is important at this point to emphasize that while reading this chapter, the reader must keep in mind that the theory of transactional distance is not a prescriptive model for instructional design. It is a transformative theory in the sense that it re-conceptualizes the process of education (teaching and learning) from a mechanical stimulus-response model to a model of education that is:

- Complex because learning and teaching consist of many interacting components;
- Dynamic as learning and teaching change in time;
- Adaptive to the needs of the learner by allowing him/her to have an input to what is worth learning, how learning should take place, and when learning has occurred;
- Self-organized by the learner as the learner progresses from being a novice to an expert; and
- Emergent as not all of the learning outcomes can be determined in advance of the learning session by the learner, instructor, or the instructional designer.

In this dynamic model, certain learning may take place by a simple stimulus-response process. That is, the instructor (or the instructional designer as proxy of the instructor) may administer a stimulus to the learner for eliciting a certain response from the learner. However, a major characteristic of dynamic complex systems is the potential for self-organization and manifestation of emergent behavior of the learner. The emergent performance of the learner includes behaviors, such as creativity, decision-making under novel conditions, and problem solving. These levels of learning are beyond obtaining predetermined learning objectives by stimulus–response teaching strategies set by the instructor or the instructional designer prior to the learner engaging in a course of study.

The theory of transactional distance does not perceive the learner as a passive being who remains inert until the instructor does something to him/her: Apply the right mix of stimuli to elicit a certain response. Learning, in this model, is what learners do! The condition of learning for the learner (i.e. autonomy) is subjective for him or her, until such subjectivity meets the objective reality of structure imposed by the instructor. If such structure is not successfully negotiated with the learner, s/he loses interest in the learning setting and moves on to another setting where structure is more conducive to her/his aptitude. Conversely, the condition of teaching (structure) is subjective for the instructor until it meets the objective reality of learner autonomy. As Whitehead (1967, p. 176) put it:

> The subject object relation can be conceived as Recipient and Provoker, where the fact provoked is an affective tone about the status of the provoker in the provoked experience. Also, the total provoked occasion is a totality involving many such examples of provocation. Again, the phraseology is unfortunate; for the word 'recipient' suggests a passivity that is erroneous.

This dynamic subject object interrelationship in Whitehead's view includes a phenomenon that he termed "prehension". In "an occasion of activity," prehension "constitute the process of becoming." In our case, object and subject are designated labels for the instructor and learner in a moment of comprehension; that is when prehension evolves to become knowledge. As such, the instructor also learns from the learner and, therefore, s/he moves under the label of subject when that happens albeit for a short period of time before s/he subjects the learner in another process of prehension to comprehension.

This dynamic view of interaction between the learner and the instructor reflects thinking about learning and teaching processes that are fundamentally different from theories that describe teaching and learning as a collection of simple stimulus-response connections. The mechanical stimulus-response view of teaching and learning, however, is entrenched in our basic understanding of education. Even descriptions of constructivist theory of learning at times are presented in the stimulus–response language in the literature of instructional design! Constructivism, in this view, is just another type of stimulus to administer to the learner to elicit desired responses. Constructivism from a TTD perspective is a call for creating educational environments for each learner to construct his or her learning according to his/her aptitude for autonomy. This shift in thinking about the design of future educational (teaching-learning) systems is essential to understanding the difference between the industrial and postindustrial design of educational systems: one that is static and does not adjust to the learner profile, and the other which is dynamic and changes in time in response to an individual learner.

In the worldview of transactional distance, "instructional design" represents the format of the overall learning space. This is in contrast to traditional instructional design, which follows a linear process from the analysis of the learner's need at one point in time to defining a set of specific objectives for him/her leading to the presentation of specific media stimuli for the learner to reach those objectives, and ultimately testing the learner to see if the objectives have been reached or not. Learning, however, is dynamic and nonlinear. It happens in real-time. Partially, because of this realization, in recent years, linear methods of instructional design have been subject to criticism. Alternative methods, such as rapid prototyping, reduce the amount of time between when learning objectives are set and when the learner is subjected to the instructional materials that are based on those learning objectives. However, the most appropriate learning environment for each individual learner is one that is capable of assessing learner needs and providing differential responses to each individual learner in real-time. Examples of such systems include simulations, serious games, or advanced highly adaptive learning systems. These systems are described in Chapter 5.

Summary

In this chapter, we demonstrated that from the perspectives of the TTD, dichotomous choices in instructional design, such as classroom instruction vs. online learning in any educational program, are a matter of degree. The degree to which students communicate synchronously or asynchronously, or are present or absent in a classroom setting, is determined by the needs of the learner and the requirements of the instructor for such forms of communication and instruction and not as an a priori design decision. In the next chapter, we will expand on this theme by examining the most prevalent instructional design models in institutions of higher education and demonstrate the continuum in which each model contributes to learner autonomy or instructor control.

Case Study 7.1 Disappointment with Moving Psych 101 Online

The Department of Psychology at Middle State University offers a course titled *Psychology 101, Foundations of Psychology*, one of the largest required general education courses online. Each semester upwards of 600 students are enrolled in this course. Three full-time faculty and two graduate assistants teach this course. In addition, each faculty holds a virtual office hour to respond to emails received from students or respond to students who have signed up in advance to participate in a chat session. Students also can reach out to one of the two graduate assistants in a synchronous chat session for an hour per day, including weekends, to resolve any problems or issues they may encounter.

For the last three years, since the course has been offered online, Dean Dorothy Hopeful of the College of Social Sciences has been tracking course enrollments and dropouts. From her point of view, after three years, the project has not met its goal. Porting the course online was supposed to reduce the rate of dropouts. The weekly office hours and the daily chat sessions were to keep students in the course and prevent them from leaving. In fact, more students have been dropping out per semester now compared to when that the course was offered offline in a classroom.

In addition, the course was now costing the college more than offering it previously on-campus. After allocating a hefty initial fund to match a grant from the provost's office to put the course online, Dean Hopeful had to put two graduate students on the payroll as well assist the faculty and offer online help to students. In addition, she has been supporting 50 percent of the time of an instructional designer (ID) to support the faculty and graduate assistants. The initial investment as well as the ongoing payroll expenditure increased the cost of the course compared to when it was offered on-campus without any appreciable return on investment in improving student grades or reducing the number of students who left the course each semester.

Also, faculty have been less enthusiastic about the entire project, as their student evaluations deteriorated. After an initial phase of eagerness to enroll in an online course, students reflected their lack of satisfaction with the course in faculty evaluations. Initially, the on-campus rumor was that the online course was going to be a lot "easier" to complete, but after the third semester, no one was claiming that the course was any simpler. If anything, students complained about the unforgiving nature of the course testing function, not to mention the few instances that the entire LMS went offline during a mid-term exam, resulting in some students receiving an automatic grade of F. It took those students several weeks to retake the test and correct their grade at the registrar's office.

Dean Hopeful called a meeting of the three faculty as well as the two graduate assistants to discuss the situation. The faculty suggested inviting the instructional designer who was assigned to them from the campus Instructional Technology Center as well.

The dean made her usual introduction about the project:

> We have received another call for reducing our budget and I am not sure where we can find any corners to cut. In the last round of budget reductions, we cut all that we could. With the economy showing some signs of general improvement, we may receive a very small increase in our budget after all these years. However, we need to think about an overall strategy about our programs, and make sure that we can carry out our general education obligations. Psych 101 is our bread and butter. We cannot lose its enrollments to another college. At the same time we have to find new ways to support the operating costs of the course, or show some results in reducing dropouts or improved grades to justify its additional cost that we incurred since it went online. I will sit back now and listen to your ideas.

Dr. Tradition spoke out first this time. Usually, he remained silent until everyone else spoke first. This time, however, he was eager to share with the group that he has considered online courses, and has talked to his friends in the College of Education who have been teaching online for several years. Dr. Tradition said:

> They all tell me that teaching online is very different than teaching in the classroom. Merely videotaping our lectures and putting them online, even with the chat sessions and the virtual office hour is not going to do the trick. The faculty in the college of education who have been successful in improving student achievement and reducing dropout have all had to redesign their courses entirely.

Dean Hopeful nodded her head approving what Dr. Tradition just said. She went on to add that she has also considered the matter and:

> Adding synchronous online time for chat sessions and virtual office hours will just increase the cost in time and money perhaps with no improvement in student achievement. This was supposed to reduce our cost not increase it! I even remember the days that I was told that distance education was going to make us money!

That comment was followed by a few chuckles from those present.

Dr. Ambivalent moved forward towards the conference table, indicating that he wanted to jump into the conversation. He said:

> Yes, I agree that synchronous communication with students will cost both money for the college, and time for us. However, despite receiving negative comments from students in my student evaluations, I would like to continue the project for another semester or two and see if we can improve our chat sessions and office hours.

Dr. Pronet who had remained silent so far, adjusted her eye glasses slightly and inquired: "I wonder what our ID has to say about all of this?"

The ID who had been part of this project from the outset said: "I am here to help all of you reach the goals you define. My job is to support you."

Dr. Pronet cut her off and said:

> Yes, that is all fine, but we asked you here to cast some light on how we are doing as compared with others that you are helping across campus. Also, we understand that the LMS just went through a major upgrade. Could you tell us about what new features were added?

The ID responded:

> Yes, well, we just had a workshop about the new features of the LMS, and we will have another one later during the semester break. So, I suggest that all of you join us for that. But to be honest with you, most of the faculty across campus are not using what we had before effectively. So, one immediate step that we can take is to make better use of the LMS to support students. But before we get into that discussion, I would like us to set a goal. Is it fair to assume that the immediate goal here is to reduce the number of students who drop out of Psych 101?

Everyone nodded in approval.

The ID then went on to say:

> The initial design of the course was to present faculty lectures online and make them somewhat interactive with office hours and chat sessions. However, the basic structure of the course has remained linear. If a student does not understand a concept or follow an instructional sequence, all s/he can do is to replay the lecture. This is woefully inadequate to make the course interactive to a point that it would make a major difference in its effectiveness in terms of increasing retention

or improving student grades. For the next academic year, I suggest that we begin to integrate some of the adaptive learning features that are now included in the Website of the textbook that students study for *Psych 101*. Some of these features, such as their slide presentations that are controlled by students, include short quizzes. We can use them as non-graded quizzes to help students prepare for their mid-term and final exams better. There are other more advanced features on the publisher's Website that use a form of intelligent tutoring technology. It may need more work to be integrated in the LMS. However, using these more advanced features will be a giant step towards the goal of making *Psych 101* fully interactive and adaptive to the needs of each individual learner.

In the meantime and until we accomplish our long-term transition to a more advanced technology, we could do the following:

1. The current LMS collects a lot of data, such as how long each student spends on the system and how well they do on the tests. These data sets could be used for identifying at-risk students. Right now we wait for students to call for help, but some students do not even know that they are in trouble until it is too late. For at-risk students, we need to be proactive to reach out to them and reengage them in the course. If you want to be more adventurous, I think the provost can help with funds to make use of a new analytics tool that we have just acquired. So far, we have used it for general campus data analysis in a college or department. But this course is very important to the university and I bet we can get some money to conduct analysis of student data at the course level.

2. The LMS also has a set of so-called intelligent agents. These are basically conditions that are set in the LMS. For example, a condition can be set for submitting a particular assignment at a specific day or time. If a student fails to meet the condition, s/he will receive an email message regarding the assignment. The agents are great not only to alert students, but for you to alert each other as a team as well about what is going on in each section of the course.

3. For some time now, the LMS also has been supporting social media, although after the upgrade the social media functions are more integrated in the LMS itself. I suggest that in addition to holding one-on-one chat sessions with students, you start creating learning circles at the very beginning of the semester so students can support each other. We must realize that although first-year or even second-year students use social media for nonacademic purposes, they are not skillful enough to organize learning circles on their own.

4. Last but not least, we need to make better use of mobile devices. We can move into mobile learning with making the LMS more accessible to students via their mobile devices. We can apply for another summer grant to work on creating some field studies to better engage students who have smart phones or tablets into the course.

Dean Hopeful said:

> These are very good ideas. I am not sure if we can implement all of them, but let's think about them and get back together in a couple of weeks to follow up on them. Some of these ideas, such as, creating learning circles can be implemented at no cost; others may cost a few dollars. I will see what I can do to get more funds for supporting the long-term integration with the textbook publisher, as well as, participating in the campus-wide analytics demonstration project.

Case Analysis

The dean and the faculty in this case decided to move *Psych 101* online with assumptions that were related to curricular and management systems levels regarding student achievement and reducing the cost of the course. Although the management of the university supported their effort with additional expenses, they were disappointed that the desired results did not materialize for students while the cost of the course increased (Instructional System and Management System levels). Now, they are making a new set of decisions regarding better use of their LMS as well as integrating the intelligent tutoring technology that the textbook publisher offers, and using the analytics technology that the university has put into use (Software System and Management System levels). Making better use of these technologies may bring about some of the results that had been anticipated originally, such as lowering student dropouts and improving grades (Instructional and Curricular Systems levels). However, the textbook publisher may require a new contract with the university for the use of its intelligent tutoring system, which in turn could increase the overall cost of the textbook for either the students or the university, depending on how the contract between the publisher and the university is structured. In using these technologies, the university must also safeguard student data, which would increase the overall cost of offering *Psych 101* online (Management System Level).

Eventually, not all of the return on this additional investment may be entirely recovered by the university. If student grades improve and dropout rates decrease, the university would certainly have benefited from these changes. Students may also save money, if they do not drop out, and reduce the time they require to complete their degree program. However, promoting better learner achievement and keeping students involved in *Psych 101* would have long-term benefits at the Societal System Level. When students do not drop out of courses, or the university entirely, the overall tax burden on society is reduced. Also, employers find better-prepared graduates for their entry-level positions, and alumni find themselves in a better situation to assimilate in the world of work (Societal System Level).

New changes in the technology platform of *Psych 101* may also result in unforeseen consequences at least at the Curricular and Management Systems levels. For example, data analysis may show that some students may need additional remedial assistance to be able to complete the course. Although providing this additional assistance may bring about more expenditure, keeping students in a course will be ultimately more beneficial to the university and society than failing them. In addition, some students may complete all the course requirements earlier than the normal 16 weeks allotted to a semester. A demonstration project may move these students to their next general education course earlier as well, thus reducing the time that it takes to complete their entire degree program (Curricular System and Management System levels). Implementing these changes require a wide range of modifications from adjusting the administrative software of the university in order to reflect student progress in a dynamic learning environment to modifying how universities are funded and student loans are structured (Societal System Level). Ultimately, the university could be compelled to redesign *Psych 101* and make it adaptable to the individual needs of learners if it is going to make its general education courses more academically relevant to each student and more cost effective for the taxpayers.

References

Bernard, R. M., Abrami, P. C., Wade, A., Borokhovski, E., and Lou, Y. (2004). The effects of synchronous and asynchronous distance education: A meta-analytical assessment of Simonson's "equivalency theory" Association for Educational Communications and Technology (pp. 102–109). Retrieved from ERIC database [485078].

Whitehead, A. N. (1967). *Adventures of ideas.* New York: Free Press.

8

INSTRUCTIONAL DESIGN MODELS
A Transactional Distance Perspective

Introduction

Contending theories of learning have had a formative influence in the field of instructional design and have brought to fore contrasting views. Instructional design models that have evolved in recent decades present dichotomous choices to instructional designers and faculty. From the vantage point of the TTD, however, individualized vs. collaborative, learner-centered vs. instructor-centered, or constructivist vs. behaviorist approaches to teaching and learning are not mutually exclusive. Each of these seemingly bifurcated choices offers a spectrum to instructors and learners for optimizing transactional distance. The choice is not selecting one over the other, but how much emphasis to put on one design criterion for an individual learner at each point in time. The value of these instructional and learning modes is determined dynamically by the autonomy that each learner exercises and the structure that the instructor brings to bear in each moment of instruction in real time. For example, the balance between individualized and collaborative learning at each moment in time depends on the following:

1. The aptitude of the learner for independent learning, as compared to joining a peer group in relation to;
2. The requirement of the instructor to engage the learner in personal interaction or assigning him/her to a peer group.

Objectivist vs. Constructivist Learning

Two views of knowledge have given rise to contrasting traditions in epistemology and by extension learning theory. The objectivist view of the world assumes that knowledge is a representation of what exists in reality, whereas the constructivist view holds that the learner constructs his or her reality based on a personal life experience. Duffy and Cunningham (1996, p. 178) quoted the influential thinker in the theory of constructivist learning, Von Glasserfeld, who stated: "Instead of presupposing knowledge is a representation of what exists, knowledge is a mapping, in the light of human experience, of what is feasible." The objectivist view of the world provides for the possibility that we are capable of understanding the reality of our world; however, our understanding may be incomplete and would be an approximation of reality at each point in time. The constructivist view presupposes that man has no direct access to reality. Our knowledge of the world is limited to a subjective construction based on our experience.

Whereas from the objectivist point of view, instruction is a method of presenting facts, concepts, procedures, and principles to enable the learner to achieve specified learning objectives and perform particular tasks, the constructivist view holds that learners build personal meaning from their experience rather than merely acquire knowledge (Duffy & Cunningham, 1996). Thus, Smith and Ragan (1993, p. 440) posited, "meaning is not resident in the medium that contains the message, but in the learner, who, in interacting with the message, constructs a personal and unique interpretation or meaning." Put simply, objectivist teaching is based on principles of behavioral psychology that requires a change in learner's overt and observable activities for learning to take place. In contrast, constructivist perspective is more concerned with the learner's cognitive, affective, and behavioral processes as they are related to the learner's entire environment as an indication that learning has occurred (Burton, Moore, & Magliaro, 1996; Duffy & Cunningham, 1996). As far as outcomes are concerned, while objectivist learning ensures that the learner has met specific learning goals, constructivist learning allows for emergent behavior as learners manifest ingenuity and creativity in contexts that may be new to them.

In recent years, constructivism has been dominant in the literature of educational technology almost to the exclusion of objectivist learning. Nonetheless, Burton et al. (1996) indicated that these two theories of learning have become closer and each has informed the other about the true nature of learning. Explaining learning from each of these perspectives to the exclusion of the other is not useful and ultimately misleading.

> Arguments such as: Cognitive psychology assumes more 'active learners'… and behaviorist more 'passive learners' or that behaviorism seeks to control behavior while cognitivist seeks to control thoughts or 'thought structures,' makes little sense and contribute little.
>
> *(p. 48)*

To further understand the relationships between these two theories from a pragmatist's point of view, Bickhard (2004, p. 94) posited:

a pragmatist, action orientation to cognition not only forces a model of the organism interacting with its environment, not just passively perceiving its environment, it also forces the modeling constraint that the mind must be active in at least three senses: (1) it must *guide* those external interactions, (2) it must *construct* those guiding schemes, and (3) it must *deploy* those guiding schemes appropriately to the situations that are being interacted with (interacting with a ball as if it were a key might be a form of creative play, but it won't open the door).

Earlier, Duffy, and Cunningham (1996, p. 171) supported the pragmatic interpretation of constructivist learning and stated:

> judge the validity of someone's knowledge, understanding, explanation, or other action, not by reference to the extent to which it matches reality but, rather, by testing the extent to which it provides a viable, workable, acceptable action relative to potential alternatives.

The hypothesis that we can draw from the analysis above is that in the paradigm of transactional distance, novice learners require objectivist instruction to develop their base of knowledge about a subject matter. Structure is high for novice learners as the instructor imposes direct control on what is to be learned and how to learn it, and also determine if learning has occurred. As learners develop expertise, they become more equipped to exercise autonomy; consequently, structure and transactional distance decrease, and dialogue and autonomy increase as learners increasingly define their own learning objectives, set the method for reaching those objectives, and assess the outcomes of their learning.

Providing Structure to Learners

In the last four decades, to structure instruction for learners, faculty and instructional designers in a wide range of universities, as well as corporate training programs, adopted one or a combination of three leading instructional design models. B. F. Skinner's operant conditioning, Gagne's conditions of learning, and Merrill's component display theory provided direct methods for instructors and instructional designers to structure the learning domain for the learner in the classroom as well as in mediated environments of programmed instruction and computer-based instruction.

Skinner's operant conditioning prescribed positively reinforcing the learner when s/he exhibited a desired learning behavior. Successive reinforcement of behaviors from small steps to more complex ones would lead the learner to perform a range of tasks from a plain response to a stimulus to solving more complex mathematics or social problems.

Gagne (1985) identified nine conditions for learning that necessitated the learner to recognize external stimuli, and respond to them for developing a range of "intellectual skills." These were:

1. Gaining attention (reception);
2. Informing learners of the objective (expectancy);
3. Stimulating recall of prior learning (retrieval);
4. Presenting the stimulus (selective perception);
5. Providing learning guidance (semantic encoding);
6. Eliciting performance (responding);
7. Providing feedback (reinforcement);
8. Assessing performance (retrieval); and
9. Enhancing retention and transfer (generalization).

Merrill's component display theory conceptualized instruction and learning in a two-dimensional matrix. One consisted of presenting facts, concepts, procedures, and principles to the learner and the other consisted of the learner's finding, using, and remembering instruction to achieve learner objectives at granular levels.

Similar to content-centered delivery of instructional information, constructivism gave life to new forms of practice that, in addition to presenting learning stimuli to the learner, was concerned with the environment of the learner. Researchers Duffy and Cunningham (1996), Savin-Baden and Wilkie (2006), and Unden and Beaumont (2006) identified case-based, problem-based and project-based methods of education under the general umbrella of problem-based learning (PBL). These methods offer the learner a context, such as a business case, a medical problem, or a class project, in contrast to presenting instructional information isolated from an applied framework. On teaching writing, for instance, Stearns, Ronald, Greenlee, and Crespy (2003, p. 214) commented, "Research on writing and writing instruction has shown for decades that skills taught in isolation, thorough exercises, or out of context do not last and do not transfer to other writing situations". Requiring students to select a context, such as writing for a particular assignment in another class, would advance their skills much better than writing the proverbial essay on how I spent my summer that could be out of context for students who are facing pressure for completing their assignments now that the summer is over.

Case-based learning (CBL) has been used in business and law schools since the 1920s. In this situated method, the instructor presents a business or legal case to students that includes details of a circumstance that closely resembles what learners might find in an actual work environment. Learners confront the dynamics of a case and move the events in a simulated environment towards a conclusion (Barbazette, 2004; Honan & Rule, 2002; Sudzina, 1999). Focusing on teacher education, Lundeberg, Levin, and Harrington (1999, p. 231) noted that "problem-based cases allow students to vicariously explore the complex world of teaching and encourage them to think about how they might resolve future dilemmas".

Problem-based learning (PBL) has been applied to medical education in the last few decades and has received attention in teaching other disciplines as well. Instructional designers make use of this method when they require the learner to analyze and solve a problem in a realistic situation. In fact, the problem-solving process is the essence of the learning that takes place in PBL. However, a discussion of PBL further highlights the polarized world of teaching methods today. PBL is not content or instructor driven; its aim is to involve the learner in resolving a situation that may occur in his or her future career. As Duffy and Cunningham (1996) explained, "Rather than 'teaching' the student in the sense of presenting or even assigning information, the goal is to support the student's learning." Engaging the learner in authentic learning activities similar to what s/he might find in a professional setting is the goal of PBL.

> It is the activity in relation to the content that defines learning; the ability to think critically in that content domain, to collaborate with peers and use them to test ideas about issues, and the ability to locate information related to the issues and bring it to bear on the diagnosis.
>
> *(p. 190)*

Other issues, such as the appropriateness of self-directed learning, emerge when educators consider implementing a PBL design for teaching and learning. Miflin (2004), in a critical analysis of the literature related to PBL in medical education, highlighted some of the theoretical and practical concerns, as well as critical factors for instructional design:

- This range seems very young for med school. The average age of first-year med students is 24. These younger students may not meet the criteria of adult learners, and as such may not be the best candidates to engage in self-directed learning.
- The way faculty interpreted adult self-directed learning affected how they implemented PBL and how they interacted with students.
- For example, when students sought to answer the questions they needed to understand the problem they were discussing in their PBL group some teachers refused to answer their questions, arguing that because this was a PBL program, teachers were not supposed to answer questions.

(pp. 43–44)

- Often what teachers and administrators meant by "self-directed" learning was "self-management" or "personal autonomy."
- Others criticized the appropriateness of and the level of such autonomy when it was expected of medical students to acquire specific skills.

As we have demonstrated, these variables are resolved in a learning environment based on the need of each learner for autonomy and the instructor's requirement for structure. While instructional design models and methods emphasize either learner control or instructor control, the question in the TTD is creating a dynamic learning environment, which is capable of striking the necessary balance between the two at each point in time for each individual learner based on his or her characteristics. Offering learner autonomy in self-directed learning or requiring a highly structured learning environment in objectivist learning at the two ends of the continuum do not have any inherent value per se. The issue is the degree to which one or the other is necessary in an instance in time for a specific learner and in the context of a particular learning activity to move the learner from prehension to comprehension leading action. It is important to note here that in many cases, self-directed or self-managed learning is applied to groups of students instead of to an individual student. In such practice, the individual learner is not evaluated or may not even be the primary focus. When these methods, which by their very nature should be individually driven, are applied to a group of students, they show no significant results in learning and at times are deemed ineffective.

Project-based learning (PrBL) involves the presentation of the learning activity to the learner with a challenging problem. Students often work in groups to face an authentic problem to which they can relate. Heckendorn (2002), for example, involved his students during an entire academic year in designing, purchasing, and building an advanced-computing cluster at Idaho State University. He explained that PrBL:

- Integrates learning into the context of a real-world problem;
- Focuses on complex problem-solving and decision-making skills;
- Engages students in multidimensional assessment;
- Helps students to integrate their various skill sets;
- Allows students to excel in their learning interests; and
- Involves students in collaborative work.

What CBL, PBL, and PrBL have in common is that they contextualize (situate) various learning tasks in an applied framework and often require the learner to collaborate with others to complete some if not all of the learning tasks. In situated learning, educators present knowledge in an authentic context and in settings that closely approximate a real-life environment.

Situated learning (SL) has antecedents in the theory of affordances presented by Gibson (1986) and the theory of social learning by Vygotsky (1978). Additionally, the theory of mathematical problem-solving by Schoenfeld (1985) embodies some of the critical elements of the SL framework. In their research, Brown, Collins, and Duguid (1989) emphasized the idea of cognitive apprenticeship, which "supports learning in a domain by enabling students to acquire, develop, and use cognitive tools in authentic domain activity."

Authentic learning, at times, requires social interaction and collaboration with others. Both in formal learning that usually takes place inside a school and in informal learning that often occurs outside of the boundaries of formal schooling, some learning advances through collaborative social interaction and the social construction of knowledge.

Lave and Wenger (1991) demonstrated that social interaction is a critical component of learning: Learners become involved in a "community of practice" that embodies certain beliefs and behaviors to be acquired as an integral part of the knowledge base. In this social context, learners usually start as novices from the periphery of a professional group, and as they gain expertise, they gradually move to the center.

Case-based, problem-based and project-based methods of instruction offer a rich menu for developing adaptive learning systems that respond dynamically to learner needs and instructor requirements. However, because their utility depends on the aptitude of the learner, their implementation is complex. Providing such a rich and diverse selection to the learner requires further integration of instructional resources, improved interoperability between computing systems, and reduction of the development cost of immersive environments employing artificial reality, augmented reality, and other similar technologies.

Individualized Learning vs. Collaborative Learning

Individualized education is not new. According to Saettler (1990), all education was individualized prior to the 1800s in the United States. As industrialization took over, individualized learning was replaced with group instruction in a classroom. Visionary educators, nonetheless, advanced several "plans" to individualize learning in the 1880s and thereafter. These plans differed in methods and implementation, but each emphasized the ability of each student to develop an understanding of the knowledge presented to him/her and the skills that are necessary for putting that knowledge to work.

In the 1960s, with a better understanding of individual differences and the ascendance of behavioral psychology, new efforts were made to individualize instruction. One of the most popular efforts was the Keller Plan, proposed by behavioral psychologist Fred Keller (1889–1996), which included:

- Introducing self-paced learning;
- Mastering a unit of instruction by the learner, before moving on to the next;
- Presenting lectures and demonstrations for motivating the learners, and not necessarily for providing information; and
- Proctoring and tutoring students closely (Saettler, 1990).

By the mid-1970s, individualized instruction in its various iterations (e.g. individually prescribed instruction (IPI), program for learning in accordance with needs (PLAN), individually guided education (IGE) declined in use and popularity. A decade later, personal computers become popular, and through the use of computer-based training (CBT)—also called computer-based instruction (CBI)—individualized instruction found a new life (Dear, 1997). However, many programs were glorified electronic page-turners. Most computers were not networked at the time, and the single computer environment was limited to simple branching of instruction. This limited capability offered some added value to the linear method of learning, but not enough to make a drastic difference in learning and training in schools, as well as in business and industry. The field had to wait a couple of decades for the Internet to be placed in the public domain, which made personal computers much more interactive through Web-based applications. In addition, the information on the World Wide Web grew at an amazing rate and provided a media-rich environment for learners. Students were no longer limited to the predetermined branching of CBI or CBT. They could browse the Web and find the information that supported and advanced learning in various formats and at different language levels appropriate for them. Also, new software applications emerged that employed new advances in cognitive science and artificial intelligence. As we demonstrated in Chapter 5, today, faculty in higher education are experimenting with various forms of adaptive learning systems that are far more advanced than their CBT and CBI ancestors. These applications can offer differentiated responses that are dynamically generated for each learner.

The strengths and virtues of individualized instruction, however, are in contrast to what students can achieve through collaborative learning. In recent years, scholars have highlighted the importance of social construction of knowledge. Pea (1993, p. 48) posited that: "Knowledge is commonly socially constructed, through collaborative efforts toward shared objectives or by dialogues and challenges brought about by differences in persons' perspectives." Harasim (1990) demonstrated how online education provides a platform for collaboration and intellectual amplification among learners, leading to:

- Increased motivation and reduced uncertainty and anxiety in groups;
- Greater cognitive development compared to the condition occurring in learners working alone;
- Better concept achievement through verbalizing to a peer; and
- Cognitive restructuring of ill-structured knowledge through controversy, disagreement, and discussion.

More recent publications on collaborative learning have noted the relationship between individual differences and group work. Ashraf (2004) described the problem of less motivated students in group work who might become "proficient free riders" when more active students compensate for them. Ochoa and Gottschall (2004) also observed "unequal contributions by individuals" in a multimedia problem-based learning module designed to develop group collaboration skills through simulated activities for special education students. Paswan and Gollakota (2004) investigated dimensions of peer evaluation in a group and found that "gender influenced group members' dependability and overall satisfaction." The likely explanation presented was that women in the study might have "attached higher importance to their academic success, were less tolerant of 'goofing off,' or were more demanding." Hancock (2004, p. 164) investigated the effects of graduate students' peer orientation on achievement and motivation to learn with cooperative learning strategies while enrolled in a one-semester educational research methods course, and found that:

> Graduate students who desire to work with others do not necessarily learn more in settings that foster student interaction and collaboration. Other variables, such as the extent to which students value learning more than social interaction and whether students allow others to dominate classroom discussions of course material, seem to influence graduate students' achievement as much as peer orientation.

Peterson and Miller (2004, p. 1) also compared learning in a large lecture setting with small collaborative discussion groups in a psychology course. They observed that "Quality of experience did not differ across instructional contexts for high- vs. low-achieving students; high-achieving students experienced greater overall quality of experience in both instructional contexts, particularly in the areas of engagement, perceived skill and self-esteem." These and other similar research results leave the question of individual differences and collaborative learning unresolved. As Hancock (2004, p. 165) suggested in his concluding remarks, "researchers should attempt to identify the specific personality and situational variables that foster graduate students' achievement in addition to fostering their motivation to learn."

Pointing to the networked environment that increasingly is defining the context of learning, Siemens (2005) suggested the theory of connectivism to explain what learning is in a "digital age." In his view, learning "is a process of connecting specialized nodes or information sources." The individual, in this theory, remains to be the starting point of learning but each person is part of a network through which s/he engages in a "cycle of knowledge development" from personal to network and back to the individual learner. This constant flow of knowledge acquisition and development keeps the learner current and leads him/her to make informed decisions. As the learner is constantly becoming aware of new information and possibilities through the network to which s/he belongs, learning leads to the instability that is required for emergent behavior and creativity. Since Siemens suggested the idea of connectivism, several scholars have explored various aspects of the theory and have tested its principles in practice. Commenting on the work of 13 scholars who contributed to a special issue of the *International Review of Research in Open and Distributed Learning* about connectivism, Siemens and Conole (2011, p. 1) said:

> New technologies that influence how information is created and shared and how people connect and socialize hold promise for adoption in education. Much like the idea of a book necessitated the development of the library or the idea of structured curriculum and domains of knowledge produced classrooms, the idea of the Internet—distributed, social, networked—influences the structure of education, teaching, and learning.

Kropf (2013, p. 1) critically analyzed several empirical studies on connectivism and concluded that the process of tapping to "reservoirs namely, (a) online classrooms, (b) social networks, and (c) virtual reality or simulated communities" does not supplant behaviorism, cognitivism, and constructivism as the current prevalent theories of learning, but it embodies all three of them at times in one form or another. Another pattern that has emerged from critical studies about connectivism is that in practice collaborative learning depends on the needs, interests, and skills of the learners. Kop (2011) determined that lurkers might learn as much as those who collaborate. Also, she questioned if learners possess all of the abilities and skills that connectivist learning requires. She posited that learners must be highly autonomous, have critical skills in using digital technologies, and be motivated by self-directed learning in a connectivist learning environment.

Milligan, Littlejohn, and Margaryan (2013, p. 157) examined the principles of connectivism in massive open online courses (MOOCs) and concluded:

> Understanding the nature of learners and their engagement is critical to the success of any online education provision, especially those where there is an expectation that the learner should self-motivate and self-direct their learning. Massive courses, by their very nature, bring in learners with a range of backgrounds, previous experience, and skill levels, and it is therefore incumbent on course organizers to design a learning experience that accommodates these diverse learner profiles.

Similar to other learning strategies discussed in this chapter, individualized instruction and collaborative learning are not mutually exclusive methods of teaching and learning. Learners, depending on their tolerance for structure and need for dialogue and autonomy, may choose to engage in self-directed and managed learning at certain points in time and seek the support of a peer or a group of peers at other times when social interaction furthers their learning.

Formal vs. Informal Learning

Historically, education has been the purview of the highest elite of society. Having a university education in particular was very rare among common people. The invention of the printing press in the 15th century began a gradual process of democratizing education by putting information in the hands of anyone who desired to be educated, thus creating the informal means of accessing knowledge. Gutenberg's invention created the modern chasm between formal and informal education and accentuated gaining knowledge through elitist educational institution or via democratic means of communication. In the 20th century, radio, television, and the Internet augmented the printing press and further opened access to educational information to almost anyone who wanted to learn.

In recent years, formal institutions of higher education took a historic step to close the gap between formal and informal education by opening their courses on the Internet to thousands of learners worldwide. Following the pioneering efforts of MIT and Stanford University in establishing MOOCs, several other top tier universities made some of their courses available to the masses on the World Wide Web as well. This use of the Internet is in the same tradition of the application of mass media that made educational opportunities more democratic in the past. MOOCs have accentuated this tradition. However, offering courses on the Internet to students who are formally registered in a university or to the masses via MOOCs have remained in the periphery. A major reason for traditional institutions of higher education to sideline distance education and only accept it in a slow and piecemeal manner is its affinity for a less elitist, more democratic form of learning (Wedemeyer, 1981).

Close to four decades ago, Charles Wedemeyer outlined the characteristics of open education. To the extent that the modern educational system is engaged in archaic practices, such as following lock-step enrollment calendars or doctrinaire opposition to distance education, it is limiting the legitimate democratic right of learners to gain an access to education, and pursue a successful program of learning. Wedemeyer, however, had a pragmatic view of the status of the individual learner in relation to the formal educational institution, i.e. a view that can be realized in a dynamic system of teaching and learning. He stated that in an open system of education, "The system acknowledges that it embodies two separate but related programs, the instructional program embodied in the institutional system; and the learning program carried on by learners with the assistance of the system" (Wedemeyer 1981, p. 3). The fundamental concept, set forward by Wedemeyer, was that open education is an effort to "expand the freedoms of learners." The questions that he posed regarding the relationship between the individual learner with the educational establishment, and its larger social system, are perhaps more pertinent today than when they were originally put forward in 1981:

Our ideas about humanity and the need or importance of learning are culture-bound. Is man a free agent in the world? A helpless victim of inherited genes? The product of social and economic conditions that force him into behavior over which he has little control? Is the individual important, or is the group, composed of conforming individuals, important? Is the individual born to serve the state, or is the state created to serve each individual? May the individual seek upward social and economic mobility through his own efforts, or are his class and status to be determined by the collective needs for the state? Who is to get an education, for how long, with what curricula and rewards, at what costs to self and state, for what purpose and at what quality levels, through what methodologies, opportunity and access systems, and under what controls?

(*Wedemeyer, 1981, pp. 7–8*)

Answering these fundamental questions orient educators and other decision-makers for designing important aspects of the future of their institution. If higher education fails to realize the importance of structuring formal education in balance with the exigencies of informal learning that are accentuated by the proliferation of various forms of media, the essence of the university as a necessary social institution would become questionable.

Face-to-Face vs. Distance Education

Research contrasting distance education with face-to-face, campus-based, or traditional education has also contributed to dichotomous thinking in the field. While research has indicated that there is no statistically significant difference between distance education and classroom instruction, issues of parity of esteem have lingered on for years. Social science research grew rapidly after World War II and led to the investigation of many novel developments, including the expansion of instructional television. Since the 1950s, comparing distance education with face-to-face education has been a favorite of education researchers. In the 1960s, Wilbur Schramm (1962) conducted studies that compared instructional television (ITV) with classroom instruction. Schramm summarized the results of more than 400 "scientifically designed and statistically treated comparisons of ITV and classroom teaching." He concluded: "we can say confidently that students learn from it, and that they learn fast and efficiently ... the conclusion has been 'no significant difference' between learning from television, and from classroom teaching" (p. 66).

Since Schramm, many other researchers have compared mediated instruction with other media, or classroom instruction. Wetzel, Radtke, and Stern (1994) summarized the results of comparative studies of video media until the mid-1990s. Johnson, Aragon, Shaik, and Palma-Rivas (2000) compared learning outcomes of an online course with a similar course taught face-to-face. Invariably, these studies showed no statistically significant difference. In a meta-analysis of 19 studies of an original pool of 700 studies that met the carefully selected criteria of the authors, Machtmes and Asher (2000, p. 43) confirmed previous conclusions that "there does not appear to be a difference in achievement between distance and traditional learners." In another meta-analysis conducted by a group of researchers, Bernard et al. (2004) revealed a slight advantage for distance education compared to classroom instruction on certain measures. However, the conclusions generally supported the lack of significant statistical difference when these two types of instruction are compared.

Despite overwhelming evidence that comparative studies of mediated instruction and classroom instruction invariably show "no statistically significant difference" in results, professionals continue to conduct them and justify why they are needed. After presenting an updated review of comparative studies and demonstrating that they have reached a point of diminishing returns by offering the same results, Meyer (2004) called for their continuation by faculty who teach courses on the Web "in the guise of a personal journey." This would, she asserted, fulfill:

> the faculty person's legitimate need to learn about the web and pursue personal evidence that it works in his or her class or discipline. The most important result will be what the faculty person learns about the process of learning and teaching online. In other words, the most likely outcome of the comparison study is a faculty person who has changed his or her understanding of the web and can now support its use.
>
> (p. 6)

This and other similar unconvincing rationalizations for the continuation of comparative studies of distance instruction with face-to-face instruction accentuate the paradigm shift that the theory of transactional distance has brought to fore. Neither of these two forms of education is superior or inferior per se. The strength of each manifests itself in the need of the learner for dialogue or structure. As we have demonstrated in this book, the dichotomy between distance education and face-to-face instruction is false. In a classroom, transactional distance can increase when dialogue is absent, and in a course that is taught on the Internet where the learner and the instructor are separated by thousands of miles, transactional distance can decrease by the presence of dialogue. The primary issue is what serves the learner best in a particular moment of instruction so that the learner can move from prehension to comprehension, and action.

Summary

In this chapter, we presented a detailed analysis of the objectivist vs constructivist learning, individualized vs. collaborative learning, formal vs. informal learning, and face-to-face vs. distance education, and we explained how each of these dynamic continua contribute to learner autonomy or instructor control.

In the next chapter, the effects of static curricular systems are presented and are analyzed from the perspective of the TTD. We will demonstrate how policies that drive contemporary curriculum systems, such as the credit hour, impede the implementation of dynamic forms of instruction that can adapt to the learner's profile and support a preindustrial form of teaching. Applying technology to preindustrial craft-oriented form of teaching contributes to increasing the cost of education without any appreciable impact on the performance of the learner.

References

Ashraf, M. (2004). A critical look at the use of group projects as a pedagogical tool. *Journal of Education for Business, 79*(4), 213–216.

Barbazette, J. (2004). *Instant case studies: How to design, adapt, and use case studies in training.* San Francisco, CA: Pfeiffer.

Bernard, R. M., et al. (2004). How does distance education compare with classroom instruction? A meta-analysis of the empirical literature. *Review of Educational Research, 74*, 379–439.

Bickhard, M. H. (2004). A challenge to constructivism: Internal and external sources of constructive constraint. *Human Development, 47*(2), 94–99.

Brown, J. S., Collins, A., and Duguid, S. (1989). Situated cognition and the culture of learning. *Educational Researcher, 18*(1), 32–42.

Burton, J. K., Moore, D. M., and Magliaro, S. G. (1996). Behaviorism and instructional technology. In D. H. Jonassen (Ed.), *Handbook of research for educational communications and technology.* New York: Macmillan.

Dear, B. L. (1997). PLATO people: A history book research project.

Duffy, T. M., and Cunningham, D. J. (1996). Constructivism: Implications for the design and delivery of instruction. In D. H. Jonassen (Ed.), *Handbook of research for educational communications and technology.* New York: Macmillan.

Gagne, R. (1985). *The conditions of learning* (4th ed.). New York: Holt, Rinehart and Winston.

Gibson, J. J. (1986). *The ecological approach to visual perception.* Hillsdale, NJ: Lawrence Erlbaum.

Hancock, D. (2004). Cooperative learning and peer orientation effects on motivation and achievement. *The Journal of Educational Research, 97*(3), 159–166.

Harasim, L. (Ed.). (1990). *Online education: Perspectives on a new environment.* New York: Preager.

Heckendorn, R. B. (2002). Building a Beowulf: Leveraging research and department needs for student enrichment via project based learning. *Computer Science Education, 12*(4), 255–273.

Honan, J. P., and Rule, C. S. (2002). *Using cases in higher education: A guide for faculty and administrators*. San Francisco, CA: Jossey-Bass.

Johnson, S. D., Aragon, S. R., Shaik, N., and Palma-Rivas, N. (2000). Comparative analysis of learner satisfaction and learning outcomes in online and face-to-face learning environments. *Journal of Interactive Learning Research, 11*(1), 29–49.

Kop, R. (2011). The challenges to connectivist learning on open online networks: Learning experiences during a massive open online course. *International Review of Research in Open and Distance Education, 12*(3), 19–37.

Kropf, D. C. (2013). Connectivism: 21st century's new learning theory. *European Journal of Open, Distance and E-Learning, 16*(2), 13–24.

Lave, J., and Wenger, E. (1991). *Situated learning: Legitimate peripheral participation*. Cambridge: Cambridge University Press.

Lundeberg, M. A., Levin, B. B., and Harrington, H. (1999). Reflections on methodologies and future research. In M. A. Lundeberg, B. B. Levin, and H. Harrington (Eds.), *Who learns what from cases and how: The research base for teaching and learning with cases*. Mahwah, NJ: Lawrence Erlbaum Associates.

Machtmes, K., and Asher, J. W. (2000). A meta-analysis of the effectiveness of telecourses in distance education. *The American Journal of Distance Education, 14*(1), 27–46.

Meyer, K. (2004). Putting the distance learning comparison study in perspective: Its role as personal journey research. *Online Journal of Distance Learning Administration, VII*(1). Retrieved from www.westga.edu/~distance/ojdla/spring71/meyer71.html.

Miflin, B. (2004). Adult learning, self-directed learning and problem-based learning: Deconstructing the connections. *Teaching in Higher Education, 9*(1), 43–54.

Milligan, C., Littlejohn, A., and Margaryan, A. (2013). Patterns of engagement in connectivist MOOCs. *MERLOT Journal of Online Learning and Teaching, 9*(2), 149–159.

Ochoa, T. A., and Gottschall, H. (2004). Group participation and satisfaction: Results from a PBL computer-supported module. *Journal of Educational Multimedia and Hypermedia, 13*(1), 73–91.

Paswan, A. K., and Gollakota, K. (2004). Dimensions of peer evaluation, overall satisfaction, and overall evaluation: An investigation in a group task environment. *Journal of Education for Business, 79*(3), 159–166.

Pea, R. D. (1993). Practices of distributed intelligence and design for education. In G. Salomon (Ed.), *Psychological and educational considerations*. Cambridge: Cambridge University Press.

Peterson, S. E., and Miller, J. A. (2004). Comparing the quality of students' experiences during cooperative learning and large-group instruction. *The Journal of Educational Research, 97*(3), 123–133.

Saettler, P. (1990). *The evolution of American educational technology*. Englewood, CO: Libraries Unlimited.

Savin-Baden, M., and Wilkie, K. (2006). *Problem-based learning online*. Berkshire: Open University Press.

Schoenfeld, A. (1985). *Mathematical problem solving*. New York: Academic Press.

Schramm, W. (1962). What we know about learning from instructional television. In W. Schramm (Ed.), *Educational television: The next ten years*. Stanford, CA: The Institute for Communication Research.

Siemens, G. (2005). Connectivism: Learning as network-creation. *European Journal of Open, Distance and E-Learning*. Retrieved from www.elearnspace.org/Articles/networks.htm.

Siemens, G., and Conole, G. (2011). Special issue—connectivism: Design and delivery of social networked learning, editorial. *International Review of Research in Open and Distance Education*, *12*(3), i–iv.

Smith, P. L., and Ragan, T. J. (1993). *Instructional design*. Upper Saddle River, NJ: Prentice Hall.

Stearns, J. M., Ronald, K., Greenlee, T. B., and Crespy, C. T. (2003). Contexts for communication: Teaching expertise through case-based in-basket exercises. *Journal of Education for Business*, *78*(4), 213–219.

Sudzina, M. R. (Ed.). (1999). *Case study applications for teacher education: Cases of teaching and learning in the content areas*. Boston, MA: Allyn Bacon.

Unden, L., and Beaumont, C. (2006). *Technology and problem-based learning*. Hershey, PA: Information Science Publishing.

Vygotsky, L. S. (1978). *Mind in society*. Cambridge, MA: MIT Press.

Wedemeyer, C. A. (1973). Characteristics of open learning systems. Report of the NAEB Advisory Committee on Open Learning Systems to NAEB Conference (New Orleans, Louisiana). ERIC Document ED099593.

Wedemeyer, C. A. (1981). *Learning at the back door: Reflections on non-traditional learning in the lifespan*. Madison: University of Wisconsin Press.

Wetzel, D. D., Radtke, P. H., and Stern, H. W. (1994). *Instructional effectiveness of video media*. Hillsdale, NJ: Lawrence Erlbaum Associates.

9

CURRICULAR SYSTEMS

Introduction

In the previous two chapters, we demonstrated that from the perspective of the TTD, dichotomous choices in instructional design, such as classroom instruction vs. online learning, in any educational program are not static binary selections. Instructional design elements are dynamic and represent a range of potential states, depending on the interaction of the learner with the instructor and the instructional environment. The degree to which students are present or absent in a classroom, or decide to communicate synchronously or asynchronously is determined dynamically by the needs of the learner and the requirements of the instructor in real time while an instructional session is in progress.

In this chapter, we will demonstrate that the static credit hour system and the fixed academic calendar that it imposes on the management of course schedules are no longer adequate to meet the curricular needs of individual students, administrators, and faculty in the postmodern time. The static academic calendar system is an artifact of standardizing products, and services in the industrial era. This preset calendar does not allow students to proceed at their own pace, which prevents them from graduating in a timely manner, and consequently increases their cost of education. The current static curricular system clashes with the needs of students who must survive and thrive in a vibrant, and dynamic postindustrial era. The case study for this chapter shows how students are directly impacted by this cultural discrepancy of curricular systems not only during the time they study at a university but also after they graduate and enter the workforce.

Professionals

In most universities, faculty, department chairs and college deans conceptualize, create and deliver educational programs that normally consist of courses offered in a set period of time (i.e. 16 weeks in a semester-based calendar) in a lock-step pace to a group of students regardless of their individual differences. This preset annual academic calendar limit professional educators to individualize curricula for learners. In this static curriculum system, either in the classroom or on the Internet, there is limited chance for learners to set the pace of their learning, and influence when to engage in learning. They must be present in a set time interval in a "class" because the university grants students credit based on the duration of their seat time but not based on how much they learn. Ironically, the initial point of this industrial lock-step academic calendar harkens back to the completion of harvest when some students had farm chores to complete in a bygone agricultural era.

Implications of the TTD for the Curricular Systems

No other policy epitomizes the industrial management structure of the contemporary curricular systems as the credit hour does, and no other structural impediment to the implementation of the principles of the TTD is as entrenched as the credit hour. The concept was formulated more than 100 years ago for the benefit of a single philanthropic organization at the height of industrialization in the United States, and it has not changed very much since. It was at the turn of the 20th century that the management of universities changed from a loosely organized arrangement to a centralized campus-based modern organization. This change occurred not for an academic reason but for the charitable purpose of steel industrialist Andrew Carnegie (1835–1919). He typified the transition of America from a rural agricultural society to a modern industrial state. He emphasized the need for a standard to justify, allocate, and assess his benevolence to academic programs and projects at a time that production methods in industry were becoming normalized by standardization of work, and manufactured goods were becoming uniformly designed so that they could be mass produced (Labaree, 1990). A prime example at the time was Carnegie's business rival John D. Rockefeller who established Standard Oil, and cornered the kerosene market by standardizing the product and streamlining its refining and distributing. Industrial standards of measurement in the form of the credit hour, therefore, were brought into the administration of higher education to facilitate accountability for the Carnegie Foundation for the Advancement of Teaching. Academic calendars were standardized on a semester or a quarter basis, and instructional time was set for 60-minute intervals with a few minutes devoted to recess.

Since then, instructors have been presenting a lecture to a group of students in one to three credit-hour courses. Although curricular systems were standardized through seat time, the lecture format remained primarily improvisational, and therein lays the lack of synchronization between the preindustrial form of the lecture and the industrial structure of the curriculum.

The Preindustrial Lecture

In classroom instruction, faculty are solo professionals who prepare and present each lecture for one classroom session at a time. They set the agenda according to what they feel is worthwhile to learn and they deliver the content to students based on a preconceived notion of what learners need to know, and they evaluate learners as a group, but not as individuals (Naidu, 2013). There is limited opportunity for learners to participate in any decisions regarding what they need to learn, how they prefer to learn, and how they should be evaluated.

In this craft-oriented practice, instructors rarely if ever have the opportunity to rely on other professionals, such as instructional designers, course developers, or evaluators, to plan and implement curricula that consider the following system components and processes:

- Standardization or customization of the lecture. Faculty members craft each lecture and present it live repeatedly. Because they work within the confine of a curricular model that is intended for providing mass education on an industrial scale, they hope that the core information in each lecture does not vary from classroom to classroom. In its pure form, classroom sessions do not follow a specific instructional strategy other than transmission of information from the instructor to the learner; as such, they do not have a design in the industrial or postindustrial sense of the word.
- Division of labor. A course team does not support the instructor as a solo worker to:
  - Determine specific learning needs of the individuals who are in a class session;
  - Evaluate prior knowledge of each learner;
  - Discern learning preferences of individual students;
  - Produce instructional materials that are customized for each learner;
  - Recommend learning activities for each individual leaner;
  - Conduct formative evaluation of incremental progress that each learner makes as a learning session progresses;
  - Conduct summative evaluation of the learner when a course of study is completed; and
  - Provide guidance to a learner to take the next step in completing a program of study.
- Capital investment. Administrators as well as policymakers assume that faculty would develop their courses for no additional compensation other than their normal salary. There is no line item in the budget of academic units of a university for course development per se.
- Individual needs of the learner. Preindustrial model of teaching practice does not consider the time, effort, and technology that are required for creating learning conditions that are needed for balancing learner autonomy

with requisite structure for each individual learner. A lecture that is presented to a group of learners in most large classrooms maximizes structure and transactional distance as the instructor-centered, content-driven presentation of educational information does not necessarily require the input of individual learners in the teaching and learning process. It is assumed that all learners enter a course with more or less the same level of prior knowledge and learning competency. In smaller graduate courses, to the extent that instructors practice various versions of the Socratic method, they have the opportunity to reduce transactional distance and structure, and increase dialogue and autonomy. However, the industrial management model of universities constantly challenges this potential.

Industrial Curricula

While deans, department chairs, and instructors have been able to mass produce course offerings and extend them beyond the walls of their campuses using information and communication technology (ICT), they have not been successful to:

- Make courses more effective by allowing learners to proceed at their own pace;
- Reduce the time that it takes for a learner to graduate; and thereby
- Reduce the overall cost of education for students.

Between the academic years 2006–2007 and 2016–2017 the tuition for public four-year institutions increased at an average rate of 3.5 percent per year (The College Board, 2016). In the 1970s and 1980s, the rate of increase in the overall cost of attending college was lower than the increase in the cost of other goods and services. Beginning in the 1990s, the cost of education has been rising above the general increase in the price of other goods and services (Schoen, 2015). Poignantly, since the 1990s, many businesses and industries have been able to employ ICT to either dramatically save time for their clients (e.g. banking on smart phones) or decrease the cost of their products and services (personalized shopping on the Internet, e.g. Amazon.com).

U.S. News & World Report set the cumulative increase in the cost of tuitions and fees for four-year public universities at a staggering rate of 296 percent between 1995 and 2015! (Mitchell, 2015). This time period coincided with the rapid expansion of the use of digital information and communication technologies in public universities across the country. Nevertheless, the correlation between deployment of information technologies and student success is proven to be very low. In an extensive report published by EDUCAUSE, Grajeck (2016) defined eight digital technology capabilities for higher education and developed assessment scales for measuring technology deployment and corresponding maturity for them. The report indicated the following: "Maturity usually correlates significantly with deployment: Institutions with higher maturity levels have deployed more related technologies." The study, however, revealed while information security had a relatively high correlation of 0.66 with maturity and deployment of digital technology, student success only correlated at 0.18. Grajeck went on to say:

> No student success technology correlated even moderately with composite student success maturity or any of its dimensions. This was true even of the maturity dimension of student success information systems. The average correlation of deployment index items with the information systems dimension is 0.13. The highest correlation between that maturity dimension and a student success technology deployment was a modest 0.23 with academic early alert system deployment.

Also, in the recent past, the time for a college student to graduate from a "four-year" institution has risen to 5–6 years, with a rate of graduation ranging between 57 percent and 59 percent in public colleges and universities (US Department of Education, 2014). Despite the clear evidence that billions of dollars of expenditure in ICT in support of the static model of curriculum has not reduced costs or time-to-degree or increased quality of learning, educators continue to maintain an industrial system of mass education that actually increases costs in money and time and impedes the progress of students. Most institutions use ICTs to achieve industrial ends with postindustrial means! Computers are used to elevate economy of scale en masse that was a true innovation in bringing costs down in the mass-manufacturing age. However, such methods, particularly in education, have shown to be counterproductive, particularly in the postindustrial economy. In the late 19th century, industrialists strived to standardize products and services and applied identical repetitive solutions to solve problems. In the postindustrial era, solutions that are customizable to each individual are in demand because of the changing nature of living and working in advanced economies. Industrial education neither in form nor in function is suitable for learners in advanced economies that have transcended the one-size-fits-all world. In addition, as we have demonstrated in the previous two chapters, the nature of teaching and learning is fundamentally different than making industrial products. Teaching and learning constitute a personal endeavor of instructors and learners. Learners are unique individuals with distinctive profiles. They are not analogous to rods of steel or barrels of kerosene that are amenable to standardization. Techniques of mass production were effective in the industrial era to reduce the cost per units of goods and services. Such techniques are proven to be highly inefficient in education, particularly in the postindustrial era.

Postindustrial Curricula

Curriculum development policies that are compatible with the TTD would provide the framework for a postindustrial practice in conceptualizing and offering academic curricula. Paradoxically, several romantic ideals of the preindustrial model of instruction are enhanced in a postindustrial model. Faculty members will actually have the time to interact with their students and spend more time on research and development or provide community service. Also, in partnership with a course team, by using adaptive learning systems, instructors will be able to craft instruction for each individual learner, as well as for groups of learners when collaborative learning is appropriate.

Hypothetically, a dynamic curricular system that is adaptable to the profile of each individual learner could:

- Increase the rate of the learner's knowledge and skill acquisition;
- Nurture a student's motivation to stay in college;
- Promote the acquisition of prior knowledge necessary for mastery of a knowledge domain;
- Increase the rate of successful course and degree completion;
- Decrease the time that it takes for a learner to complete a course or a degree program;
- Increase the ability of learners to master all of the required competencies; and as a result,
- Reduce the cost of attending college.

In such a system, students can move forward at their own personal pace. Some would progress faster, thus saving time and money for themselves and the university. Others would move slower. However, they receive personal attention and would acquire all of the objectives in a course of study, thus realizing the intended value of investment in their education, and reducing the overall cost of education that is incurred by underachieving, or simply dropping out. The majority of students, who show up in a bell-shaped curve as a specific data point and receive a B, or a C grade, receive the personal attention they deserve. In a learning space in which they can excel, they would not only master the course criteria but also show emergent behavior as well and exhibit creativity above and beyond predetermined learning objectives. Simply assigning these learners the label of being mediocre would serve neither them well nor the postmodern society in which they live.

Capital resources in this model are allocated to support members of course teams who will be engaged in performing specialized tasks. Supported by a course team, faculty will benefit from services of professional instructional designers, curriculum developers, tutors, evaluators, librarians, media production staff, computer specialists, LMS managers, and guidance counselors in supporting students. In addition, each course team includes professional administrators who provide support to the faculty to navigate the increasingly complex tasks of managing the teaching process from taking care of simple clerical chores managing the funds that are allocated to designing, developing, presenting, and evaluating courses that are adaptable to the individual needs of students. Currently, faculty members are compelled to perform specialized tasks of a course team for which they have little or no training, and no long-term professional interest in acquiring the skills that are required to perform these tasks! In addition, the contributions of course team members, if they are available to an instructor, evaporate when students are standardized in how they are taught and normalized in how they are evaluated.

Tracking the progress of a student is the primary task of a course team, as students who may start together in a cohort, may not progress together in a linear fashion. In the current curriculum system, regardless of the time that a learner is ready to engage in a new academic program, s/he must wait until the institution is ready for the learner. Once in a program of study, the learner must move in lockstep with other learners regardless of his or her individual pace, prior knowledge of the subject, aptitude for performance and other personal characteristics. Students must wait the duration for enrolling in their next course even if they have mastered all the objectives before the end of a semester or a quarter. Others who have been left behind in a one-size-fits-all model of instruction simply receive a lower or a failing grade for the course!

In a postindustrial model of curriculum, students may belong to a "home" class; however, they may engage in entirely different learning activities depending on their individual profile, including prior knowledge and academic and career goals. In this model, the faculty would be similar to surgeons who are supported by an anesthesiologist, as well as a team of specialized nurses and paramedical professionals who assist the surgeon through pre-operation to operation and post-operation procedures. To accomplish this, faculty development programs and workshops not only must emphasize the use of technology and integration of instructional strategies to teaching but they should also include key concepts of the TTD as well as the management skills that are required to work with members of a course team. Perhaps more importantly, the faculty must become cognizant of the changing culture of their work from a preindustrial craft effort to a postindustrial collaborative enterprise in a primarily technological environment.

At first glance, a staffing formula for academic departments in which a course team would support each faculty member may seem to be a costly proposition. However, the overall cost of education is bound to decrease when:

- Learning becomes much more appropriate to the needs of each learner;
- Learners are allowed to move ahead when they complete a set of learning objectives;
- Time-to-degree is reduced;
- Ineffective and costly remedial education programs are eliminated;
- Many more students complete their curriculum and graduate from an institution; and
- Graduates can lead highly satisfactory and productive lives.

While a university may not directly benefit from every aspect of a postindustrial curricular system, the overall expenditure for parents and other taxpayers would substantially decrease as fewer students drop out of courses, and more students complete their degree programs in less time with higher proficiency.

In moving an institution to a postindustrial curricular model, administrators must find acceptable answers to the following questions:

To what extent do the curricular systems

1. Balance the need of the learner for autonomy with the requirement of the institution for structure for each individual learner?
2. Increase the relevancy of education to each individual learner by optimizing the rate of autonomy?
3. Decrease the overall cost of education to the university as well as to students and parents by optimizing the stock of transactional distance for each individual learner?

Summary

Curriculum development policies that complement the TTD would provide the framework for a postindustrial practice in managing institutions of higher education. In this framework, information and communication technologies are not deployed to support the industrial management system of a university. With the use of adaptive learning systems and in collaboration with a course team, faculty members will be able to craft instruction for each individual learner as well as for groups of learners when collaborative learning is appropriate. This dynamic practice in designing and offering curricular systems result in decreasing the dropout rate and increasing the number of students who graduate with fully realized competencies. As a result, the overall cost of education for society decreases as its value and benefits increase. In the next chapter, we will revisit the idea of structure, as it was defined by Moore, and suggest that administrative structure in a university is a measure of an institution's responsiveness to a learner's individual needs in establishing academic objectives and lifelong goals.

Case Study 9.1 Curriculum of the College of Professional Studies

The College of Professional Studies (CPS) had not seen this level of student activism since the 1970s. Students had gathered in the largest lecture hall to accommodate everyone who wanted to participate. Yet, for the latecomers, it was standing room only. Three students were leading this protest meeting. They were sitting at a table in front of the packed lecture hall as a student was trying to set up a microphone for them and ensure that the sound system was working properly.

Finally, one of the student leaders tapped on the microphone and called the meeting to order. She said:

> We are here today to make our voices heard. We have had numerous discussions with the associate dean for student affairs Dr. JoAnn Friendly (the name was followed by a long boo from the audience) over the past two semesters but we have seen little action. Our courses are not relevant to our needs. Many of the recent graduates still do not have a job. People with no college degree can get an entry level job if they know how to work a computer software or if they have the basic skills to perform specific tasks.

Then she raised her voice and shouted into the microphone "and they do not have any student loans to pay back year after year either!" The crowd roared and booed again, this time many were standing up, too.

CPS was established in the 1960s at a time of economic growth and optimism for new professions. Its mission was to bring together professionally oriented courses and programs that had appeared throughout the university over the previous decade and establish a new college. Since then, the college had mushroomed to a behemoth that offered programs ranging from environmental technology to hospitality and tourism management, to electronic journalism, new media production and broadcasting, and public relations and communication.

Prior to student discontent reaching its highest pitch in the lecture hall, department chairs of the CPS had been receiving feedback regarding the curriculum of the college from students, alumni, and CEOs of national and international corporations that had offices in the Middle State University geographic area. The general tenor of the feedback was that since the 2000s when the College had gone through its major curriculum revision, the programs and courses have become less relevant to the real needs of the graduates for securing jobs.

The department chairs had tried to deal with this issue as much as they could on their own in their respective disciplines. However, they had to keep a balance between general requirements of the university regarding providing a liberal arts education to all students and the needs of the alumni for being competitive in the job market. After all, competencies relevant to available jobs always had changed. However, a broad background in the chosen discipline of students remained with them throughout their entire career.

CPS's reputation was stellar nationwide, at least up to now. Students learned about the history and development of the profession in which they were interested and mastered some of the practical skills on which they could build a career. A few even did internships with local government agencies as well as businesses and industries. Nevertheless, the College had not been able to keep up with technological changes, particularly in environmental technologies, journalism, and broadcasting. Technologies related to these professions were changing too quickly for the College to respond in a timely manner. The procurement cycle of the university was between 12 months and 18 months from the time that a particular hardware or software system had become available to the time that they were installed in college laboratories. Often, once the college received a technology, it was already obsolete. This lack of equipment replacement was highly evident in the professional hotel-sized kitchen that the college had operated to train chefs since the early 1970s. While the Department of Broadcasting received equipment donated from local television stations when they upgraded their facilities every two years or so, other programs were not as fortunate to receive free equipment.

Students were still booing and cheering, when Dean Charles Adamant entered the lecture hall, and stood next to the table at which student leaders were sitting. He raised both his hands and lowered them together several times signaling to the crowed to quiet down and let him speak. The crowd finally obliged and quieted down. Dean Adamant took the microphone and said:

> I understand your concerns and fully agree with some of your criticisms. If you think my colleagues and I are not aware of your issues, you are sadly mistaken. You are here to receive an education and follow prosperous lives after graduation. But you also have to understand our limitations.

The crowd booed again, this time even louder. Dean Adamant signaled the students with hand gestures again to quiet down. After a while, the jeering died down and the dean reached into his coat pocket, pulled out a paper and said:

> So, here in my hand I hold a summary of your suggestions or as you put it 'demands'. Let's review and analyze them. I will be very upfront with you in this process. I will let you know here and now, which ones are doable and which ones are not and why. Implementing some of these suggestions are not wise and some others are even beyond the purview of the college:

1. Reducing required credit hours to graduate. My guess is that this is more about the time that it takes to graduate and not necessarily the number of credit hours that you need in order to graduate. I know that when some of you have completed your general education requirements and are ready to take courses in your major areas, some of those courses are not offered and that has been a source of frustration for you. Well, we can do something about this. We need better tracking of your general education progress, and we need to collect better data on the demand for courses in upcoming semesters in your major areas. I will be working with the chief information officer of the university to see how we can better track data related to these matters and make sure that we can better match course offerings with the demand. I cannot promise that we can come up with one-to-one matches; however, in general, we will have a much better matching of your needs with course offerings in the near future. I have already asked department chairs to think about how we can better collect and sort out this kind of data. So, don't be surprised if you are asked to fill out online forms. I hope all of you will cooperate in this matter. Progress depends on the accuracy and quality of the data you provide.
2. Making courses more hands-on. I believe this issue is related to the competencies you need to succeed in your chosen professions. Our college was established to provide you with these skills. That is why we are here in this university. However, there must be a difference between the education you receive in a university and one that you may receive in a trade school. Our aim is to provide you with a broad liberal arts background that would serve you for many years to come. We are not a so-called vocational school. I hope you agree that what you learn here is much more comprehensive and valuable to you than just a set of skills for doing a job. Having said that, I think we can take some steps to make sure that you are also well served in acquiring work-related competencies you need. I have asked department chairs to look into setting up mastery-based micro-courses for you to deal with this matter. In

these short courses, we begin to offer more of the hands-on skills that you need. Some of them will be worth one credit hour, and depending on their content area, some may be even worth less. In any case, in these courses, you will earn electronic badges that indicate you have gained a new skill and have earned credit towards your degree program for acquiring that skill. When you earn enough badges to equal one credit hour, then that will be reflected in your transcript. You still need to accumulate enough credit to graduate based on the catalog of the year in which you were admitted to the college. Nevertheless, I think micro-courses will reduce the time that you would normally stay in college. This is a step towards making courses more personalized, too. You can take as many micro-courses as available during a semester, since most of them will be online. These courses will inevitably reduce the time that you need in order to graduate.

Another step in this regard is forging better relationships with businesses and industries near Middle State University and even those that are not so close to us. We will need to expand our internship program dramatically to provide you with better hands-on skills. Our internship program is going to be more robust and better integrated in the course structure in each program. Department chairs are already meeting with CEOs of companies near us to see how we can place more of you in internship programs.

A third area of concern is software and equipment acquisition. I know that very often equipment that you need in your professional area is not available in the lab. Some of you have had to spend a few hundred dollars to buy recent versions of the software you need in a course. The fact of the matter is that the procurement cycle from the time that a hardware, software, or service comes to the market to the time that we get it in a lab is between 18 and 20 months! This is one of those areas that the College simply does not control. Some of you graduate and leave before you see any of the new technologies. To accelerate the ordering and purchasing process, I am going to meet with the Vice President for Business Affairs to see what we can do about this important issue. We live in an age when software or equipment can be bought with one click and delivered the next day. Going through the state procurement protocol, which compels us to wait months to receive bids, is just not acceptable. I will see what I can do about it. But I also want you to know that this is an area that is controlled by several layers of bureaucracy.

3. Changing the college e-Portfolio platform. Some of you have sent me emails, or placed messages on the college Facebook page asking for a change in the e-Portfolio platform. I understand that your e-Portfolios are very important to you, not only while you are here studying but

also when you leave us and engage in a job search. So, I take this issue very seriously. I also know that we are working with a diverse group of programs in this college and the e-Portfolio platform that we selected and put in place some five years ago may not serve everyone well now. I have done some research about this issue before this meeting and asked lots of questions about the state-of-the-art e-Portfolios from our colleagues in other colleges. We have basically two choices: We can either go back to the commercial market and see what is available and adopt a new platform. The other option is to use some of the outstanding resources that we have in the computer science department and the university IT services to create our own e-Portfolio platform. This is an area that we need to work closely together. I am asking your leaders to join a committee that I have set up under the leadership of Associate Dean JoAnn Friendly (mild boos from the crowd) to select a strategy that we all agree on and move forward.

4. Dropping the requirement for English proficiency. Now here is an area that we have a deep disagreement. We simply cannot do this (this statement of the dean was followed by jeers and boos, however, not as loud as before). English is a basic skill. You need that in any job in the future. So, the requirement for taking the proficiency test before we allow you to take upper division courses in your major area shall remain. However, I am in discussion with the chair of the English department to make the course that you take in preparation for taking the proficiency test more relevant to technical and professional writing. I understand you are not served well by some of the courses that you take in the English department. Sometimes you have no choice but to take courses that are simply not relevant to your needs. Studying a certain era in the English literature, or a certain genre or style of poetry or prose, or a particular distinguished poet or author does not provide you with what you need to succeed in your upper division courses. So, we are going to make a concerted effort with the English department to provide the types of competencies you need in this area, but we cannot drop the requirement altogether. The English proficiency requirement will stay.

5. Fire the associate dean of student affairs. This is another matter that I strongly disagree with you. Associate Dean Friendly cannot be more understanding and responsive to your concerns. However, in some cases, she is not authorized to do what you are asking her to do. Reducing the credit hours is not an area that she or I can directly control. This is something that is set at the university level. All the deans must agree with the number of credit hours and we also must meet the

conditions of our accreditation and state policies. Firing JoAnn and replacing her is not going to solve any of these issues because these are baked into accreditation criteria, and state rules and regulations. So, the appropriate thing to ask is not to fire her but to understand what the rules are and help her to try to modify them when we are going through regular legislative or accreditation review processes. I understand that this may take longer than either you or I want, but this is the nature of higher education; it moves slower than we want it to move. I hope I have dealt adequately with these issues, and I look forward to sitting down with your leaders later today and review what we discussed.

Dean Adamant, then, left the lecture hall amid a smattering of applause.

Case Analysis

Similar to other cases that we have presented in previous chapters, the issues and decisions regarding the Curricular System Level directly relate to other system levels and are affected by them. However, as we move up in the hierarchical model, resolving problems becomes more complicated. Firing an associate dean is not simply a Curricular or Management System level issue; it is a political matter. Such a decision not only defines the relationship between the dean's office and the students, it ripples through the news media, and the entire political strata of the state, if not the entire country (Societal System Level). It establishes the extent to which a social system would permit students to engage in decision-making and exercise autonomy regarding their own educational process. Allowing students to participate in governing a college is at a higher level of complexity than engaging them in learning decisions at the Instructional System Level. In this case, the dean agreed to consider the following:

- Setting up micro-courses (Instructional System Level);
- Establishing a better relationship with local businesses for offering internships to students (Societal System Level);
- Trying to change the procurement process for hardware and software acquisition (Management System Level); and
- Changing the e-Portfolio platform (Software System Level).

However, he refused to drop the requirement for English proficiency (Instructional and Curricular Systems levels) and fire his associate dean (Management and Societal Systems levels). These decisions establish the level of administrative transaction as the dean exercises his management structure in relation to the feedback that he received from students trying to exercise their autonomy. (For an explanation of the concept of administrative structure, see the next chapter.)

In the past, students have been able to participate in making decisions regarding what society expects from higher education only when they have vocally protested. This is perhaps because there is no established mechanism for students to have an ongoing, organized, and legitimate dialogue with university administrators about curricular and management issues that impact them. The promise of the TTD is to engage students in matters related to their learning and education on a continuous basis before mass discontent arises and paralyzes the normal working of an institution.

Issues regarding the number of credit hours needed for graduation or changing the procurement protocol of the university involve several stakeholders at various levels of complexity: Curricular, Management, and Societal Systems levels. For example, if the dean in consultation with student leaders and IT specialists decides to design and produce a new e-Portfolio software, his task would be much more complex than selecting a solution that is already available in the market. Creating a new e-Portfolio platform from scratch is at a much higher plane of complexity as compared to merely selecting one, even though just selecting a platform is a complex task by itself.

References

Grajeck, S. (2016). *The digitization of higher education: Charting the course.* Retrieved from http://er.educause.edu/articles/2016/12/the-digitization-of-higher-education-charting-the-course.

Labaree, D. F. (1990). A kinder and gentler report: Turning points and the Carnegie tradition. *Journal of Education Policy, 5*(3), 249–264.

Mitchell, T. (2015). Chart: See 20 years of tuition growth at national universities. Retrieved from www.usnews.com/education/best-colleges/paying-for-college/articles/2015/07/29/chart-see-20-years-of-tuition-growth-at-national-universities/.

Naidu, S. (2013). Instructional design models for optimal learning. In M. G. Moore (Ed.), *The handbook of distance education* (3rd ed., pp. 268–280). New York: Routledge.

Schoen, J. W. (2015). Why does a college degree cost so much? Retrieved from www.cnbc.com/2015/06/16/why-college-costs-are-so-high-and-rising.html/.

The College Board. (2016). *Trends in college pricing 2016.* Retrieved from https://trends.collegeboard.org/sites/default/files/2016-trends-college-pricing-web_1.pdf/.

US Department of Education. (2014). *The condition of education 2014 (NCES 2014-083), institutional retention and graduation rates for undergraduate students.* Retrieved from https://nces.ed.gov/fastfacts/display.asp?id=40.

10

MANAGEMENT SYSTEMS

Introduction

In the previous chapter, we demonstrated that the static credit hour system and the fixed academic calendar that it imposes on the management of course schedules are no longer adequate to meet the curricular needs of individual students, administrators, and faculty in the postindustrial era. In this chapter, we will revisit the idea of structure, as it was defined by Moore, and we suggest that administrative structure in a university is a measure of an institution's responsiveness to a learner's individual needs in establishing academic objectives and lifelong goals. This is to formalize the dynamic relationship of each learner with the university administration in the TTD.

The case study for this chapter illustrates contemporary issues that are in play to make higher education administrations more responsive to the needs of individual learners not only when they are enrolled in a university but after graduation as well.

Professionals

Presidents, vice presidents, associate vice presidents, provosts, deans, and their professional staff who work at the Management System Level face multiple challenges in the complex environment in which colleges and universities operate today. Some of these challenges stem from a lack of synchronization between the modern industrial policies of their institution and the dynamic academic needs and lifelong personal aspirations of students who are preparing to live in a postindustrial economy and a postmodern society.

Implications of the TTD for Management Systems

To resolve this overarching problem, we suggest that the definition that Moore (1983, p. 157) set forward for instructional structure be extended to include administrative structure as well. Based on Moore's definition, we propose administrative structure as a measure of an institution's responsiveness to the learner's academic objectives, career goals, and lifelong ambitions as they relate to his/her personal profile.

Similar to instructional interaction, learner-administrator interaction influences the stock of transactional distance. In a highly structured institution, deans, department chairs, and faculty predetermine the academic objectives for groups of learners as they may relate to their career goals and a general notion of their lifelong aspirations. Learners do not have the opportunity to interact with administrators on an ongoing basis to discuss career choices and possibly modify their broad academic goals to position them well for future professional prospects. Administrative structure in this instance is high and learner autonomy is low. As the learner is given an opportunity to engage in dialogue with an administrator and exercise his or her autonomy to shape lifelong objectives, career goals, and a program of study, administrative control decreases and learner control increases. Today, this dynamic process does not pass the threshold of effective transactional distance for each learner in most colleges and universities because learner-administrator interaction is infrequent and inadequate. The dynamic interplay between administrative structure and learner autonomy does not include a formative assessment process in which a learner's academic goals are reviewed on an ongoing basis in relation to his/her lifelong ambitions and career goals. In an ideal implementation of the TTD, each student would benefit from frequent interactions with advisors to optimize the flow of administrative structure, and thereby the stock of transactional distance. This process would synchronize the managerial functions of the university with the social and career objectives of the learner, thus removing one of the most vexing obstacles in making higher education directly relevant to not only the needs of students but also to the requirements of others who have a stake in institutions of higher education. These include employers who cannot find talent with skills relevant to their needs, state governments that are challenged with budget allocations to higher education, and parents who question the value of higher education for their daughters and sons.

Optimizing the flow of administrative structure for each learner is of utmost importance as long as the legitimacy of the university as a vital social institution for responding to career goals and lifelong aspirations of learners is in dispute. The roots of this contention trace back to the demonstrations of 1968 in Paris, when university students challenged the rigid administrative structures of French universities and their legitimizing power of arts and sciences (Rosenau, 1992). Similar protests occurred in American universities in the 1960s. However, participating in the civil rights movement and dissenting the war in Vietnam perhaps had a higher priority for American students than reorganizing the management structure of the university (Readings, 1996). French postmodernists confronted the administrative structure of the academy, how it put knowledge in discrete disciplines, and how it failed to relate to the needs and ambitions of students. They strongly argued that the postmodern institution is formless, and that it has no method, analytical approach, or critical processes to move its project forward. In fact, the postmodern idea essentially has no project! Yet, the semantic deconstruction of "text" emerged as the unmethod of postmodernism in search of imbedded meanings in a work (e.g. the text of a document) that as yet has remained unnoticed. Thus, new categories for representing "the other" may emerge in a text by various readers and interpreters, regardless of the original intent of the author. In the context of managing institutions of higher education, one might see how deconstruction of text would lead, for example, to revising and ultimately dismantling policies that govern the day-to-day machination of a university. Taking the French postmodern attitude, each interpreter of a policy may discover hitherto unnoticed and unacknowledged ideas in it. The logical conclusion of such an approach would be that text of the policy as a set of commonly agreed on rules to manage an institution gradually becomes a formless, meaningless, and useless document. Ultimately, the unmethod of the French school of postmodernism directs any sustained effort in assigning meaning to a text towards futility and nihilism (Dickens, 1994; Rosenau, 1992).

Postmodernism Revisited

In contrast, the American school of postmodernism, as put forward here, is pragmatic in outlook, and tends to reconcile divergent views. Its system method is constructive for each individual learner, as it is the instrument by which learners, instructors, academic advisors, and administrators optimize the stock of transactional distance at each moment in time for each student.

Towards the end of the 19th century, American pragmatic philosopher William James defined the constructive attitude of American postmodernism by acknowledging the limitation of empiricism in the scientific tradition for offering a more comprehensive method of inquiry, particularly in liberal arts and social sciences. This was long before the current usage of the term postmodern had entered the lexicon of contemporary discourse, but James's slouching towards postmodernism—at least in the eyes of the authors of this book—is unmistakable. Decades before French postmodernists realized the limitations of the modern approach to inquiry in the 1970s, James offered the concept of "radical empiricism" for expanding traditional empiricism and transcending its limitation at the turn of the 20th century. Described by

Cornel West (1989), radical empiricism recognizes the limitation of theory as a static knowledge product, and offers it as a method (process) for knowledge acquisition. In the case of Management Systems, knowledge acquisition occurs between the learner and the administrator to optimize transactional distance, while at the Instructional Systems Level, knowledge acquisition occurs between the instructor and the learner, and among learners to influence the stock of transactional distance.

Radical empiricism also acknowledges the shortcomings of scientific empiricism by including and reconciling qualitative information with quantitative data. While American postmodernism recognizes individual differences among learners as pedagogically legitimate, it does not continue to deconstruct an instructional strategy, or an educational institution for that matter, to oblivion in order to accommodate the diversity of students. First, it discovers such diversity and then it includes newly recognized divergent categories in a wide net of systemic feedback loops to respond to the unique needs and requirements of each learner. The concrete manifestation of this systemic net consisting of myriad influences is a system dynamics flow diagram in which newly discovered processes are included and are tested for their validity in contributing to learner control, instructor control, and administrative control.

In summary: the American approach to postmodernism is:

- Constructive, as it reconciles seemingly divergent or dichotomous system variables in relation to each individual learner. This is in sharp contrast to the deconstructive unmethod of the French school of postmodernism that recognizes divergent system variables but offers no means for resolving them. It merely continues its deconstructive trajectory.
- Radically empirical, as its approach offers a remedy to the narrowness of traditional empiricism that might neglect the discovery of learner's "subjective" needs and lifelong aspirations as represented in their speech acts or written narratives.
- Convergent, in the sense that it casts a wide net to systemically embrace seemingly divergent categories, ideas, viewpoints, learning styles, instructional strategies, and managerial practices in a dynamic system that is responsive to the background of an individual learner. It does not identify the "otherness" from a reductionist and divergent perspective—it includes the other in the feedback net of an open, dynamic, inclusive, and seemingly unlimited but purposeful, teleological, and responsive system to resolve the personal learning needs of each student.

As we demonstrated in Chapter 7, at the Instructional System Level, the test for the validity of the concept of transactional distance occurs in moments that prehension turns to comprehension for each individual learner throughout a course of study. Similarly, the test of validity of transactional distance at the Management System Level occurs when objective data points regarding a learner's progress in completing a program of study coincide with subjective data points collected from the learner regarding his or her hopes and ambitions for lifelong goals, career objectives, and academic aims. Some of these administrative data are collected quantitatively and objectively by how a learner behaves. Other data are qualitatively collected by how a learner describes his/her intuitive understanding of lifelong aspirations, career goals, and academic objectives verbally or in writing.

The ability of administrators to shape the learning space for optimizing administrative structure for each learner is limited when academic schedules are predetermined and curricula are fixed. Grounding the learner in a solid foundation that would serve her/him for years to come is difficult if not impossible if the primary intention of the university is to place learners on an assembly line made of courses in which they receive the same standard treatment regardless of their individual differences in mastering immediate learning objectives and reaching future lifelong goals.

Current principles of good practice in education that are rooted in the industrial concept of economy and society constrain administrators to dynamically create academic schedules that are responsive to the needs of each learner. Administrators are also limited in creating learning environments that would be conducive for implementing dynamic personal academic calendars. Dynamic personal academic calendars allow individual learners to set their pace for mastering a set of universal predetermined learning objectives balanced with their emergent learning outcomes. These nascent outcomes are personal for each learner and may be perceived by others as "relative" or "local" or "unconventional" modes of knowing. Achieving optimal transactional distance for each learner, in part, depends on balancing the dynamic interplay between:

- The structured requirements of an academic institution and the disciplines that form a curriculum, and
- The personal, cultural, and local modes of knowledge for each individual learner. This dynamic interplay would resolve many cultural issues that challenge American universities to successfully respond to the local and social needs of the learners domestically, as well as those who study in other countries of the world. (See Chapter 12, Global Systems.)

As the 21st century unfolds, the university leadership will find itself increasingly challenged by divergent views and actions taken by faculty, parents, legislators, and other stakeholders (Table 10.1). Illustrating divergent thinking between the modern and the postmodern university, Ford (2002, p. 97) commented:

Because the postmodern university will rest on a postmodern metaphysics and because it will have a very different objective than the modern university, it will require a different structure and a new curriculum. The differences between the two can be summarized as follows:

TABLE 10.1 Differences between the Modern and the Postmodern University

Modern	Postmodern
Disciplinary/vocational	Problem-based/place-based
Ostensibly value-neutral	Explicitly value-laden
Abstract and narrowly practical	Complex and broadly practical
Anthropomorphic and individualistic	Biocentric and social
Apolitical	Democratic forms of government favored
Universal	Localized
Education for rootlessness	Education for rootedness
Status quo reinforced with aim to augment it	Substantial change aimed for

Not everyone may agree on the categories presented by Ford above, and many more contrasting views of the structure and the role of the postmodern university in contrast to its current form and function may arise in the future. Nevertheless, resolving conflicting choices is one of the most important tasks for administrators to keep American universities in their position of global leadership. The university needs to put in place managerial practices and resources that treat all stakeholders as individuals and develop dynamic mechanisms for interacting with them. In the future, administrator-parent communication as well as communication between university leadership and individual political decision-makers become as important as administrator-learner interaction. Such managerial practices would mitigate student discontent before it boils over and appears as headlines in the media.

Summary

A reorganization of the modern industrial management style of universities is needed to synchronize its relations with learners who are bound to live in a postindustrial economy and a postmodern society. If the American system of higher education is to maintain its global leadership, a pragmatic approach is needed to optimize the administrative structure of a university as a measure of an institution's responsiveness to a learner's individual academic needs, career objectives, and lifelong aspirations. Postmodern system thinking in the tradition of William James provides the methodology for imagining the future of the university administration as a dynamic, adaptive, and responsive process to meet the needs of not only learners but the many other constituencies of universities that include parents, lawmakers, employers, and others.

Case Study 10.1 The Future of Middle State University

President Jorge Enlightened was deep in thought in his office as he was trying to compose an email to the campus community. This is probably the most important email he would be sending out as he was completing his fifth and last year of presidency at Middle State University. The memo he was trying to commit to email was about asking the help of everyone on campus to develop a vision for the future of Middle State University. He wanted to leave this vision statement as his legacy to the next person who would take the helm. He wanted the institution that he had come to love and respect to have a clear picture for how it would evolve in the next ten years.

In the last five years, President Enlightened had worked diligently to diversify the student body as well as the faculty. While some of the other universities in the country were still grappling with this issue, Middle State was in a sweet spot in this regard. Academically, almost all programs were in good stead in terms of their accreditation. Several departments and research centers had gained national if not international recognition as well. The tough budget years were also behind now, and the university could look forward to a decade of growth and prosperity.

However, there was a sense of unhappiness that permeated the campus community. The unease was in the air, in the nonverbal realm. Occasionally, the discontent would bubble up to the level of verbal communication as presented in Case Study 4.1, when students in the college of professional studies went on strike to show their dissatisfaction with the curriculum. Even the college of business administration and leadership and the college of engineering, which usually remained calm and generally silent under adversity, were showing signs of dissatisfaction. The sociology, English, and philosophy departments, however, were outright gloomy. President Enlightened's academic home department was philosophy. The glumness there bothered him perhaps more than any other academic area. A few months ago, he invited his colleagues in the department to a weekend retreat to get to the bottom of their unhappiness. After a day and a half of intense discussion and deliberation, the attendees coalesced around three groups with somewhat differing ideas about the future. On behalf of her discussion group consisting of three other faculty members, Dr. Sharp presented the first point of view to the entire group as summarized below.

Middle State University has created new knowledge, taught countless students, and provided services to its immediate communities and many others around the world in the last 125 years. We have had many outstanding faculty members who excel in conducting research and attracting grants while maintaining a tradition of distinction in teaching. I think we can all agree that in our institution, most of us are teacher-scholars. The university has had a strong culture of service, too. We not only have kept a high profile in assisting farmers and small businesses in our community, we have also been extremely influential in K–12 schools through research and demonstration projects, as well as supervising teachers and assisting schools in complying with state and federal standards. We have been truly a model institution for keeping a healthy balance between engaging in research, teaching our students, and offering a wide range of community services.

In the last two decades or so, technology has crept in to our lives very slowly, but it has changed everything drastically. We feel we are under attack by technology. So far, the department of philosophy has been somewhat immune to this disease. However, there are rumors that the College of Human Sciences may join a consortium of other colleges throughout the country, pull their resources together, and adopt one online course for each of the lower division courses in philosophy that all would share. That will take the teaching of a course completely out of our hands. Our faculty would have little or no control over these courses. The teaching process for the majority of students would be automated through technology, and relegated to a MOOC. These courses would be homogenized for all the participating universities, and there would be no diversity of thought or viewpoints expressed in them.

The overwhelming feeling is that the university is moving towards a dystopian future in which the faculty will have little or no role to play. Robots will take over and will be in charge of presenting a uniform curriculum to all students. The faculty would become merely slaves to MOOCs. All there would be left for them to do is to follow the results of data crunching and analytics by computers and ensure that students fall in the brackets that the machine recommends for them. They never see any students or converse with them. They would spend their time in a control room following data sets about each student that are reflected on large video screens. They would intervene through an agent (a bot) if a student shows deviation from the normal path that the big robot has anticipated. The bottom line is that it is unrealistic to expect faculty to excel in teaching when they are merely control room operators for a giant automaton.

President Enlightened thanked Dr. Sharp for presenting her summary. He scratched his forehead as he thought how to respond to such a frosty scenario. He said that he understands the totalizing power of technology as Jacques Ellul (1964) explained more than 50 years ago. However, he was sure that robots are not already in charge. He asked Dr. Karim Aalem to present the view of the second small group before he made further comments.

Dr. Aalem took over the meeting and summarized the results of his group discussion as follows:

> Our small group does not think that the future is as bleak as robots ruling the university, although we share the views of our colleagues that there is a possibility for such a scenario to materialize if we do not plan for the future we want. If we remain passive and let hardware, software, and telecommunication technologies proliferate without a specific design in mind, robots will take over. However, we think that there is a place for technological innovation if we plan for it. We need to expand our current reductionist definition of technology that has permeated among some of our colleagues throughout the university. This definition has been limited to the use of hardware, software, and telecommunication. We need to include design, development, implementation, and evaluation of instructional, curricular, and organizational units to the definition of technology as well. Our group feels that we must become active in planning for our future with this expanded view of technology in mind. Some of our colleagues in the school of education have demonstrated that technology can assist us in individualizing instruction to the point that we would be able to respond to the personal learning needs of every single one of our students. Our group thinks that such a prospect would liberate faculty from the burden of repeating lectures, and all the other mechanical things that we must do to support the rigid administrative structure of the university. If we relegate repetitive processes to machines, we can establish a more personal relationship with our students. Surely, we need to track some data about them and know where they stand vis-à-vis the instructional objectives they must master. However, our group views technology as a means of developing a more desirable future in which we as instructors can attend to the academic needs of each of our students instead of viewing them as a mass of people sitting in our 200-seat lecture halls. This of course means that we need to change our management philosophy as well. We need to make sure that the inflexible administrative rules do not stand in the way of our progress towards such an ideal future.

President Enlightened thanked Dr. Aalem for presenting a hopeful future. Before turning the meeting to Dr. Helen Smart to present the case of the third group, he commented that his main purpose for this retreat was to explore the possibility for developing a comprehensive plan for the future of the university. However, in universities, the faculty pursue their unique areas of interest and developing a comprehensive plan for implementing it is not an easy task to achieve.

Dr. Smart, realizing that the time for ending the retreat is nearing, stood up signaling that it is her turn now to present the case for her group. She opened her remarks by thanking her colleagues in the other two groups. She indicated that in her group, both of the previous scenarios for a utopian and a dystopian future were discussed. The views of her group, in a sense, included both of these ideas. Her group also concluded that a comprehensive planning effort for the future of the university is needed. However, they arrived at this conclusion from a different cataclysmic point of view compared to the dystopian view in which robots would rule the institution. We felt that the effect of technology would serve the purpose of disintegrating the university. We know that the seed of such a breakup was planted in the protests of the 1960s. However, today, there is a strange confluence of business interests with the ideas expressed by postmodernist philosophers. These two groups have nothing in common, except that the end result of their objectives is the same! The business community wants us to unbundle programs and courses to smaller units so they can be more responsive to the needs of businesses and industries for a trained workforce. We see this idea being implemented at the university in certain programs through competency-based education, and through digital badges offered to those who can perform specific tasks very well. Our group felt that the future is not towards robots taking over and homogenizing courses in MOOCs and offering them to masses of faceless students. In contrast, the future might bring disintegration of what in academia we call a "discipline" or organized knowledge articulated in a specific coherent aesthetic language. I cannot even imagine what this world would look like and I expect that it might be upon us sooner than we think. Would we need universities anymore if we deconstruct knowledge to granular texts that are only useful for carrying out specific tasks for a particular employer? This totally discombobulated future is different from robots regimenting faculty and students in data-driven strands of courses and programs. However, its prospects are as distasteful.

Case Analysis

A confluence of Hardware, Software, and Telecommunications Systems has impacted higher education institutions in unprecedented ways. It has caused faculty and administrators to review and reconsider the mission and vision of their institutions and begin to envisage their future mission in novel ways. Technology not only has affected instructional practices and curriculum development (Instructional and Curricular Systems levels), it has also brought about internal and external conditions that require taking a second look at the organization structure of the university and its management practices (Management System Level). The unplanned use of technology may support the current inflexible management structure of the university. Data-driven regimentation of students, courses, and programs would not prepare them for a future in which their unique ability in creativity, decision-making, and problem solving would be in demand.

Unbundling the academic structures of universities, opening up their curriculum to meet the needs of specific employers, and deconstructing their disciplined approach to science and humanities are not a desirable future either.

However, comprehensive universities may be able to keep their current general framework and offer outstanding teaching, cutting-edge research, and world-class service. To do so, they must integrate into their management practice a constant process of envisioning, planning, and simulating the future of such visions and plans as President Enlightened has begun to do so in this case.

References

Dickens, D. R. (1994). North American theories of postmodern culture. In D. R. Dickens & A. Fontana (Eds.), *Postmodernism & social inquiry*. New York: Guilford Press.

Ellul, J. (1964). *The technological society*. New York: Vintage Books.

Ford, M. P. (2002). *Beyond the modern university: Towards a constructive postmodern university*. Westport, CT: Praeger.

Moore, M. G. (1983). The individual adult learner. In M. Tight (Ed.), *Adult learning and education* (pp. 153–168). London: Croom Helm.

Readings, B. (1996). *The university in ruins*. Cambridge, MA: Harvard University Press.

Rosenau, P. M. (1992). *Post-modernism and the social sciences: Insights, inroads, and intrusions*. Princeton, NJ: Princeton University Press.

West, C. (1989). *The American evasion of philosophy: A genealogy of pragmatism*. Madison, WI: University of Wisconsin Press.

11

SOCIETAL SYSTEMS

Introduction

In the previous chapter, we proposed that administrative structure is a measure of an institution's responsiveness to a learner's individual needs. It expresses the extent to which lifelong goals, career objectives, and selection of an academic program of study can be adapted to a learner's personal profile. In this chapter, we will demonstrate how the social environment affects universities and how expectations of other institutions of society influence their management structure which, in turn, affect the ability of an institution to be responsive to each learner. The case study for this chapter shows the impact of public policy on universities and how institutions balance their academic responsibilities towards students with the expectations of the societal system in which they operate.

Professionals

Aspirations, visions, policies, and decisions of political leaders at the state and federal levels, as well as those who lead businesses and various institutions in civil society, form the intricate web of influences that set the social policies under which universities function. Government executives and legislators affect the internal affairs of universities through direct financial and regulatory decisions and set the stage for their success in responding to learners. Today, the environment of universities is changing rapidly and is challenging their ability to adapt to new social and economic conditions. Some of the changes, ironically, are the hand-maiden of universities. Basic research and development in information technology, for example, has greatly impacted the world of work, and what employers must expect from university graduates to perform. These expectations, in turn, inform the decisions of government executives and lawmakers in demanding that universities be more responsive to the needs of employers.

Implications of Societal Systems for the TTD

Living systems must adapt to their environment or they would wither away and die. Today, the ecosystem of colleges and universities is heavily influenced by the rise of a postindustrial economy and a postmodern society that depends on knowledge and practical skills. To the extent that universities respond to their changing environment, their administrative structures can also be responsive to the needs of their students. A major challenge for university administrators, therefore, is keeping the academic independence of their institution while balancing the needs and expectations of students with the requirements of employers, the expectation of taxpayers, the aspirations of lawmakers, and the mandates of government executives.

There is, however, a widespread and entrenched reluctance among university administrators to respond decisively to the changing environment of higher education. Typically, cautious decision-making rather than decisive action is higher education's salient feature. The hesitancy to make timely adjustments is not new. It goes back to the inherently cautious nature of decision-making in universities from their inception (Cohen, 1998). This is a trait that colleges and universities inherited from the earliest formal institutions of higher education that were originally established in the Mediterranean coast during the Middle Ages. A drawn-out process of decision-making served the university well from the 10th to the 20th century, when institutions did not have a direct impact on the day-to-day affairs of other social units in the private sector or the government. In the contemporary era, however, business, industry, government, and other major social institutions rely heavily on basic scientific and applied research in universities. Also, employers depend on university graduates to perform highly specialized tasks. Institutions of higher education have become indispensable for the economic prosperity and national security of the United States. Their well-being has a direct impact on other social institutions.

The Role of Higher Education

Higher education is a vital and integral part of the social and economic life in the United States. The relationship between the university and a robust socioeconomic condition can hardly be overstated. The importance of innovation to vital social functions, the value of intellectual property to the public and the private sector, and the significance of a workforce capable of higher-order thinking and problem solving are drivers of this symbiotic relationship between the university and other social institutions. Examples of the contributions of university research and public service to contemporary life and society are too numerous to list here. They range from vital progress in medicine, resulting in a steady increase in life expectancy worldwide, to an increase in food production that has made the United States not only self sufficient but also a major exporter of foodstuff, and the creation of the Internet that has transformed how we live, learn, and work.

Wages are higher for better-educated workers

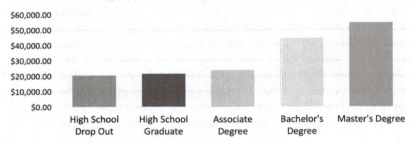

Median annual earnings of U. S. Workers, age 25+, by education 2011

FIGURE 11.1 Wages as a function of education.
Source: Economic Analysis and Research Network.

On a personal level, those who earn a bachelor's or a master's degree earn considerably more than those who graduate from high school, as indicated in Figure 11.1 (Berger & Fisher, 2013).

Colleges and universities in the United States are academic leaders in the world in instruction, research, and public service. Of the top 100 universities ranked by *Times Higher Education*, 42 are located in the United States, with six listed in the top ten (*Times Higher Education*, 2017). However, certain developments in recent years point towards chronic trends that undermine the leadership of U.S. universities. These range from a steady increase in the cost of education to the inability of colleges and universities to synchronize their administrative structure with the academic needs of their learners.

Much of the debate about higher education at the Societal and Management Systems levels is tied up in the notion that higher education is not producing students who are ready for particular jobs. This issue points to a major shift in the society's perception of the role of higher education. The traditional purpose of a university has been to offer a broad liberal arts education to students. Today, the taxpayers, as well as state governments and local businesses and industries, are asking universities why their graduates are not ready to be placed in specific job functions. A major challenge for university administrators, therefore, is to balance the traditional academic needs and expectations of faculty and students with those of the multiple public constituencies that support them.

Is the university to:

- Respond to the needs of the job market? Or
- Educate a person with
  - a comprehensive liberal arts background,
  - higher-order problem solving and decision-making skills,
  - the ability to be creative in novel situations, and
  - the ability to lead a satisfactory life?

Responding to these questions will define the role that universities play in society in the foreseeable future.

Purpose of Higher Education

Although some employers believe that college graduates may not be ready for assuming the positions that they have available for them, they are not arguing for industry-specific vocational education, at least at the four-year university level. CEOs of U.S.-based corporations have argued for more emphasis on liberal arts education in colleges to bolster the foundational skills that are required in the postmodern workplace that is increasingly dependent on information, knowledge, and wisdom. A study conducted by Hart Research Associates (2015) and released by the Association of American Colleges & Universities echoed these sentiments. The majority of employers (60 percent) have agreed that it is important for students to learn a broad range of knowledge and skills, whereas only 15 percent were in favor of students learning skills that applied only to a specific field or position. In this survey, employers valued the following areas of knowledge and skills among university graduates:

- Problem-solving skills in relation to people who have differing views;
- Ability to work with people from different cultural backgrounds;
- Holding democratic ideals;
- Capacity for civic mindedness; and
- Possessing a broad liberal arts and sciences education.

Today, skills such as designing new products and services, analytical and critical thinking, decision-making, and leadership have gained exceptional significance because of the changing nature of tasks at most workplaces. Since nearly all new employees receive industry-specific on-the-job training, those who are equipped with higher-level cognitive competencies and applied analytical skills can succeed compared to those who have some level of technical training but little or no background in liberal arts and sciences.

Demand for Higher Education

Regardless of the debate about the appropriate social function of the academy, enrollment in higher education has steadily risen in the last thirty years (Snyder, 2013). If the projection of the US Department of Labor (2013) is accurate, there will be increased demands in the job market for individuals with the following higher levels of educational attainment until 2020:

- Master's degree close to 18.4 percent;
- Associate's degree by 17.6 percent;

- Doctoral or professional degrees by about 16 percent;
- Post-secondary non-degree programs by 15.6 percent; and
- Bachelor's degree by 12.1 percent.

In contrast, occupations in the high school category are expected to grow by just 7.9 percent, while occupations in the less than high school diploma or equivalent category are projected to grow by 10.9 percent.

As far as the student population is concerned, until 2023, undergraduate enrollment at four-year institutions is projected to increase by 12 percent to 11.9 million students, while enrollment at two-year institutions is projected to increase by 16 percent to 8.3 million students (Kena et al., 2014). Although a more recent report reaffirmed these general trends until 2024 (Hussar & Bailey, 2016), they are subject to annual variations as factors, such as increase in the demand for labor, might attract young adults to earn money instead of going to school. For example, a survey by the National Student Clearinghouse Research Center (2015) indicated a drop of 1.7 percent in general higher education enrollment between 2014 and 2015.

Depicting a more complex picture, a study by Hanover Research (2014) revealed the interplay between several factors that have impacted enrollment trends in recent years. These included:

- Perceived value of a college degree in relation to employment opportunities for college graduates;
- Market saturation of degree holders in certain fields for which there is no employment;
- Lack of degree holders in fields for which there are employment opportunities;
- Dramatic increase in total student loans leading to a potential collapse of a "bubble" with negative effects on the U.S. economy similar to but perhaps not as extensive as the recession of 2008; and
- Regulatory trends impeding necessary reforms in colleges and universities.

Hanover's study showed that although the demand for higher education may continue to be strong in future years, each institution, depending on its mission and goals, may be more subject to variability in general economic conditions compared to previous decades when higher education enjoyed a steady increase in enrollments since the 1960s.

Lack of Synchronization between Higher Education and Employers

An analysis of youth unemployment and available professional positions in the job markets worldwide by Mourshed, Farrell, and Barton (2012) indicated that there is a discrepancy between what education providers believe regarding the value of their programs for employability of graduates, how students perceive the usefulness of their education in relation to future employment, and how employers look at the value of a college degree. While 72 percent of education providers think that their programs prepare students for the job market, only 45 percent of the youth surveyed, and 42 percent of the employers agreed with the education providers. Using the metaphor of a highway as it intersects with the interest of three stakeholders, namely, students, providers, and employers, the authors stated:

> There are significant challenges at each intersection. At the first (enrollment), cost is the top barrier, with 31 percent of high-school graduates indicating they did not continue their education because it was too expensive. Among those who do enroll, 46 percent are convinced they made the right choice in their selection of institution or field of study. At the second intersection (building skills), about 60 percent of youth say that on-the-job training and hands-on learning are the most effective instructional techniques, but fewer than half of that percentage are enrolled in curricula that prioritize those techniques. At the third intersection (finding a job), a quarter of youth do not make a smooth transition to work; their first jobs are unrelated to their field of study and they want to change positions quickly. In emerging markets, this number rose to as much as 40 percent.
>
> *(p. 19)*

Varying perceptions of the social role and function of higher education among students, providers, and employers have brought the purpose of higher education under the sharp scrutiny of policymakers, university administrators, and employers.

Public Policy

Because of the complex conditions described above, it is imperative that public policymakers establish the legal and regulatory framework that universities need to respond to their fast-evolving environment. The increasing cost of higher education coupled with a lack of synchronization between the needs of employers and the skills acquired by students has raised serious questions in the minds of parents and students alike concerning the worth of a university degree (Mourshed et al., 2012; Selingo, 2015). Nonetheless, innovative approaches to making education more responsive to the needs of learners continue to be constrained by policies that were formulated in the modern era. Rules that were formulated and put in place in the previous century are no longer applicable to opportunities that are present in the postmodern era.

In their sweeping review of federal and state policies from the perspective of competency-based education, Lacey and Murray (2015) indicated that despite the fact that in 2005 Congress authorized the U.S. Department of Education to offer financial aid to those students who are enrolled in programs with no ties to the credit hour standard, many federal and state regulations for public and private institutions are still closely linked to policies that are dictated by seat time. Ultimately, the authors implied that genuine innovations under the current regulatory regime, such as alternative models for the assessment of learners' competencies, are square pegs that would not fit in the round hole of credit hour.

Other informed critics have also commented on federal and state policies that impact implementation of academic innovations. Judith Eaton (2015), President of the Council for Higher Education Accreditation, presented her views in *The Hill* on the proposed bill H.R. 970 titled *Supporting Academic Freedom Through Regulatory Relief Act* and the U.S. Senate's companion bill S. 559. She wrote:

> The House and Senate bills call for the rollback of some of the most egregious regulatory interference in higher education by the federal government in the past decade. These are regulations that mandate a federal definition of credit hour; judge the worth of academic programs by gainful employment or non-academic factors such as student earnings and debt; and tell states how to authorize higher education institutions. The bills also halt work underway to establish a federal quality review capacity to be implemented in 2015–2016, a Postsecondary Institutions Ratings System to judge the performance of colleges and universities. The combined impact of these regulations is to position government officials in the U.S. Department of Education to function as de facto faculty and academic administrators on a daily basis.

Despite the increasingly onerous higher education regulatory framework, a few institutions have been able to receive exemption from U.S. Department of Education and experiment with more flexible models of instruction and management. An early example of an inventive institution to offer flexible educational programs is Western Governors University (WGU). Founded in 1996 by the governors of 10 western states, WGU operates on a competency-based educational model. Learners receive credit for what they know and can do and not necessarily based on how much time they spend in a course. The U.S. Department of Education defines competency-based education as:

> Transitioning away from seat time, in favor of a structure that creates flexibility, allows students to progress as they demonstrate mastery of academic content, regardless of time, place, or pace of learning. Competency-based strategies provide flexibility in the way that credit can be earned or awarded,

and provide students with personalized learning opportunities. These strategies include online and blended learning, dual enrollment and early college high schools, project-based and community-based learning, and credit recovery, among others. This type of learning leads to better student engagement because the content is relevant to each student and tailored to their unique needs. It also leads to better student outcomes because the pace of learning is customized to each student ("Competency-based learning or personalized learning").

Besides WGU, The U.S. Department of Education has allowed a few other institutions of higher education to offer experimental educational programs. Students in these institutions can receive federal loans while they are enrolled in flexible learning programs that are based on learners' demonstrated competency and not seat time. However, these institutions, such as, Cappella University, University of Maryland University College, Northern Arizona University, and the University of Wisconsin, are exceptions. Transformational changes in policies and regulations governing higher education are needed at the federal and state levels to expand the possibility for innovation and change in all colleges and universities.

More than 40 years ago, Wedemeyer (1975) outlined the general features of such policies by describing the characteristics of open educational systems. We slightly modified Wedemeyer's framework for this chapter to match it with the current technological possibilities. The following proposed policies, however, reflect the essence of Wedemeyer's thinking:

- Allow colleges and universities to function anytime, anyplace;
- Provide comprehensive admission criteria by offering credit for previous learning, including recognition of authentic life and work experience as well as informal and independently acquired learning, particularly for adult learners who are already in a career path;
- Accept the learner as an equal partner by allowing each student the autonomy to participate in selecting learning objectives, learning activities, and assessment methods commensurate with the structure that an academic discipline or an institution requires;
- Broaden the role of the instructor to a critic, guide, advisor, mentor, and problem solver;
- Augment academic staffing by forming course teams consisting of professionals with the skills needed to support instructors and learners;
- Employ multiple instructional and learning strategies depending on the profile of each individual learner;
- Expand the learning environment to multiple settings (e.g. museums, libraries, theme parks, and community organizations) using mobile learning systems;

- Seek multiple accreditation models and agencies for review and valuation of academic programs;
- Seek funding from multiple resources; and
- Plan academic programs in direct consultation with as many stakeholders as possible, including students, faculty, administrators, parents, community leaders, political decision-makers, business trailblazers, and entrepreneurs.

Developments in Hardware, Software, and Telecommunications Systems levels have made the implementation of the TTD based on Wedemeyer's framework viable on a system-wide scale. However, unless the legislative and regulatory barriers at the Societal System Level are removed, the implementation of needed changes at the Management and Curricular Systems Levels will remain impeded. This will result in a steady increase in costs not only in financial terms but in social cohesiveness, and general quality of life as well.

Summary

In this chapter, we demonstrated the social importance of higher education in the contemporary economic environment, and discussed how the university has become an integral part of the social and economic fabric of the United States. Because of this crucial role, socioeconomic developments, such as the demand for higher education and the need for a workforce with some level of higher education credentials, have a direct influence on how universities respond to the needs of students. Universities, however, are also directly influenced by public policy. While policies that support the credit hour system may impede the responsiveness of institutions of higher education to their students, rules that reinforce educational programs, such as competency-based education, dynamically respond to the needs of multiple stakeholders including learners, employers, and parents. Charles Wedemeyer conceptualized a policy framework that would keep the institutions of higher education responsive to the needs of the learner, as well as others who have an interest in the success of higher education. The framework is broad and comprehensive and is applicable now more than when Wedemeyer formalized it in 1975, as information technologies have caught up with his vision for the future.

The case study below will explore these social policies affecting higher education in a setting that university administrators and faculty frequently find themselves.

In the next chapter, we will turn our attention to higher education in the global arena and how variables, such as cultural characteristics of students who study in different countries, influence other system levels, such as creating new curricula (Curricular Systems Level) or course materials (Instructional Systems Level).

Case Study 11.1 Regional Higher Education Council

It was on a bright Spring morning when President Jorge Enlightened headed towards a lakeside resort near the campus of Middle State University. In a few hours, the plush conference center at the resort with heavy doors, wood-paneled walls, and ornate 19th-century American style furniture would be hosting the annual meeting of the Regional Higher Education Council (RHEC).

The conference agenda for RHEC indicated that this year the plenary session of the conference was going to be dominated by presentations by CEOs, chief information officers, chief engineers, and marketing managers of regional businesses and industries. If previous memos from state governors to state university presidents were any indication, these business and industry representatives were going to complain about the "output" of the institutions of higher education and their inability to fill many open positions in their companies, particularly in advanced manufacturing and software engineering jobs.

As the plenary session got underway, Larry Sedulous, President of Clean Chemicals, splashed one slide after another on the large conference room screens showing the number of unfilled positions in his plant over the last three years. These ranged from entry-level programming and software design jobs to positions for experienced senior chemical engineers who were also familiar with the oil industry worldwide.

In the Education to Work Subcommittee that followed the plenary session, President Enlightened was surrounded by several of his colleagues who presided over public and private colleges and universities in neighboring states. A dozen staff members working for legislators as well as officers of state boards of higher education were also attending the Subcommittee. The back seats of the conference room were, however, occupied by faculty members from area campuses who have been attending this conference for the last two decades or so.

President Earnest who had guided a community college from being a rudderless institution to a purposeful organization opened the session. In his brief remarks, he stated that his college has been able to place at least two generations of graduates in entry-level positions at Clean Chemicals as well as several nearby oil refineries and environmental assessment companies. "I am truly puzzled why there are still so many open positions and why private sector managers are still complaining about a mismatch between the so-called 'output' of colleges and universities and the job opportunities that they have in their companies." He continued to say that, as a relatively recent university graduate himself, he is also appalled by the fact that all the governors are more or less in sympathy with the demands of the private sector regarding this issue. Perhaps the governors have forgotten that over the past 10 years, they have reduced the contribution of their states to the budgets of colleges and universities, compelling them to increase tuitions and rely on donations from local and regional businesses more than ever before. Some programs in his community college, Earnest reminded the audience, are only sustainable because of the strategic alliances that he has forged with businesses and industries. Graduates of these programs are sought by the local and regional manufactures, oil refineries, and their affiliated chemical plants. That is why they support students in these programs while they study in his college.

Professor Eliot who has attended this subcommittee for at least the last 25 years raised his hand and asked permission to speak. He said:

> President Earnest is absolutely right. We have been put under tremendous pressure to look for money from sources other than the state government, yet we seem to be still indebted to governments that do not support the lion's share of our budgets anymore. Furthermore, our dear governors, for whom I have great respect, may have forgotten that besides software and chemical engineers, they need other kinds of people, people who understand liberal democracy. Ironically, democracy is an important concept for governors who would like to get re-elected by the people of their states.

As he paused to catch his breath, several attendees chuckled sheepishly. Eliot cleared his throat and continued:

> We need young people who not only understand the political system of our country, but also possess a deep understanding of her history, and her position in the world. If some foreign policy experts are correct, we are just about to lose our position as a superpower and assume the second or perhaps even the third rank among the nations in certain areas, such as, international commerce. Clean Chemicals may face at least stiff competition, if not lose its markets abroad altogether, if the United States loses her leadership in international commerce. How can we safeguard our global position if students no longer are required to take courses in history, geography, literature, and dare I say philosophy? This does not bode well for our future.

Elizabeth Antediluvian who teaches English literature asked to be recognized by the chair. In a calm and deliberate tone, she said:

> I am truly concerned about some of the words, and phrases that have been introduced to our lexicon in recent years. Our teaching is now going to be assessed by return on investment, or ROI. Last week, I was asked how I am going to brand my courses from now on. It conjured up the image of a calf being branded in a cowboy movie! Why does my course on Shakespeare need to be branded? How do we calculate ROI on teaching Hamlet? Can anyone explain this brave new world to me? The other phrase that I keep hearing is disruptive technology. I understand that technology, as a tool, could possibly support my teaching. It can also assist my students learn better. But if it keeps disrupting us, would it be useful? We need continuity not disruption.

"Thanks, Elizabeth," said Chairperson Earnest. "As usual, you brought up a lot of issues in a few well-spoken sentences. Is there anyone who wants to respond to Elizabeth?" A long period of silence followed that question. Fran Insightful broke the silence and said:

> I am not sure if I can address Elizabeth's concerns, but the reality is that these words and phrases have become part of our conversation because the environment of higher education has changed. There are more private institutions now than 10 years ago when I started my career. These new so-called universities brand their courses and calculate their ROI. Don't ask me how they do it but, apparently, they do. Last week, I had an entrepreneur in my classroom speak to students in the higher education leadership seminar. He said that he has invested in a worldwide university that is going to unbundle its courses, and let students choose from a menu of competencies that they feel is important to them. Students in my seminar were somewhat enthusiastic about the idea. However, during the Q&A session, it became clear that this unbundling of courses is not going to lead to any structured curriculum that would prepare someone to become a lawyer or a surgeon. This will lead to dismantling not only disciplines but also the idea of the university as a whole. We won't be just unbundling our courses, but our universities.

At this point, the meeting was deteriorating in cohesion and focus. Several side discussions had erupted as attendees started talking to each other in whispers. The chairperson tapped on his microphone to get everyone's attention. He asked everyone to pay attention and said:

> What I have heard so far in this subcommittee has far-reaching implications for the future of our universities, the education of our students, and the general well-being of the states we serve. I think we need more time to discuss these issues in smaller groups. I am asking you to form groups of 3–5 people and develop scenarios that would encapsulate your vision for the future of universities. We need to think about developing agile institutions that can respond to changes in their environment. There are many questions to which we need to find answers and fast. Are we going to go down the road of becoming vocational education institutions? Are we to provide a wide range of foundational skills to our students in the tradition of a liberal arts education? Is there a right mix in blending liberal education and providing business and industry with the skilled workforce they need? If there is a right mix, how can we determine what the mix should be and how do we achieve it? Finally, what would be our posture towards the issues that Elizabeth and Fran brought up? Our universities cannot be isolated from social and technological changes that are occurring at a dizzying speed. Every day, there is a new communication or information technology that can impact how we teach and learn. How can we cope with these disruptive technologies and their intended and unintended consequences? We cannot deny that private institutions have had some degree of success, and as a result, they have brought new measures of success to our profession. They measure success by ROI and it will be just a matter of time that we will be asked to demonstrate to the state that our public universities are worth the taxpayers' money. I know that our research in science and technology brings huge returns on the investment that states and the federal government make in us. Our farmers, physicians, and those who work in industries benefit immensely from our research and development in basic sciences. But we have not been successful in articulating our worth to the public to the point that now some young people even doubt that they need a university education. So, with these issues in mind, I look forward to getting back together this afternoon so that we can all learn from our collective wisdom.

Let's share our thoughts when we come back and see if we can take a few good ideas in coherent and practical solutions back to the plenary session.

References

Berger, N., and Fisher, P. (2013). A well-educated workforce is key to state prosperity. Retrieved from http://www.epi.org/publication/states-education-productivity-growth-foundations.

Cohen, A. M. (1998). *The shaping of American higher education: Emergence and growth of the contemporary system.* San Francisco, CA: Jossey-Bass Publishers.

Competency-based learning or personalized learning. Retrieved from www.ed.gov/oii-news/competency-based-learning-or-personalized-learning.

Eaton, J. (2015). New bills protect academic quality through calls for reducing regulation. *The Hill.* Retrieved from http://thehill.com/blogs/pundits-blog/education/237329-new-bills-protect-academic-quality-through-calls-for-reducing/.

Hanover Research. (2014). Higher education's enrollment bubble: A trends analysis. Retrieved from http://www.hanoverresearch.com/insights/higher-educations-enrollment-bubble-a-trends-analysis/?i=higher-education/.

Hart Research Associates. (2015). *Falling short? College learning and career success.* Retrieved from www.aacu.org/leap/public-opinion-research/2015-survey-results.

Hussar, W. J., and Bailey, T. M. (2016). Projections of education statistics to 2024. Retrieved from http://nces.ed.gov/pubs2016/2016013.pdf/.

Kena, G., et al. (2014). *The condition of education 2014.* Washington, DC.

Lacey, A., and Murray, C. (2015). *Rethinking the regulatory environment of competency-based education.* Washington, DC: American Enterprise Institute.

Mourshed, M., Farrell, D., and Barton, D. (2012). *Education to employment: Designing a system that works.* New York: Mckinsey & Company.

National Student Clearinghouse Research Center. (2015). Current term enrollment estimates, fall 2015. Retrieved from https://nscresearchcenter.org/currenttermenrollmentestimate-fall2015/.

Selingo, J. J. (2015). Why are so many college students failing to gain job skills before graduation? *The Washington Post.* www.washingtonpost.com/news/grade-point/wp/2015/01/26/why-are-so-many-college-students-failing-to-gain-job-skills-before-graduation/.

Snyder, T. D. (2013). *Digest of education statistics 2012.* (NCES 2014-015). Washington, DC: National Center for Education Statistics. Retrieved from http://nces.ed.gov/pubs2014/2014015.pdf/.

Times Higher Education. (2017). World university rankings 2016–2017. Retrieved from https://www.timeshighereducation.com/world-university-rankings/2017/world-ranking#!/page/0/length/25/sort_by/rank/sort_order/asc/cols/stats/.

U.S. Department of Labor. (2013). Employment 2012 and projected 2022, by typical entry-level education and training assignment. Retrieved from www.bls.gov/emp/ep_table_education_summary.htm.

Wedemeyer, C. A. (1975). *Implications of open learning for independent study.* Brighton, UK Retrieved from ERIC database [ED 112 766].

12

GLOBAL SYSTEMS

Introduction

In the last chapter, we discussed how the domestic social environment affects universities in the United States. In this chapter, we will discuss how global events, in turn, influence and dramatically impact domestic social environments in which universities function. Teaching students on the Internet worldwide, the influx of students from abroad, the migration of scholars, and the general global exchange of research findings and theoretical ideas are among the global events that directly impact universities. Overarching global social and economic developments create the conditions in which these events take place. Currently, major multinational trade agreements, administrative and economic unification/disunification of Europe, dramatic upheavals in the Middle East, and the global economic emergence of countries such as China and India have dramatic sways on the lives of learners and educators. These profound changes are still unfolding and influencing universities in multiple ways. Undoubtedly, global events of the future will be different, and they would influence various countries in different ways. However, as far as the model for the technology-based institutions of higher education is concerned, the imperative remains that global developments have a direct impact on the ability of universities to optimize transactional distance for each learner.

The case study for this chapter demonstrates how universities will need to adjust their goals and functions for their academic units to respond to their changing international environment.

Professionals

Professional educators and students are critical nodes in a wide network of formal and informal communication, collaboration, and competition among universities worldwide. At the Global System Level, they also represent cultures; national, local, and personal histories; economic statuses; and a wide spectrum of educational, scientific, and technological accomplishments and ambitions. Because of the vastness of academic and professional activities of universities throughout the world and their interplay with international events, Global Systems are the most complex and perhaps the least understood level of the hierarchical model discussed in this book. Innumerable political, economic, and cultural relations among nations influence how universities function domestically and globally. What makes this situation even more complex is that these relations are currently revised and redefined in a historically pivotal era as world leaders are attempting to establish the post–Cold War status of the world in the inaugural decades of the 21st century (Burrows, 2014; Hass, 2017).

Implications of Global Systems for the TTD

As powerful information and communication technologies have shrunk the world to a global village, issues related to personal identity have become of paramount importance. Learners focus on their self-concept when they are exposed to multiple cultures and experience similarities and differences between their local and national cultures with that of other civilizations (Jensen, 2003). A learner's distinct self-concept influences the interaction between the instructor and the learner, and among learners, thus directly affecting the stock of transactional distance.

Gunawardena (2014) demonstrated that in certain cultures, personal identity is directly related to a sense of community. If the TTD is based, in part, on empowering the individual learner, in such cultures educators involved in personalized learning must consider how learners perceive their individual growth and development in relation to the dominant culture of the community to which they belong. Furthermore, Gunawardena and Jung (2014) emphasized how individuals in certain cultures interact in social settings. Referring to research conducted by Edward Hall in anthropology and cross-cultural communication, Gunawardena and Jung highlighted that in "high context" cultures, in addition to verbal communication, much is left to the situation of the interaction, as well as body language—what is unsaid is as important as what is verbalized or written. At the other end of the spectrum, in "low context" cultures, what is verbalized or written is important and there is not much attention paid to reading in between the lines. Further complexity arises when we realize "Culture is a variable concept and understandings of ostensibly the same culture will differ from one person to the next. Consequently, how that culture is represented and understood by others will differ" (Levy, 2007, p. 6). Each learner, therefore, has a unique cultural identity that is dynamically influenced by the social, and ethnic community in which s/he lives, as well as cultural traits of where s/he studies or works. Unique cultural identities of each learner are not among the factors that are assessed by most current LMSs and ALSs.

This adds to the burden of the instructor to optimize transactional distance for each learner. Other information technologies have enhanced learner control as well as the ability of the instructor to respond to each learner. In recent years, videoconferencing and social media have increased learners' exposure to various cultures and civilizations, further empowering individuals to self-organize around ideas and causes. These technologies have distributed more power to a greater number of people worldwide, empowered the individual vis-à-vis national governments, and as a result diffused the structure of power within and among nation states. Nye and Joseph (2017, pp. 13–14) observed:

> Complexity is growing, and world politics will soon not be the sole province of governments. Individuals and private organizations—from corporations and nongovernmental organizations to terrorists and social movements—are being empowered, and informal networks will undercut the monopoly on power of traditional bureaucracies. Governments will continue to possess power and resources, but the stage on which they play will become ever more crowded, and they have less ability to direct action.

Among the ironies of the postmodern experience is that the very technologies that have empowered learners to participate in cross-cultural and international learning are moving democratic societies towards governances that are riddled with insecurities and uncertainties, thus compromising the control that learners can bring to bear in their own learning experience.

Burrows (2014, p. 40) explained:

> Individual empowerment is part of a broader trend of diffusion of power. It is both cause and effect. Many of the effects of the Internet-based technologies, for example, have been to favor the individual, putting capabilities into the hands of individuals that even governments did not possess two decades ago. At the same time, there is greater insecurity because the churn is continuous. It's not as if anyone can feel secure—from the worker being displaced through Internet-driven automation to the CEOs and political leaders who now have markedly shorter careers than their predecessors.

Globalization

A major ingredient in the continuous churn of technological and postindustrial innovation is the contemporary trend towards globalization—a process that is increasingly tested by new developments, such as, Britain's exit from the European Union, or the United States leaving the Trans-Pacific Partnership (TPP). Nonetheless, globalization has brought turmoil to labor markets and is testing the ability of universities to prepare the workforce of the future. In commerce and education, globalization is as old as ancient mariners who navigated the high seas and travelers who traversed the Silk Road and other land routes to connect early civilizations of Asia, Africa, and Europe. However, the numbers of ancient travelers were limited, and their cultural and material exchanges were with very few individuals. Contemporary globalization is at a different scale and magnitude. It has reached millions of individuals and hundreds of thousands of institutions in all continents and has profoundly affected the international role of education. Nerad (2010, p. 2) asserted that globalization is "a force more powerful than industrialization, urbanization, or secularization combined." This force has set in motion many developments by which millions of individuals have lost their jobs in some parts of the world, while many millions have gained employment in other regions; individuals have ascended from poverty to the middle class in one country, while others have descended economically to a poorer status; corporations have grown to achieve a worldwide status, while small businesses have been put out of business. To say that a global force at this scale and with this magnitude has created turmoil the world over is not an overstatement.

In this volatile global environment in which sovereign countries both collaborate and compete with each other, institutions of higher education are faced with fundamental questions. These include:

- To what extent does a country have the capacity to attract the skills of the graduates of its universities to the workforce in meaningful and productive positions?
- How well are university graduates prepared to respond to the needs of the country of their origin?
- Under what circumstance can university graduates leave their country of origin and migrate to another country?
- Under what circumstance can university graduates become electronic migrants and take positions that are outsourced by another country?

Nerad (2010) outlined four choices for countries to respond to these questions:

1. Increasing the number of higher education graduates at home to meet the domestic economic and social needs;
2. Increasing the number of immigrants endowed with skills that a country needs to compete in the global economy, when the "production" of local universities is inadequate to meet the national demands;
3. Outsourcing work to other countries where skilled workers live; and
4. Adopting a combination of the above policies.

As the current news headlines indicate, these policies are discussed at various levels of decision-making domestically and internationally on a daily basis.

However, adoption of any of the four policies above creates dramatic consequences for university graduates, employers, and the society in which they live.

While globalization has empowered many individuals both in advanced and emerging economies, it has also dislocated many and disrupted hitherto stable cultural communities, ranging from the nuclear family unit to that of the workplace and the society at large (Adres, Vashdi, & Zalmanovitch, 2015; Dodson, 2015; Fulu & Miedema, 2016). Disparities are apparent within countries among those who represent the global knowledge-based economy, and those who still live in local economies that are untouched by the worldwide markets. In fact, such local economies can be found in certain neighborhoods of New York, Chicago, and Los Angeles in which conditions are no better than villages located in underdeveloped countries. In contrast, in cosmopolitan cities of Jakarta, Cairo, and Abuja to name a few, the educated elite are thoroughly engaged in the new global knowledge economy.

> Either in the countryside, far away from the "new economy" which deals with the exchange of knowledge and ideas, or in urban squalor, where old and new knowledge, ideas and values collide: East meets West and high-tech meets low-tech, causing a great cultural rift and the makings of revolution. Here we envision old catchphrases that divide people into "winners" and "losers," societies of widening disparities, much worse than the United States because of government corruption and a lack of fair laws. We call it the gap between "rich" and "poor." Asians and Africans call it "light" and "darkness." Call it what you want. Extreme disparities and huge inequities hinder mobility around the world.
>
> *(Ornstein, 2015, p. 148)*

Lack of mobility is for those who, because of inadequate higher education, cannot participate in the global economy. Similar to financial capital, intellectual capital circulates around the world and goes where it is appreciated and is put to satisfying work. Those who do not possess intellectual capital remain stationary in the new world economy. Historically, this phenomenon has led to brain drain from the underdeveloped countries to those with developed economies. An emerging trend in the postmodern economies of the 21st century points to the fact that brain circulation (either physically or via the Internet) is among regions of the world that enjoy a vibrant economy regardless of where they fall within the boundary of a nation state (Khan & Bashar, 2016; Kolesnikova, Ricaud, Kamasheva, & Zhao, 2014). As the concept of the Westphalian nation state is challenged, national boundaries do not necessarily define the status of their population as they did in centuries past. Possessing intellectual capital is becoming an important distinguishing characteristic of individuals, no matter where they live. The intellectual elite circulates around the world on jet airplanes or the Internet, while those who have less access to opportunities to develop intellectual capital remain stagnant.

This "disembedding" process from the nation state is not only among individuals but also among institutions as well. Transnational flows of the educated class coupled with circulation of research and instructional information, as well as technical and financial recourses, tend to displace the university from its national origin and replace it in a global environment, too. A report by The Organisation for Economic Co-operation and Development (OECD) (2009, p. 47) hypothesized that:

> higher education institutions are becoming and will become "disembedded" from their national contexts because some driving forces of globalisation exceed the strength of national factors. The disembedding hypothesis characterises the relationship between global and national elements not as symbiotic (as in the notion of the national domain as a filter of global effects) but as zero–sum.

Individual disparities and institutional displacements are among both the causes and the effects of insecurity and instability within and among countries.

A Volatile Future

The uncertainty and volatility of globalization affects directly individuals, corporations, civil organizations, and governments and has a profound effect on the relations among nations. Commentators have described the current unstable state of global affairs as "a new world *disorder*" (Hass, 2017); realignment of the global balance of power (Kissinger, 2014); a clash of civilizations (Huntington, 1996); an erosion of the liberal democratic world order, giving rise to fundamentalist and dictatorial regimes (World Economic Forum, 2016); or aging of modernity in the West (Copely, 2012), while postmodern institutions are still embryonic to bring order to art, culture, governments, societies, and the world. As Copley concluded: "We are entering a period which as yet has no firm horizon let alone goals, and under such conditions it is difficult to plot a course" (p. 31). In this unpredictable environment, maintaining the academic integrity of universities becomes of paramount importance for educators. Universities that can face the current rebirth of world order with determination and resolve to deal with its inconsistencies, contradictions, and conflicts will thrive in the 21st century and contribute to bring order out of the current chaos. Global conflicts start when education fails.

Summary

Profound changes in the relations among nations have had a direct and paradoxical effect on each learner. As universities find themselves competing in a global arena, the personal and cultural identity of each learner has become front and center in his or her relation with instructors and higher-education organizations. As such, balancing the need of the individual learner to assert his/her cultural autonomy with the requirements of instructors and the educational organizations for academic and administrative structure becomes of paramount importance. How the world system of relations among nations is going to resolve discrepancies of the postmodern realities is not very clear at this point. This ambiguity necessitates a focused and continuous effort on system planning to ensure academic integrity and financial viability of the American system of higher education. We will explain this system planning in the next chapter and introduce resources that include detailed instructions about system design and implementation.

Case Study 12.1 New Realities, New Goals in Global Education

The International Training and Development Center (IT&DC) at Middle State University has been active in different countries since 1945. It responded to President Truman's Point Four program and helped several countries in Europe and Asia build new capacities in industrial, agricultural, and rural development. In the 1960s, its programs had synergy with the Peace Corps in several countries in Africa and Asia through a variety of community health and educational programs. In the 1970s, the Center shifted its focus to higher education and provided consulting services and technical assistance to several universities in Indonesia, South Korea, and The Republic of China (Taiwan) to elevate their academic standing, broaden their research profile, and integrate principles of instructional design in their teaching practices. Some of these efforts also led to the development of instructional television programs for K–12 schools as well as regional universities. Middle State University benefited from collaborative work with instructors and researchers in these countries, and developed a wide spectrum of expertise in providing educational and technical assistance in countries with developing and emerging economies. Some of the contracts with universities in Asia were lucrative and brought badly needed funds to the university, especially when state funds were not as generously available in the last decades of the 20th century. Since 2000, however, the need for consulting services abroad decreased and IT&DC faced difficulty in supporting its staff and even justifying its existence. In a 50-page report to President Enlightened, Dr. Rondure, the longtime director of IT&DC, listed several reasons for this dwindling demand. These included:

1. Self-sufficiency of leading universities in some Asian countries in academic, research, and instructional development. These universities

now have faculty and staff who were either educated in some of the best American and European universities or received years of technical assistance and training from Middle State University and other institutions, including the United Nations and the World Bank.

2. Greater regional exchanges among institutions of higher education. Donor universities in India, Japan, China, and Australia are supplanting the role of Middle State University in providing technical assistance and consulting services in Asia and beyond.

3. Increased contribution by faculty and staff of leading universities in Asia to prestigious refereed publications. This trend indicates a general progress and maturation in research and development projects. The flow of scientific knowledge that was unidirectional from the "North" to "South" during the 20th century has now become multidirectional. Faculty members in many countries that were previously deemed as "underdeveloped" are now making substantial contributions to the body of scholarly literature.

4. Decreasing availability of federal funds allocated to foreign aid. It has become increasingly difficult in recent years to attract federal funds through grants for providing technical assistance and consulting services to universities abroad.

Dr. Rondure stated that in the past, IT&DC has changed its focus and direction when domestic and international developments demanded letting go of past practices and taking new directions. He suggested that it is time for IT&DC to redirect its efforts to a new area. Middle State University should drop its traditional practice of placing faculty and technical advisors abroad and use its technology infrastructure and expertise in instructional design and development to reach out to students abroad. Given the rapid rise of a middle class in countries with emerging economies, and the inevitable increase in demand for higher education among families with higher incomes, Middle State University should shift its attention from assisting universities abroad to providing direct educational services to students in countries throughout the world. He reasoned that in the coming ten to fifteen years, literally, millions of young people would be added to the number of those who would need some form of higher education in Asia, Africa, Latin America, and Eastern Europe. Eventually, indigenous universities will expand their ability to respond to this demand. However, it will be years before they can build up their capacity in all of the scientific and technical fields to accommodate the large group of young people who would be added to the ranks of those in search of a program at a university. To be sure, there will be several obstacles that the Middle State University must overcome. These include:

1. Students in many countries may not be able to afford standard tuitions for some years to come, despite the fact that income in emerging economies are increasing at a moderate rate. Tuitions for these students must be adjusted and lowered to match the affordability of the average income level of families in countries that are enjoying a healthy degree of economic growth and development, but still may find the cost of education in American universities unaffordable.

2. Courses must be offered in the language of each country as much as possible. Some courses could be easily translated into other languages. However, some languages lack the range of technical vocabulary that is needed for teaching science, engineering, and technology courses.

3. Providing English language competency at a low or no cost at all would be necessary to offer courses in English.

4. Although offering courses in the language of a country goes a long way to establish cultural rapport, it is not enough. Instructional designers and instructors must be sensitive to local cultures in creating and presenting courses. Therefore, each course must go through a process of cultural adaptation. Language is intertwined with culture. Great care must be taken in translating course materials from English into other languages.

5. Telecommunication services have improved throughout the world, and in certain countries, such as South Korea, they are exceptional. However, services are not uniformly available in different countries and even in those that enjoy access to high-speed Internet, the quality of connectivity varies considerably between rural and urban areas. Media production values embedded in these courses, as well as requirements for high-end video conferencing, must be considered in the design and development of new courses directed to countries with emerging economies.

6. The digital divide between families with access to computers and those families that do not own a computer or can access one has decreased in recent years. However, some software applications may not be available in some countries. Such limitations must be considered in course development.

7. Price structure, language requirement, cultural issues, and technology limitations will have a direct impact on the feasibility of offering courses directly to students in other countries. These issues must be addressed using effective strategies. These would include:

a. Dynamic analysis of students' needs and requirements of employers in target countries;

b. Automated translation of course content with quality control provided by professional translators;

c. Implementation of adaptive learning systems;

d. Adapting course content to observe cultural subtleties;

e. Providing ongoing support and feedback to students through social media; and

f. Integrating learners to Middle State University student life and learning environment.

8. In addition to exploring opportunities in countries with emerging economies, Middle State University should continue its tradition of responding to major international problems, particularly those that affect disadvantaged people. We should explore funding offered by the U.S. government, as well as the European Union, the United Nations, the World Bank, and private foundations to provide programs to millions of people who have become economically or politically displaced in recent years. An entire generation of young people in refugee camps are in danger of losing the opportunity to become economically viable and lead independent lives.

These considerations will place Middle State University at the forefront of modeling the future of global education. Our expertise in developing this unique model will be in demand by other institutions that wish to be globally relevant.

Case Analysis

The changing world conditions has had a major impact on the need and demand for international programs offered by the faculty and staff of Middle State University to the point that it has almost made one of its most active and lucrative centers irrelevant (Global System Level). The worldwide changes that ushered in the era of globalization and multipolar relations among nations were not only in the realm of economics and politics but they had an academic dimension as well—i.e. in the form of increased competition by universities in other countries. Maturing of academic institutions in formerly developing countries put the existence of the International Training and Development Center in Middle State University in jeopardy. Unless the university changed its vision and the mission of IT&DC, there would be no reason for its existence. The university would also lose a major source of income if IT&DC simply closed its doors. Changing its approach from providing consulting services to offering programs and courses to individual learners in their indigenous language in countries with emerging economies is a major shift in the vision and mission of IT&DC (Curricular and Instructional Systems levels). A major portion of the Center's work would be to provide instructional design and development as well as learner support in the future.

In doing so, it is going to make use of hardware and software technologies, such as learning management systems with adaptive capabilities, automated translation of course contents, dynamic learner needs assessment and analysis of learning outcomes (Hardware and Software Systems levels). Telecommunication systems, particularly in areas of the world where such services are not readily available or perform poorly, would also impact the international posture of Middle State University.

Providing instruction in languages other than English will differentiate Middle State University from other universities based in the United States. Providing instruction in the language with which students are most familiar would put the University in a good competitive position worldwide at least for a few years until other universities catch up with this innovative approach. However, translating course content will increase the cost of instructional development. The cost of this approach must be analyzed in relation to its benefit in attracting students (Management Systems Level). The status quo is no longer an option for IT&DC. It must respond to a rapidly changing world or become passé and wither away. Only time will tell if venturing into offering courses in different languages on a worldwide scale would become successful. These and similar approaches must be considered for Middle State University to remain competitive in a globalized academic environment.

References

Adres, E., Vashdi, D. R., and Zalmanovitch, Y. (2015). Globalization and the retreat of citizen participation in collective action: A challenge for public administration. *Public Administration Review, 76*(1), 142–152.

Burrows, M. (2014). *The future declassified: Megatrends that will undo the world unless we take action*. New York: Palgrave McMillan.

Copely, G. R. (2012). *Uncivilization: Urban geopolitics in a time of chaos*. Alexandria, VA: The International Strategic Association.

Dodson, K. (2015). Globalization and protest expansion. *Social Problems, 62*(1), 15–39.

Fulu, E., and Miedema, S. (2016). Globalization and changing family relations: Family violence and women's resistance in Asian Muslim societies. *Sex Roles: A Journal of Research, 74*(11), 480–494.

Gunawardena, C. N. (2014). Online identity and interaction. In I. Jung and C. N. Gunawardena (Eds.), *Culture and online learning* (pp. 34–44). Sterling, VA: Stylus.

Gunawardena, C. N., and Jung, I. (2014). Perspectives on culture and online learning. In I. Jung and C. N. Gunawardena (Eds.), *Culture and online learning: Global perspectives and research* (pp. 1–14). Sterling, VA: Stylus.

Hass, R. (2017). *A world in disarray.* New York: Penguin Press.

Huntington, S. P. (1996). *The clash of civilizations and the remaking of world order.* New York: Simon and Schuster.

Jensen, L. A. (2003). Coming of age in a multicultural world: Globalization and adolescent cultural identity formation. *Applied Developmental Science, 7*(3), 189–196.

Khan, H., and Bashar, O. K. M. R. (2016). Does globalization create a "level playing field" through outsourcing and brain drain in the global economy. *The Journal of Developing Areas, 50*(6), 191–207.

Kissinger, H. (2014). *The world order.* New York: Penguin Books.

Kolesnikova, J., Ricaud, C., Kamasheva, A., and Zhao, Y. (2014). Current trends of realization of the intellectual capital and problems of intellectual migration. *Procedia Economics and Finance, 14,* 326–332.

Levy, M. (2007). Culture, culture learning and new technologies: Towards a pedagogical framework. *Language Learning & Technology, 11*(2), 104–107.

Nerad, M. (2010). Globalization and the internationalization of graduate education: A macro and micro view. *Canadian Journal of Higher Education, 40*(1), 1–12.

Nye, J. S. Jr. (2017). Will the liberal order survive? The histoy of an idea. *Foreign Affairs, 96*(1), 10–16.

Ornstein, A. C. (2015). The search for talent. *Society, 52*(2), 142–149.

The Organisation for Economic Co-Operation and Development (OECD). (2009). *Higher education to 2030: The new global landscape of nations and institutions.* Retrieved from www.oecd.org/edu/ceri/highereducationto2030volume2globalisation.htm.

World Economic Forum. (2016). Strengthening the liberal world order. Retrieved from http://www.brookings.edu/wp-content/uploads/2016/07/strengthening_liberal_world_order_wef-1.pdf/.

13

FROM THEORY TO PRACTICE

Introduction

In this book, we:

- Described the principles of the theory of transactional distance;
- Stated that the world of higher education is complex;
- Established that the TTD offers a fresh approach towards understanding this complexity;
- Demonstrated the application of system dynamics for understanding the principles of the theory of transactional distance;
- Advanced the idea that higher education is transitioning from a modern industrial system to a postmodern and postindustrial era; and
- Recommended that educators plan a unique future for their university based on the TTD principles by using system dynamics modeling methodology.

In this chapter, we will present the rationale for using system dynamics modeling for strategic planning and outline how to implement and manage the planning process. A companion website to this book at http://distance-educator.com/planning/ expands this outline and offers more details. We hope the resources in this website would facilitate easy access to seminal articles about system dynamics, simplify sharing information among the planning team, and engage more stakeholders in the planning process.

Strategic Planning for Higher Education

Universities are unique institutions. Their history traces back to the Middle Ages. They have survived the test of time and have become increasingly successful in scholarship, knowledge generation, teaching, and community service. Over the centuries, they have changed and reformed some of their basic organizational structures, but change has been slow, incremental, decentralized, and in many occasions ad hoc and not systematic and holistic. Methodical and sweeping enterprise-wide change in a university is very rare. As we demonstrated in this book, today, this hesitancy to change that made institutions strong over the centuries is not serving them well anymore and is at odds with the new realities of their technological, social, economic, and global environments.

System dynamics modeling provides a holistic approach to assessing the current status of complex organizations at the current time, deciding what kinds of changes must be implemented to improve organizational performance in the future, and determining if the modifications in policies and procedures have resulted in obtaining the desired effects. To put in motion such a comprehensive planning process, it is important that as many stakeholders as possible be included in the modeling and implementation process. Planning for the future of any institution of higher education and implementing it is, therefore, a major effort. Depending on the number of stakeholders involved and the boundary of the system model one chooses to build, the entire process may take several months. Also, in more complex institutions, it is more difficult to agree on a set of common goals among the many stakeholders. Priorities in different institutional units compete for resources and often conflict with each other. As a result, forming consensus on taking one set of action becomes difficult to achieve. Furthermore, in most situations, priorities are not clearly defined and cannot be quantified for system-wide decision-making. At times, the resolution of issues or ideas languishes in the labyrinths of interconnected committees and workgroups because assumptions based on which priorities may be established differ widely among the participating decision-makers. Mental models that stakeholders have about the organization differ widely, and as Sterman (1992, p. 4) among many other system dynamics scholars and professionals have reminded us over the years, "Mental models are not explicit. They are not easily examined by others. Their assumptions are hard to pin down in debate or discussion. Interpretations differ. Ambiguities and contradictions can go unresolved."

In addition, deadlines imposed by institutional exigencies do not always match the time lines set for a planning project, and even if they do match, the onset of a change process often requires an incubation period to mature and develop to its potential before its results become apparent for everyone to see. Frequently, during the gestation process, leaders who are pressed to show results in a short period of time succumb to political pressure, change direction, and do not let the change process mature and show results.

Investment in time and effort, however, becomes rewarding as stakeholders assess how their university is functioning now and how it could change for the better in the future. System dynamics modeling is a means of decision-making that can enhance evaluation of ongoing projects and programs and provide additional insights to the future behavior of an organization. It is also a tool for demonstrating the trajectory of decisions and policies to everyone involved and recruiting their assistance in resolving foreseeable issues and problems before

Planning and Model Building Tasks

The process of planning and model building using system dynamics requires undertaking several specific tasks during a relatively long period of time. Some of these tasks are related to clarifying current policies and procedures that are already in place in an institution and developing consensus for future goals. Other tasks include constructing the system dynamics model on a computer, and collecting and coding the data to make the model work. Several system dynamics planners have outlined these tasks in the projects they managed in education and in other arenas (Groff, 2013; Martinez–Moyano & Richardson, 2013; Senge, 2006; Sterman, 1992, 2002). In addition, we found the suggestions made by Yaure (2004) for strategic planning to implement technology-based projects in higher education useful. Our direct participation in the planning and decision-making processes in several institutions of higher education over the last three decades led us to combine and update suggestions made by these authors, as summarized below:

- Plan broadly for change but implement such changes in demonstration projects on a smaller scale to pilot the change before expanding it to all institutional units.
- Understand that people do not want the achievement of their aspirations be left to happenstance when planning and implementing a change process. It is imperative that all interested parties be involved not only in the planning process but in implementing the plan as well.
- Recognize the constraints of individuals affected by change in terms of:
  - Their knowledge of the substance and subject of change;
  - Resources available to them to make the change;
  - Consensus among individuals affected to make the change; and
  - Additional demands for making the change while dispensing normal work.
- Include representatives of all constituents (on and off campus) so that their needs are not marginalized and are included in the planning process.
- Provide an open decision-making process so that those who wish to participate can do so.
- Inform stakeholders about decisions made in the planning process, especially those who are directly affected by its results.
- Educate all stakeholders about the subject and substance of the decisions.
- Integrate technology decision-making (in this case, application of the technology of system dynamics) into other decision-making processes in the entire campus, or in the unit that is the subject of planning and organizational change.

Implementing System Dynamics

Researchers have used system dynamics to study many types of social institutions, including education, since Jay Wright Forrester (1961) developed it at MIT more than five decades ago. Examples of the application of system dynamics in a variety of educational and business settings are provided in the publication *System Dynamics Review* since 1985 when its first issue appeared. Current information about the field and its practitioners is also available at the website of the System Dynamics Society (www.systemdynamics.org). Over the years, Forrester, as well as his colleagues, students, and followers, have presented detailed instructions for implementing a system dynamics planning and modeling project (Roberts, Andersen, Deal, & Shaffer, 1994). For the purpose of this book, we have streamlined these procedures in fifteen steps in the following outline:

1. Selecting an organizational unit. This step involves an initial decision to choose a university system as a whole, a single campus, or a number of colleges or academic departments for the planning and modeling process. As such, it defines the boundary of the system to be modeled.
2. Identifying system components. Depending on the selection of the organizational unit in step one, the planning and modeling project may include many components or a few. If a university were the primary unit for modeling, the components would include larger units with many subcomponents, such as colleges, departments, programs, and courses. Components in smaller units, such as a division or an academic department, may be smaller and include courses, instructors, learners, projected enrollments in each course, etc.
3. Determining system components. A thorough analysis of the organization, as well as its policies, and practices is needed at this step to determine the extant components that form a university or one of its smaller units, as well as the variables that relate the components to each other.
4. Illustrating causal loops. The purpose here is to depict the relationship among components that were determined in step three in the form of cause-and-effect information feedback and feedforward loops.
5. Developing a flow diagram. A flow diagram is developed at this point. It would be based on the causal loop diagram in step four. The diagram would illustrate the relationship of components in system dynamics functions, such as stocks flows, and delays.
6. Developing system equations. In this step, equations are written to represent the model's stocks, flows, and other functions in mathematical terms.
7. Simulating the behavior of the model. Once the equations are written, the model is run with data shown at a steady state to test the validity of the model.
8. Comparing the behavior of the model with the actual referent organization. At this stage, the behavior of the model in step seven is compared with the behavior of the actual referent organization. The comparison is made to determine to what extent the model represents the behavior of the referent organization.

9. Revising the model. Depending on the results of the comparison in step eight, the model is revised and refined to better reflect the current components, operations, and behavior of the referent organization.

10. Running the simulation. The model then is run under specific assumptions determined by stakeholders and other participants in the planning process, using the data that are collected from the referent organization.

11. Reviewing results. The stakeholders and others in the planning process review the results of the runs of the model to understand their ramifications for current practices and future plans.

12. Experimenting with model assumptions. This is the step in which the detailed work undertaken so far finally pays off. To improve the performance of the organization, the participants in the planning process can experiment with future visions, as well as new policies and procedures. They can run the model under several assumptions to assess the effects of the varying scenarios before they are implemented in the referent organization.

13. Assessing the results of the runs of the model. In this step, the stakeholders review the results of the runs of the simulations and agree on a new set of policies and procedures to implement in the referent organization in order to improve its performance. It is important, however, for the stakeholders to decide on what changes they want to make to their university. Arriving at a consensus would be ideal, as difficult and time consuming as it may be.

14. Altering policies and procedures in the real (referent) organization. This is when the stakeholders have the opportunity to make the necessary changes in the policies and procedures of their organizational units to move its actual behavior towards the ideals on which everyone agreed in step thirteen.

15. Rerunning the model. Systemic organization development requires frequent assessment of its behavior. Once changes have taken place in the organization, in appropriate time intervals (every six, nine, or twelve months), it is necessary to collect new data and run the model again to see how the organization is behaving now and if its performance can be further improved in the future.

Managing the Model Building Process

A professional team is required for managing the planning process and creating a system dynamics model based on the steps that were outlined above. Managing the planning process requires tact and sensitivity in order to include and reflect the viewpoints and needs of all the stakeholders involved. It is imperative that faculty, students, administrators, parents, alumni, and political and community leaders be invited to take an active role in conceptualizing the future of the institution, determining the trajectory of its current policies, and deciding on how they should be modified to achieve a more desirable future. The planning team also must undertake the technical tasks of developing causal loops, flows, and diagrams, as well as writing equations, and running and testing the model.

The following list reflects the personnel needed for the planning team and the tasks they typically perform. This list is based on the experience of the authors in model building as well as the contributions of others in the field (Bala, 2016; Roberts, Andersen, Deal, & Shaffer, 1994; Schoenberg & Bean, 2012), including the following:

- *Planning manager*—The planning manager is in charge of the entire process of planning and modeling.
- *Facilitator(s)*—Depending on the size of the project and the number of stakeholders involved, one or more facilitators are required to engage all participants in planning meetings, focus groups, brain-storming sessions, scenario building, data collection, and reviewing the results of simulation runs during the entire process.
- *Model Designer*—The model designer's task is to facilitate the deliberations of the participants to determine the components that constitute the institution: that is, the subject of planning and how these components relate to each other.
- *Model Builder*—Creating the flow diagram based on the causal loop diagrams and developing the equations that represent the flow diagram are the primary tasks of the model builder. The main deliverable of the model builder is a working model on a computer with initial hypothetical values for each component.
- *Model Technician*—Tasks of the technician include entering the collected data into the databases of the model, running and testing the model, and working with the model builder to ensure that it runs according to its design.
- *Data Manager*—The task of the data manager is to collect, classify, and code the quantitative and qualitative data that are necessary to build and run the model. Collecting data from stakeholders requires close coordination with the facilitators.

The roles of the members of the planning team are further explicated in the companion website. It is sufficient to say here that the planning manager and facilitators must have a solid background and experience in organization development and supervising related techniques, such as conducting focus groups, developing future scenarios, and other similar tasks. They must gain the respect and confidence of all the participants in the planning process and be able to relate to them on a personal basis to carry out their important mission.

As we have neither presented nor advocated dogmatic ideas for planning the future of institutions of higher education, the skills of the planning team become of utmost importance in carrying out a pragmatic systems approach for visualizing and implementing a future that reflects the goals and ambitions of members of an institution. The result of such planning and implementing must reflect the collective wisdom of stakeholders in a college or a university that is specific to that institution. The ultimate objective is optimizing transactional distance for each individual learner.

References

Bala, B. K. (2016). *System dynamics: Modelling and simulation*. New York: Springer Berlin Heidelberg.

Forrester, J. W. (1961). *Industrial dynamics*. Waltham, MA: Pegasus Communications.

Groff, J. S. (2013). Dynamic systems modeling in educational system design & policy. *New Approaches in Educational Research*, 2(2), 72–81.

Hadjis, G. P. A. (2011). Strategic management via system dynamics simulation models. *International Journal of Social, Behavioral, Educational, Economic, Business and Industrial Engineering*, 5(11), 1331–1336.

Martinez-Moyano, I. J., and Richardson, G. P. (2013). Best practices in system dynamics modeling. *System Dyamics Review, 29*(2), 102–123.

Roberts, N., Andersen, D. F., Deal, R. D., and Shaffer, W. A. (1994). *Introduction to computer simulation: A system dynamics modeling approach*. New York: Productivity Press.

Senge, P. M. (2006). *The fifth discipline: The art and practice of the learning organization* (Rev. and updated ed.). New York: Doubleday/Currency.

Sterman, J. D. (1992). *System dynamics modeling for project management*. Cambridge, MA: Massachusetts Institute of Technology. Retrieved from http://web.mit.edu/jsterman/www/SDG/project.pdf/.

Sterman, J. D. (2002). System dynamics: Systems thinking and modeling for a complex world. Retrieved from https://esd.mit.edu/WPS/internal-symposium/esd-wp-2003-01.13.pdf/.

Yaure, R. G. (2004). *A case study analysis of technology decision making at a higher education institution*. (Unpublished doctoral dissertation.) University of Maryland at College Park. College Park, MD.

APPENDIX

REVIEW OF SELECTED LITERATURE ABOUT THE THEORY OF TRANSACTIONAL DISTANCE

A brief review of selected literature is presented below to highlight conceptual and methodological issues concerning scholarship about the theory of transactional distance. The review provides examples of two types of studies: (1) research that has focused on primary constructs of the TTD, and (2) studies that have focused on the perception of or satisfaction with the primary constructs of transactional distance. A third section in this review is devoted to the role of system dynamics research in studying the TTD.

1. Studies about the Primary Constructs of the TTD

    a. *Shearer's study on the refinement of the definition of dialogue.* Shearer (2009) conducted an exploratory study to further understand the concept of dialogue and refine its definition. His method of study was to analyze the discourse of individual learners using an ethnographic approach. The study resulted in developing a classification scheme for dialogue in online learning environments as presented in Table A1.

    The importance of this study is threefold:

    1. The study provided a more refined understanding of the concept of dialogue in educational settings, offered a more precise definition of the concept, and presented a matrix of analysis for future researchers to examine dialogue as a construct.
    2. Shearer's use of discourse analysis in this study was consistent with his earlier study (Saba and Shearer, 1994) in which the content of the conversation of learners with their instructors was analyzed based on certain validated and reliable categories. In both studies, the researchers measured directly the constructs under study.

TABLE A1 Classification Scheme for Dialogue in Online Learning Environments

		Theme		
		Interactional unit		
			Dialogic qualifiers	
Who	Primary dialogic category	Dialogic form	Dialogic move	Dialogue outcome
	Dialogic intent	Dialogic form	Dialogic move	Dialogue outcome
	Dialogue towards understanding	Inquiry—Indirect/Active Debate—Indirect/Active Instruction—Direct/Indirect Gestalt	Questions Responses Building Redirecting Examples	Understanding of assignments, activities, etc.
	Dialogue towards conversation	Conversation	Regulatory Classroom Management Communication Maintenance Learning Activity—formatting Structuring—advanced Organizer Structuring—guidance Social presence Close off dialogue	Feel connected and supported in learning process Isolation
	Passive/silent	Reflective		

They did not measure the perception of such constructs by learners or teachers or their degree of satisfaction with them. Measuring perception and satisfaction is not the same as gauging the systemic and dynamic interplay and outcome of dialogue, structure, or transactional distance. Therefore, studies of perception and satisfaction do not contribute to the paradigmatic growth and development of the TDD. As we demonstrated in this book, dialogue is subjective for the learner, as structure is subjective for the instructor. Perception and satisfaction with dialogue and structure, however, are objective measurements of these constructs and fall outside of the proper system in which dialogue and structure are negotiated subjectively by the instructor and the learner to determine the level of transactional distance at each moment in the duration of teaching and learning.

3. Shearer also analyzed the data for each individual subject, compared to aggregating the data collected from all learners. The paradigm of the TTD is built on the idea of the uniqueness of each individual learner. When the data from a group of learners are aggregated and analyzed, individual differences are lost and, therefore, the study would not shed any light on the concepts of dialogue, autonomy, and transactional distance which are unique for each learner. Looking at these constructs from the lens of aggregated data is meaningless. Thus, the methodology that Shearer selected for his study was as significant as the subject of the inquiry.

b. *Sandoe's study on measuring structure in instructional materials.* Sandoe (2005) focused on the concept of structure as a component of the design of instruction and defined it as "a variable of the transactional distance theory that refers to how the instructional program is designed" (p. 6). She developed and validated the Structure Component Evaluation Tool to measure the structure component of online courses and distinguish between courses that are structurally sound and those that are not. The instrument had 47 descriptors, which determined the value of three major categories. As shown in Table A2, one category had four subcategories and two had three subcategories: Content Organization, Delivery Organization, and Course Interaction Organization.

Sandoe used statistical analysis that aggregated data that were collected about the features of a course. In this case, aggregating data was justified since she was focusing on the standard features of inanimate objects that were identical—e.g. a course syllabus—in learner-instructional materials interaction. In this case, she was not concentrating on the learner per se. In the future, as each learner would be able to generate personalized instructional materials in real time, aggregating data collected about an instructional material might

TABLE A2 Categories of the Structure Component Evaluation Tool

Content organization	
Subcategories	
	Overall
	Syllabus
	Sequencing
	Course schedule
Delivery organization	
Subcategories	
	Overall
	Consistency
	Flexibility
Course interactions organization	
Subcategories	
	Student to instructor
	Student to student
	Student to interface

Source: Adapted from Sandoe, C. (2005). *Measuring transactional distance in online courses: The structure component*. University of South Florida, Tampa, FL.

not be appropriate anymore. Methods of data collection and analysis on individual artifacts (e.g. different versions of a course syllabus generated for each individual learner) might be needed when instructional materials have gained some intelligence to adapt to individual learners, however minor such adaption might be. Had Sandoe studied the concept of structure in learner-instructor interaction, the case would have been different, as aggregating data would have introduced theoretical and methodological issues regarding the individuality of each instructor. It would have raised the question: To what extent is each individual instructor responsible for strictly adhering to design features incorporated in course materials prior to the onset of instruction? Since that was not the case, her study was conducted within the paradigm of the TTD.

    c.   *Shin's study of the concept of transactional presence.* Shin (2001) introduced the concept of transactional presence in terms of how learners relate to their instructors, peers, and the educational institutions in which they study. Transactional presence is an intriguing concept. Shin could have hypothesized that it has an inverse relationship with transactional distance: An increase in transactional presence (e.g. availability of learning support service personnel to learners and the degree of connectedness of such personnel as a function of dialogue) would decrease transactional distance. However, the study was not conducted within the paradigm of the TTD. The study did not:

1. Put forward the concept of transactional presence as a function of the rate of dialogue.
2. Pose a hypothesis in terms of the relationship of transactional presence with transactional distance in a system dynamics model.
3. Proceed to measure availability and connectedness in terms of variation in the frequencies of inquiries fulfilled for each student by a support staff, or a qualitative analysis of the discourse that took place between an individual learner and a support staff.

Instead, the study:

1. Focused on the perception of availability and connectedness, compared to actual availability and connectedness in duration, frequency, or quality.
2. Aggregated and analyzed the data for all learners, which obscured individual differences among the learners. The data collected from all learners were combined to show if learning outcomes were statistically correlated with the perceived availability and the degree of connectedness between learners and their instructors, between learners and their institutional support staff, and among all participating learners.

Although the result of Shin's study is statistically valid for groups of learners, it does not reflect the measure of autonomy, dialogue, and structure for each individual learner. Had the data been analyzed for each learner, patterns of variability for each individual learner at each moment of "connectedness" would have surfaced. The study used key constructs of the theory nominally, but it was conducted outside the paradigm of the TTD conceptually and methodologically. A native method of data collection and analysis for this study within the paradigm of the TTD would have included:

1. Measuring each construct directly—e.g. frequency, duration, and quality of fulfilled learner inquiries by a teacher or a support staff compared to perception of or satisfaction with such variables; and
2. Analyzing data on each individual learner separately so individual differences would have remained intact and would not have been lost in aggregated data.

Commonly used statistical procedures in physical sciences that have been widely adopted in social sciences may be applicable to analyzing variables that can be isolated from their environment. However, in living systems, including learning environments, many variables are operating at the same time and one cannot assume that while the effect of one variable on another is analyzed statistically, the values of the rest of the variables remain fixed. Another issue is time. Living systems change in time, and data that are collected at one instance in a time interval may change in the next time interval. System dynamics is the preferable method of study in the pre-paradigm of the TTD as it allows for studying the effect of several variables on each other as they work together, for each individual learner, and over an extended duration of time. In other words, dynamic and nonlinear methods of data analysis are more suitable to the study of living systems and organizations than linear and static methods of statistical data analysis. Researchers who collect one set of data which reflect a snapshot of the status of the learner or the instructor at one moment in time and proceed to subject the data to linear statistical methods of analysis completely ignore this dynamic nature of learning, and the cybernetic relation between the learner and the instructor, particularly in online learning.

d. *Vasiloudis, Koutsouba, Giossos, and Mavroidis* (2015) studied transactional distance between students in a Counseling Group Session (CGS) and their tutor, as well as the autonomy of students in a postgraduate course at Hellenic Open University. They concluded that:

> there is little evidence that the learning process affects the relation between transactional distance and autonomy, at least within the framework of the Hellenic Open University. This could also be regarded in the overall framework of the different critiques and interpretations of Moore's theory.
>
> *(p. 120)*

The research design and method of data collection in this study also ignored one of the key tenets of the theory of TTD: focusing on each individual learner. Single subject method of data collection and analysis is an integral part of the pre-paradigm of the TTD to assure that the rate of autonomy as well as the level of transactional distance—that are unique for each individual learner—are reflected in the results of any study. We assume that if the data for each individual learner would have been collected and analyzed individually, the results of this study would have been different.

2. Studies on Perception and Satisfaction
   Several studies in recent years have focused on perception of transactional distance, or satisfaction with it in instructional settings (Giossos, Koutsouba, & Mavroidis, 2016; Hughes, 2010; Jung, 2006; Mathieson, 2012; Nwankwo, 2013; Rabinovich, 2009; Shin, 2001; Stein, Wanstreet, Calvin, Overtoom, & Wheaton, 2005; Wengrowicz & Offir, 2013). These studies furthered analytical discussion of the key constructs of the theory of transactional distance. However, they did not move the scholarship forward as

much as they could have because they measured perception of or satisfaction with transactional distance, but not transactional distance itself. These studies hearken back to evaluation of distance education programs in the 1970s and 1980s when administrators conducted atheoretical surveys of students' satisfaction with distance education programs or their perception of the programs. The difference between the older evaluation studies and those cited here is that contemporary researchers invoke the TTD in their studies nominally, but ignore its key concepts and continue to measure student satisfaction and perception as in the past. Studying satisfaction with or perception of transactional distance is not studying the phenomenon of transactional distance as a function of three variables of structure, dialogue, and autonomy. These studies, therefore, fell outside the paradigm of the TTD as researchers ignored the operational definition of the key concepts of the TTD in system dynamics language as set forward by Moore (1973, 1983, 2013).

3. Role of System Dynamics Research
   Very few studies have addressed the role of systems research in scholarship regarding transactional distance. Although systems modeling methods are widely used in social sciences, they are rarely taught in schools of education: This shortcoming has limited scholarly work about transactional distance using its native method of study. Shaffer (2005) called for the development of standard models of distance education using the system dynamics method and proposed a preliminary model of the socioeconomic environment of distance education. Another scholar who has used system concepts and methods for his studies in transactional distance is Jon Dron (Dron, 2007; Dron & Anderson, 2014; Dron, Seidel, & Litten, 2004). Focusing on social interaction in online learning environments, Dron (2007, p. 62) clearly described social software in systems terminology as being "organic," "self-organizing," and "stigmergic" with emergent properties that are formed from the bottom up instead of from the top-down. In discussing transactional distance in a blended learning environment, Dron, Seidel, and Litten (2004) described the complex variables that had an impact on how instructors and learners decided on allocating their time to different tasks. Their study also focused on the impact that the course environment had on the problems that learners and instructors faced. These researchers used systems thinking and terminology to explicate these variables. They stated:

   The complex system that we recognize as a course is made of the interactions of its own parts and with other systems, including those of which it is a constituent. Like many complex systems, it learns and develops with an internal dynamic very different from the sum of its components, not always in the ways that its leaders expect or intend. The movement from structure to dialogue and back again is one that can be strongly influenced, but seldom fully controlled. That control arises at least in part from the systemic interactions within the system itself.

(p. 173)

In another study, Dron and Anderson (2014, p. 71) expressed their deep understanding of the nature of systems research when they advocated expanding the concept of transactional distance from measuring a single dimension of communication between the learner and instructor to measuring multiple dimensions that are in play in social forms of communication.

These studies are essential in further understanding the complex systems that are present in educational settings, but they are hardly adequate to explore all of the complex systems that work in the eight hierarchies that we have presented in this book. Much more is needed to identify and explore the fundamental system components in technology-based higher education organizations and understand the intricate feedback networks among them.

References

Dron, J. (2007). Designing the undesignable: Social software and control. *Educational Technology & Society, 10*(3), 60–71.

Dron, J., and Anderson, T. (2014). The distant crowd: Transactional distance and new social media literacies. *International Journal of Learning Media, 4*(3–4), 65–72.

Dron, J., Seidel, C., and Litten, G. (2004). Transactional distance in a blended learning environment. *ALT-J, Research in Learning Technology, 12*(2), 163–174.

Giossos, Y., Koutsouba, M., and Mavroidis, I. (2016). Development of an instrument to measuring learner-teacher transactional distance. *The American Journal of Distance Education, 30*(2), 98–108.

Hughes, W. G. (2010). *Transactional distance theory: The effect of disseminating educational messages to frontline nurses in an acute care hospital setting.* (Unpublished doctoral dissertation), Southern Louisiana University.

Jung, H. Y. (2006). *Transactional distance and student motivation: Student perception of teacher immediacy, solidarity toward peer students and student motivation in distance education.* (Unpublished doctoral dissertation) West Virginia University.

Mathieson, K. (2012). Exploring student perceptions of audiovisual feedback via screen-casting in online courses. *American Journal of Distance Education, 26*(3), 143–156.

Moore, M. G. (1973). Toward a theory of independent learning and teaching. *Journal of Higher Education, 44*(9), 661–680.

Moore, M. G. (1983). The individual adult learner. In M. Tight (Ed.), *Adult learning and education* (pp. 153–168). London: Croom Helm.

Moore, M. G. (2013). The theory of transactional distance. In M. G. Moore (Ed.), *Handbook of distance education* (pp. 66–85). New York: Routledge.

Nwankwo, V. I. (2013). *The relationship between faculty perceptions and implementation of elements of transactional distance theory and online web-based course completion rates.* (Unpublished doctoral dissertation), Florida International University.

Rabinovich, T. (2009). *Transactional distance in a synchronous web-extended classroom learning environment*. (Unpublished doctoral dissertation), Boston University.

Sandoe, C. (2005). *Measuring transactional distance in online courses: The structure component*. (Unpublished doctoral dissertation) University of South Florida.

Shaffer, S. C. (2005). System dynamics in distance education and a call to develop standard models. *International Review of Research in Open and Distance Learning, 6*(3), 1–13.

Shin, N. (2001). *Beyond interaction: Transactional presence and distance learning*. (Unpublished doctoral dissertation), The Pennsylvania State University.

Stein, D. S., Wanstreet, C. E., Calvin, J., Overtoom, C., and Wheaton, J. E. (2005). Bridging the transactional distance gap in online learning environments. *The American Journal of Distance Education, 19*(2), 105–118.

Vasiloudis, G., Koutsouba, M., Giossos, Y., and Mavroidis, I. (2015). Transactional distance and autonomy in a distance learning environment. *European Journal of Open, Distance and E-Learning, 18*(1), 114–122.

Wengrowicz, N., and Offir, B. (2013). Teachers' perceptions of transactional distance in different teaching environments. *American Journal of Distance Education, 27*(2), 111–121.

INDEX

Taylor & Francis eBooks

Helping you to choose the right eBooks for your Library

Add Routledge titles to your library's digital collection today. Taylor and Francis ebooks contains over 50,000 titles in the Humanities, Social Sciences, Behavioural Sciences, Built Environment and Law.

Choose from a range of subject packages or create your own!

Benefits for you

» Free MARC records
» COUNTER-compliant usage statistics
» Flexible purchase and pricing options
» All titles DRM-free.

Benefits for your user

» Off-site, anytime access via Athens or referring URL
» Print or copy pages or chapters
» Full content search
» Bookmark, highlight and annotate text
» Access to thousands of pages of quality research at the click of a button.

REQUEST YOUR FREE INSTITUTIONAL TRIAL TODAY

Free Trials Available
We offer free trials to qualifying academic, corporate and government customers.

eCollections – Choose from over 30 subject eCollections, including:

Archaeology	Language Learning
Architecture	Law
Asian Studies	Literature
Business & Management	Media & Communication
Classical Studies	Middle East Studies
Construction	Music
Creative & Media Arts	Philosophy
Criminology & Criminal Justice	Planning
Economics	Politics
Education	Psychology & Mental Health
Energy	Religion
Engineering	Security
English Language & Linguistics	Social Work
Environment & Sustainability	Sociology
Geography	Sport
Health Studies	Theatre & Performance
History	Tourism, Hospitality & Events

For more information, pricing enquiries or to order a free trial, please contact your local sales team: www.tandfebooks.com/page/sales